NOTE.

The names of those places in the neigh
-bourhood of which the views have been
taken are underlined thus —Hudson.
The line of Route is Colored Red

PART OF
VIRGINIA AND MARYLAND
on the same Scale.

Greenwich.

Drawn and Engraved by W.Hughes.

AMERICAN SCENERY

Yours truly

W H Bartlett

AMERICAN SCENERY

BY N. P. WILLIS, ESQ.

With 121 *steelplate engravings*

from drawings by W. H. BARTLETT

ASCENT TO THE CAPITOL, WASHINGTON.

IMPRINT SOCIETY BARRE, MASSACHUSETTS 1971

10/94

Library of Congress Catalog Card Number 79-142582

International Standard Book Number 0-87636-018-5

Printed in the United States of America

PREFACE

EITHER *Nature has wrought with a bolder hand in America, or the effect of long continued cultivation on scenery, as exemplified in Europe, is greater than is usually supposed. Certain it is that the rivers, the forests, the unshorn mountain-sides and unbridged chasms of that vast country, are of a character peculiar to America alone—a lavish and large-featured sublimity, (if we may so express it,) quite dissimilar to the picturesque of all other countries.*

To compare the sublime of the Western Continent with the sublime of Switzerland—the vales and rivers, lakes and waterfalls, of the New World with those of the Old—to note their differences, and admire or appreciate each by contrast with the other, was a privilege hitherto confined to the far-wandering traveller. In the class of works, of which this is a specimen, however, that enviable enjoyment is brought to the fire-side of the home-keeping and secluded as well; and, sitting by the social hearth, those whose lot is domestic and retired, can, with small cost, lay side by side upon the evening table the wild scenery of America, and the bold passes of the Alps— the leafy Susquehanna with its rude raft, and the palace-gemmed Bosphorus with its slender caique. So great a gratification is seldom enjoyed at so little cost and pains.

In the Letter-press, it has been the Writer's aim to assemble as much as possible of that part of American story which history has not yet found leisure to put into form, and which romance and poetry have not yet appropriated—the legendary traditions and anecdotes, events of the trying times of the Revolution, Indian history, &c. &c. It is confidently hoped, that the attempt to assemble a mass of interesting matter under this design, has not failed; and that, in the value of the intellectual portion, as well as in the beauty and finish of the embellishments, the Work will be thought worthy of the patronage of the public.

CONTENTS & LIST OF ENGRAVINGS

AMERICAN SCENERY

ENTRANCE TO THE HUDSON HIGHLANDS, NEAR NEWBURGH.

AMERICAN SCENERY

IT strikes the European traveller, at the first burst of the scenery of America on his eye, that the New World of Columbus is also a new world from the hand of the Creator. In comparison with the old countries of Europe, the vegetation is so wondrously lavish, the outlines and minor features struck out with so bold a freshness, and the lakes and rivers so even in their fulness and flow, yet so vast and powerful, that he may well imagine it an Eden newly sprung from the ocean. The Minerva-like birth of the republic of the United States, its sudden rise to independence, wealth, and power, and its continued and marvellous increase in population and prosperity, strike him with the same surprise, and leave the same impression of a new scale of existence, and a fresher and faster law of growth and accomplishment. The interest, with regard to both the natural and civilized features of America, has very much increased within a few years; and travellers, who have exhausted the unchanging countries of Europe, now turn their steps in great numbers to the novel scenery, and ever-shifting aspects of this.

The picturesque views of the United States suggest a train of thought directly opposite to that of similar objects of interest in other lands. There, the soul and centre of attraction in every picture is some ruin of the *past*. The wandering artist avoids every thing that is modern, and selects his point of view so as to bring prominently into his sketch, the castle, or the cathedral, which history or antiquity has hallowed. The traveller visits each spot in the same spirit—ridding himself, as far as possible, of common and present associations, to feed his mind on the historical and legendary. The objects and habits of reflection in both traveller and artist undergo in America a direct revolution. He who journeys here, if he would not have the eternal succession of lovely natural objects—

"Lie like a load on the weary eye,"

must feed his imagination on the *future*. The American does so. His mind, as he tracks the broad rivers of his own country, is perpetually reaching forward.

[3]

Instead of looking through a valley, which has presented the same aspect for hundreds of years—in which live lords and tenants, whose hearths have been surrounded by the same names through ages of tranquil descent, and whose fields have never changed landmark or mode of culture since the memory of man, he sees a valley laden down like a harvest waggon with a virgin vegetation, untrodden and luxuriant; and his first thought is of the villages that will soon sparkle on the hill-sides, the axes that will ring from the woodlands, and the mills, bridges, canals, and railroads, that will span and border the stream that now runs through sedge and wild-flowers. The towns he passes through on his route are not recognizable by prints done by artists long ago dead, with houses of low-browed architecture, and immemorial trees; but a town which has perhaps doubled its inhabitants and dwellings since he last saw it, and will again double them before he returns. Instead of inquiring into its antiquity, he sits over the fire with his paper and pencil, and calculates what the population will be in ten years, how far they will spread, what the value of the neighbouring land will become, and whether the stock of some canal or railroad that seems more visionary than Symmes's expedition to the centre of the earth, will, in consequence, be a good investment. He looks upon all external objects as exponents of the future. In Europe they are only exponents of the past.

There is a field for the artist in this country (of which this publication reaps almost the first-fruits) which surpasses every other in richness of picturesque. The great difficulty at present is, where to choose. Every mile upon the rivers, every hollow in the landscape, every turn in the innumerable mountain streams, arrests the painter's eye, and offers him some untouched and peculiar variety of an exhaustless nature. It is in *river scenery*, however, that America excels all other lands: and here the artist's labour is not, as in Europe, to embellish and idealise the reality; he finds it difficult to come up to it. How represent the excessive richness of the foliage! How draw the vanishing lines which mark the swells in the forest-ground, the round heaps of the chestnut-tops, the greener belts through the wilderness which betray the wanderings of the watercourses! How give in so small a space the evasive swiftness of the rapid, the terrific plunge of the precipice, or the airy wheel of the eagle, as his diminished form shoots off from the sharp line of the summit, and cuts a circle on the sky!

The general architecture of the United States cannot pretend, of course, to vie with that of older countries; yet, taken in connexion with the beautiful position of the towns, no drawing will be found deficient in beauty, while many of the public buildings especially are, as works of art, well worthy the draughtman's notice. The curiosity now generally excited with regard to this country, by its own progress, and by the late numerous books of travels, will throw a sufficient interest around every point that the pencil could present.

—— " The green land of groves, the beautiful waste,
　　Nurse of full streams, and lifter up of proud
　　Sky-mingling mountains that o'erlook the cloud.
　　Erewhile, where yon gay spires their brightness rear,
　　Trees waved, and the brown hunter's shouts were loud
　　Amid the forest; and the bounding deer
Fled at the glancing plume, and the gaunt wolf yell'd near.

" And where his willing waves yon bright blue bay
　　Sends up, to kiss his decorated brim,
　　And cradles, in his soft embrace, the gay
　　Young group of grassy islands born of him,
　　And, crowding nigh, or in the distance dim,
　　Lifts the white throng of sails, that bear or bring
　　The commerce of the world;—with tawny limb,
　　And belt and beads in sunlight glistening,
The savage urged his skiff like wild bird on the wing.

　　　*　　*　　*　　*　　*　　*

" Look now abroad—another race has fill'd
　　These populous borders—wide the wood recedes,
　　And towns shoot up, and fertile realms are till'd;
　　The land is full of harvests and green meads;
　　Streams numberless, that many a fountain feeds,
　　Shine, disembower'd, and give to sun and breeze
　　Their virgin waters; the full region leads
　　New colonies forth, that toward the western seas
Spread, like a rapid flame, among the autumnal trees.

　　　*　　*　　*　　*　　*

" But thou, my country, thou shalt never fall,
　　But with thy children—thy maternal care,
　　Thy lavish love, thy blessing shower'd on all—
　　These are thy fetters—seas and stormy air
　　Are the wide barrier of thy borders, where
　　Among thy gallant sons that guard thee well,
　　Thou laugh'st at enemies: who shall then declare
　　The date of thy deep-founded strength, or tell
How happy, in thy lap, the sons of men shall dwell."

BRYANT

[5]

NIAGARA FALLS, FROM THE FERRY

Niagara Falls, from the Ferry

THE best way to approach Niagara is to come up on the American shore, and cross at the ferry. The descent of about two hundred feet by the staircase, brings the traveller directly under the shoulder and edge of the American fall—the most imposing scene, for a single object, that he will ever have witnessed. The long column of sparkling water seems, as he stands near it, to descend to an immeasurable depth, and the bright sea-green curve above has the appearance of being let into the sky. The tremendous power of the Fall, as well as the height, realizes here his utmost expectations. He descends to the water's edge, and embarks in a ferry-boat, which tosses like an egg-shell on the heaving and convulsed water; and in a minute or two he finds himself in the face of the vast line of the Falls, and sees with surprise that he has expended his fullest admiration and astonishment upon a mere thread of Niagara—the thousandth part of its wondrous volume and grandeur. From the point where he crosses, to Table Rock, the line of the Falls is measurable at three quarters of a mile; and it is this immense extent which, more than any other feature, takes the traveller by surprise. The tide at the Ferry sets very strongly down, and the athletic men who are employed here, keep the boat up against it with difficulty. Arrived near the opposite landing, however, there is a slight counter-current, and the large rocks near the shore serve as a break-water, behind which the boat runs smoothly to her moorings.

It may be remarked, that the well-known stanzas on the "Fall of Terni," in the fourth canto of "Childe Harold," are, in many respects, singularly and powerfully descriptive of Niagara.

> "The roar of waters!—from the headlong height
>   Velino cleaves the wave-worn precipice;
>   The fall of waters! rapid as the light
>   The flashing mass foams shaking the abyss;
>   The hell of waters! where they howl and hiss,
>   And boil in endless torture; while the sweat
>   Of their great agony, wrung out from this
>   Their Phlegethon, curls round the rocks of jet
> That gird the gulf around, in pitiless horror set,
>
> "And mounts in spray the skies, and thence again
>   Returns in an unceasing shower, which round,
>   With its unemptied cloud of gentle rain,
>   Is an eternal April to the ground,
>   Making it all one emerald:—how profound

The gulph! and how the giant element
From rock to rock leaps with delirious bound,
Crushing the cliffs, which, downward worn and rent
With his fierce footsteps, yield in chasms a fearful vent

"To the broad column which rolls on, and shows
More like the fountain of an infant sea
Torn from the womb of mountains by the throes
Of a new world, than only thus to be
Parent of rivers, which flow gushingly,
With many windings through the vale:—Look back
Lo! where it comes like an eternity,
As if to sweep down all things in its track,
Charming the eye with dread,—a matchless cataract,

"Horribly beautiful! but on the verge,
From side to side, beneath the glittering morn,
An Iris sits, amidst the infernal surge,
Like Hope upon a death-bed, and, unworn
Its steady dyes, while all around is torn
By the distracted waters, bears serene
Its brilliant hues with all their beams unshorn:
Resembling, 'mid the torture of the scene,
Love watching Madness with unalterable mien."

BYRON

View from West Point

OF the river scenery of America, the Hudson, at West Point, is doubtless the boldest and most beautiful. This powerful river writhes through the highlands in abrupt curves, reminding one, when the tide runs strongly down, of Laocoon in the enlacing folds of the serpent. The different spurs of mountain ranges which meet here, abut upon the river in bold precipices from five to fifteen hundred feet from the water's edge; the foliage hangs to them, from base to summit, with the tenacity and bright verdure of moss; and the stream below, deprived of the slant lights which brighten its depths elsewhere, flows on with a sombre and dark green shadow in its bosom, as if frowning at the narrow gorge into which its broad-breasted waters are driven.

Back from the bluff of West Point extends a natural platform of near half

VIEW FROM WEST POINT

a mile square, high, level, and beautifully amphitheatred with wood and rock. This is the site of the Military Academy, and a splendid natural parade. When the tents of the summer camp are shining on the field—the flag, with its blood-bright stripes, waving against the foliage of the hills—the trumpet echoing from bluff to bluff, and the compact batallion cutting its trim line across the greensward—there are few more fairy spots in this working-day world.

On the extreme edge of the summit, overlooking the river, stands a marble shaft, pointing like a bright finger to glory, the tomb of the soldier and patriot Kosciusko. The military colleges and other buildings skirt the parade on the side of the mountain; and forward, toward the river, on the western edge, stands a spacious hotel, from the verandahs of which the traveller gets a view through the highlands, that he remembers till he dies. Right up before him, with the smooth curve of an eagle's ascent, rises the "old cro' nest" of the culprit Fay, a bright green mountain, that thrusts its topmost pine into the sky; the Donderbarrak, or (if it is not sacrilege to translate so fine a name for a mountain,) the *Thunder-chamber*, heaves its round shoulder beyond; back from the opposite shore, as if it recoiled from these, leans the bold cliff of Breknock; and then looking out, as if from a cavern, into the sun-light, the eye drops beyond upon a sheet of wide-spreading water, with an emerald island in its bosom; the white buildings of Newburgh creeping back to the plains beyond, and in the far, far distance, the wavy and blue line of the Cattskills, as if it were the dim-seen edge of an outer horizon.

The passage through the highlands at West Point still bears the old name of Wey-gat, or Wind-gate; and one of the prettiest moving dioramas conceivable, is the working through the gorge of the myriad sailing-craft of the river. The sloops which ply upon the Hudson, by the way, are remarkable for their picturesque beauty, and for the enormous quantity of sail they carry on in all weathers; and nothing is more beautiful than the little fleets of from six to a dozen, all tacking or scudding together, like so many white sea-birds on the wing. Up they come, with a dashing breeze, under Anthony's Nose, and the Sugar-Loaf, and giving the rocky toe of West Point a wide berth, all down helm, and round into the bay; when—just as the peak of Crow Nest slides its shadow over the mainsail—slap comes the wind aback, and the whole fleet is in a flutter. The channel is narrow and serpentine, the wind baffling, and small room to beat; but the little craft are worked merrily and well; and dodging about, as if to escape some invisible imp in the air, they gain point after point, till at last they get the Donderbarrak behind them, and fall once more into the regular current of the wind.

[10]

Trenton Falls

(View Down the Ravine)

TRENTON FALLS (called Cayoharie by the Indians) are formed by the descent of a considerable stream, known by the name of West Canada Creek, through a mountainous ravine of singular formation and beauty. The Creek, which is swollen to a tremendous torrent by rains in the mountains, or by the spring thaws, has evidently worn through the strata which now enclose it, and runs at present over a succession of flat platforms, descending by leaps of forty or fifty feet from one to the other, and forming the most lovely chain of cascades for a length of three or four hundred miles. The walls that shut it in are either perpendicular, or overhanging it in broad table ledges; the wild vegetation of the forest above, leaning over the chasm with an effect like foliage of a bright translucent green, painted on the sky.

Although but fourteen miles distant from a town containing twelve or fourteen thousand inhabitants, Trenton Falls were unknown till within a very few years. They were discovered by an artist in search of the picturesque, and are now visited, like Niagara and Terni. A quiet but excellent inn, which contrasts strongly, by its respectful service, and its neat and secluded air, with the noisy and carelessly kept hotels of the country, stands on the edge of the pine forest, a little back from the brink of the chasm; and being off the business line of travel, and requiring a little time and expense to reach, it is frequented principally by the better class of travellers, and forms a most agreeable loitering place, either for the invalid, or the lover of quiet leisure.

In company with the artist to whom the public is indebted for these admirable drawings, I lately visited the ravine by moonlight. We had passed the day in rambling up and down the creek, (a term, by the way, that, differing from its use in England, describes usually in America the finer class of streams;) and I had already made myself familiar by many visits in former years with every turn and phase of its matchless waters, as seen by the light of day. The moon rose about ten, and lifted her perfect orb, without a mist or a cloud, over the shoulder of the mountain which turns the outlet of the ravine. The fine and majestic wood, through which winds the narrow footpath to the Falls, let in the white light in silvery and broken masses—sometimes sliding a long argent line down the dark body of a pine, sometimes pouring in upon the horizontal branches of the hemlock, like an open hand sprinkled with snow; and here and there lighting up a broad circle upon the carpet of tassels

TRENTON FALLS, VIEW DOWN THE RAVINE

and dead leaves, which, in contrast with the heavy shadows of the surrounding wood, looked illuminated with the special brightness of a fairy ring.

We descended the long ladder leading into the ravine, and were soon below the reach of the moonlight, which came slant as yet, and only rimmed the black wall above us with a long strip of white, which, where the wavy line of moss and creepers ran into it, resembled the edging of lace upon a velvet coat in a dark old Flemish picture. The water in this part of the gulf quite fills up the chasm, and rolls, even by daylight, in a black and sullen stream between the bare cliffs which frown over it. The only path here is a giddy ledge, half way up the precipice, which is passed with the aid of a chain run along the rock; and, as we stood on this, looking over into the uncertain darkness below, with the murmur of the far-down and invisible current ascending faintly to our ears, and the light of heaven ceasing so far above us, it seemed to us not an inapt image of the infernal river. We crept on till we came to the foot of the principal Fall, and sat down on the platform below, to wait the gradual descent of the moon.

The mist over the Fall began to show like a film of gauze waving in the air; the sharp angles and crevices in the precipice caught the light one by one, and soon the whole upper ravine was illuminated, while through the gorge below the stream still made its way darkly and solemnly to the outlet.

No pencil, no language, can describe the splendour with which the moon drew her light across the face of the Fall. The other objects in the ravine drank her beams soberly, and gave back only their own calm outlines to the eye; but, from this wall of waters, every spray-drop gave back a diamond—every column of the descending element, a pillar of silver. If there were gates to fairyland opening from this world of ours, and times when they are visible and recognizable by the chance passing eye of man, I should have believed that we had fallen on the hour, and that some inner and slowly opening portal was letting the brightness of a fairy world through these curtains of crystal.

View from Mount Holyoke

PROBABLY the richest view in America, in point of cultivation and fertile beauty, is that from Mount Holyoke. The bald face of this mountain, which is turned towards Northampton, is about one thousand one hundred feet above the level of the Connecticut river, (or Quonnecticut, as pronounced by the Indians,) and commands a radius of about sixty miles. The ascent at the side is easy; and it is a fashionable climb for tourists, whose patronage of ginger-beer and sunrises maintains a shanty and a hermit on the top, and keeps in repair a series of scrambling but convenient ladders at the difficult points of the enterprise. The view immediately below presents a singular phase of the scenery of the river, which seems here to possess a soul for beauty, and loiters, enamoured and unwilling to flow on, in the bosom of a meadow which has no parallel in New England for loveliness and fertility. Four times the amorous stream turns to the west, and thrice to the east, threading its silver tide through the tender verdure as capriciously as a vein in the neck of beauty, and cheating twelve miles of direct course into twenty-four of coil and current. The meadow is almost entirely unfenced, and the river is fringed in all its windings with weeping elms, wild flowers and shrubs, while up toward the town the fields rise in slightly swelling terraces—forming a foreground to one of the most sunny and cheerful villages in Massachusetts.

The more extended view embraces a great variety of mountain range—Monadnoc in the north-east, Saddle Mountain in the north-west, Mount Tom (between which and Mount Holyoke the Connecticut seems to have broken with the outlet waters of an immense lake) close on the south-west, and spurs of the Green Mountains advancing and receding in the course of the Connecticut in the north. Geologists speculate extensively on the lakes that once existed in the bosoms formed by these mountains—but we have not time to go back to the deluge.

There is a small hamlet at the foot of Mount Holyoke, on the eastern side of the river, called by the Indian name *Hoccanum*, and another at the foot of Mount Tom, on the western side, called *Pascommuc*, both of which were burnt by the savages in the early settlement of the country, and the inhabitants killed or taken captive. The early history of all these towns on the Connecticut river is filled with events of Indian warfare. Northampton, by its rich alluvial land allured the first settlers of Massachusetts long before most of the country between it and the sea-coast possessed an inhabitant. These adventurous pilgrims seated themselves in the midst of an unprotected wilder-

VIEW FROM MOUNT HOLYOKE

ness, and surrounded by populous Indian tribes; and, first purchasing the land at the Indians' valuation, they defended themselves afterwards as they might from the aggressions of these and others. The township of Northampton (called Nonotuc by the aborigines) was first bought in 1653. It was conveyed to John Pyncheon for the planters by Wawdillowa, Nenessahalant, Nassicochee, and four others (one of whom was a married woman), who were styled the "chief and proper owners." The price was "one hundred fathom of wampum by tale, and ten coats," to which was added an agreement to plough for the Indians, in the ensuing summer, sixteen acres of land on the east side of Quonnecticut River. These "all bargained for themselves, or the other owners by their consent." All the aborigines of this country, observes a correct writer on this subject, are owners of the lands on which they dwell—men and women alike. This property in lands, held by the Indian women, is a singular fact in the history of the savage nations.

Three years after, a rich interval near Northampton, called Capawanke, and containing eight or nine hundred acres, was sold to these same planters by an Indian, named Lampancho, for fifty shillings, at two payments, "to his entire satisfaction."

These two purchases give a very fair idea of the Indian purchases made by our forefathers. In the former, ninety square miles were sold for a hundred fathom of wampum and ten coats! Within this tract were near five thousand acres of interval land, worth at the present time perhaps eight or nine hundred thousand dollars. Unjust as the transaction seems, however, the price was ample to the Indian, who could not have got so much by keeping it, and for whom there was no other purchaser.

The settlers of Nonotuc lived in comparative harmony with the tribe about them; but in the subsequent Indian wars they lived in perpetual fear and agitation. The town was surrounded with palisadoes, "the meeting-house" was fortified, as were most of the private houses, and several forts were built within the town. Still their dwellings were often burnt, their women and children carried into captivity, and their time was divided between war and agriculture.

Outlet of Niagara River

THIS view is taken from the American side, and presents the *debouchure* of the waters of Niagara into Lake Ontario, from a point of great advantage. The vastness of the lake beyond, the tremendous agony which the still foaming waters have just escaped at Niagara, and the remoter journey of three thousand miles by which they have sought the sea from their fountains in the west, form a back-ground of imagination to this view, which, realised on the spot, give it a very thrilling interest. It is in itself, however, a landscape of unusually bold character; and the lofty and curving banks of the river are in keeping with its powerful flow, and the immense volume it pours into the lake.

Fort Niagara, on the opposite side, was erected by the French so late as 1751, and was looked upon by them as the key to all these inland seas. They had possession of it about eight years. In the beginning of July, 1759, General Prideaux, with his troops, reinforced by the Indian auxiliaries under Sir William Johnson, advanced to Niagara without the least hinderance—the enemy here not being in sufficient force to throw any impediments in the way. About the middle of July he commenced the siege, which he carried on with great vigour till the twentieth, when he was killed in the trenches. Sir William Johnson, who succeeded him, pressed the siege with great vigour. The enemy, alarmed with the apprehension of losing a place of such importance, resolved to make a last effort for its relief. For this purpose, they assembled about twelve hundred men, drawn from Venango, Presque Isle, and Detroit; and these, with some Indian auxiliaries, were detached, under the command of M. d'Aubry, on an attempt to reinforce the garrison. Sir William Johnson having received intelligence of their design, made a disposition to intercept them in their march. He accordingly detached a considerable body of troops for this service, who, falling in with the enemy very near the lines of the besiegers, a battle was fought, which resulted in the entire defeat of the French, with the capture of their commander, and most of his officers. This battle happened the twenty-fourth of July, and was fought in sight of the French garrison at Niagara. Sir William Johnson immediately after sent Major Harvey to the commandant of the fort, with an order, exhorting him to surrender, which being complied with, the garrison, consisting of about six hundred men, surrendered prisoners of war.

The following letter from Sir William Johnson, reporting his victory, is preserved in the Historical Journal kept by Captain Knox, and printed at the time:—

[17]

THE OUTLET OF NIAGARA RIVER

(LAKE ONTARIO IN THE DISTANCE)

"I have the honour to acquaint you, by Lieutenant Moncrief, that Niagara surrendered to his Majesty's arms, on the twenty-fifth instant. A detachment of twelve hundred men, with a number of Indians, under the command of Messieurs Aubry and Signery, collected from Detroit, Venango, and Presqu'-Isle, made an attempt to reinforce the garrison, the twenty-fourth in the morning; but as I had intelligence of them, I made a disposition to intercept them. The evening before, I ordered the light infantry and piquets to take post on the road upon our left, leading from Niagara Falls to the fort; in the morning, I reinforced these with two companies of grenadiers, and part of the forty-sixth regiment. The action began about half an hour after nine; but they were so well received by the troops in front, and the Indians on their flank, that, in an hour's time, the whole was completely ruined, and all their officers made prisoners, among whom are M. d'Aubry, de Signery, Marin, Repentini, to the number of seventeen. I cannot ascertain the number killed, they are so dispersed among the woods; but their loss is great. As this happened under the eyes of the garrison, I thought proper to send my last summons to the commanding officer, for his surrendering, which he listened to. I inclose you the capitulation: M. Moncrief will inform you of the state of our ammunition and provisions; I hope care will be taken to forward an immediate supply of both to Oswego. As the troops that were defeated yesterday were drawn from those posts which lie in General Stanwig's route, I am in hopes it will be of the utmost consequence to the success of his expedition. The public stores of the garrison, that can be saved from the Indians, I shall order the Assistant Quarter-Master General, and the Clerk of the stores, to take an account of, as soon as possible. As all my attention at present is taken up with the Indians, that the capitulation I have agreed to may be observed, your Excellency will excuse my not being more particular. Permit me to assure you, in the whole progress of the siege, which was severe and painful, the officers and men behaved with the utmost cheerfulness and bravery. I have only to regret the loss of General Prideaux and Colonel Johnson; I endeavoured to pursue the late General's vigorous measures, the good effects of which he deserved to enjoy."

THE PALISADES—HUDSON RIVER

The Palisades—Hudson River

THE first feature of the celebrated banks of the Hudson, which arrests the eye of the traveller after leaving New York, is this singular wall of rock, extending as far onward as he can see, and forming a bold barricade against the river on the side of New Jersey. This singular precipice varies in height from fifty to two hundred feet, and presents a naked front of columnar strata, which gives it its descriptive name. The small sloops which lie along under the shore, loading with building stone from its base, and an occasional shed, diminished to the size of a dog-kennel, across the breadth of the river, are the only marks of life and habitation it presents to the traveller's eye.

With most persons, to mention the Palisades is to recall only the confusion of a steamer's deck, just off from the wharf, with a freight of seven or eight hundred souls hoping to "take tea" in Albany. The scene is one of inextricable confusion, and it is not till the twenty miles of the Palisades are well passed, that the bewildered passenger knows rightly whether his wife, child, or baggage, whichever may be his tender care, is not being left behind at the rate of fifteen miles in the hour.

I have often, when travelling alone, (for "reflection with folded arms" consorts only with the childless and baggageless bachelor), I have often flung my valise into a corner, and sure that the whole of my person and personal effects are under way, watched the maniform embarrassments and troubles that beset the uninitiated voyager on the Hudson. Fifteen minutes before the starting of the boat, there is not a passenger on board; "time is moving," and the American counting it as part of the expense, determines to pay only "on demand." He arrives on the narrow pier at the same instant with seven hundred men, ladies, and children, besides lapdogs, crammed baskets, uncut novels, and baggage for the whole. No commissioner in the world would guarantee to get all this freight on board in the given time, and yet it is done, to the daily astonishment of newspaper hawkers, orange-women, and penny-a-liners watching for dreadful accidents. The plank is drawn in, the wheels begin to paw like foaming steeds impatient to be off, the bell rings as if it was letting down the steps of the last hackney-coach, and away darts the boat, like half a town suddenly slipping off and taking a walk on the water. The "hands," (who follow their nomenclature literally, and have neither eyes nor bowels) trip up all the little children and astonished maids, in coiling up the hawser; the black head-waiter rings a hand-bell as if he were crazy, exhorting "them passengers as hasn't settled to step to the Cap'n's office, *and* settle," and angry people who have lost sight of their portmanteaus, and selfish people who *will not* get up to let the young gentleman see if his penny trumpet is not under them, play in a real-life farce better than Keeley or Liston. A painted notice and a very fat black woman in the door-way, inform the gentleman who has not seen his wife since the boat started, and is not at all sure that she is on board, that "no gentleman is permitted to enter the ladies' cabin," and spite of his dreadful uncertainty, he is obliged to trust to this dark Hebe to find her, among three hundred ladies, by description, and amuses all the listeners with his inventory of her dress, features, and general appearance. The negress disappears, is called twenty ways in twenty seconds, and an hour after, the patient husband sees the faithless messenger pass with a glass of lemonade, having utterly forgotten him and the lady in the black bonnet and grey eyes, who may be, for ought he knows to the contrary, wringing her hands at that moment on the wharf at New York. By this time, the young ladies are tired of looking at the Palisades, and have taken out their novels, the old gentlemen are poring over their damp newspapers, and the captain has received his fourteen hundred or two thousand dollars, locked up his office, and gone up to smoke with the black funnel and the engineer. The broad waters of the Tappan Sea open before the flying cut-water; those who have never been up the river before, think of poor André as they pass Tappan and Tarrytown, and those who love gentle worth and true genius begin to look out for Sleepy Hollow, and the house of Washington Irving. It is a quiet little spot, buried in trees, and marked with an old Dutch vane. May his latter days, when they shall come, find there the reverence and repose which are his due!

The Rapids Above the Falls of Niagara

DURING the last Canadian war, General Putnam, the famous partisan soldier, made the first descent upon Goat Island. A wager had been laid, that no man in the army would dare to cross the Rapids from the American side; and with the personal daring for which he was remarkable, above all the men of that trying period, he undertook the feat. Selecting the four stoutest and most resolute men in his corps, he embarked in a batteau just above the island, and

THE RAPIDS ABOVE THE FALLS OF NIAGARA

with a rope attached to the ring-bolt, which was held by as many muscular fellows on the shore, he succeeded by desperate rowing in reaching his mark. He most easily towed back, and the feat has since been rendered unnecessary by the construction of the bridge from which the accompanying view is taken.

Many years since, a Tonemanta chief, after a violent quarrel with his squaw, lay down to sleep in his canoe. The little bark was moored just out of the tide of Niagara river, at the inlet to the creek which takes its name from his tribe, and the half-drunken chief, with his bottle of rum in his bosom, was soon fast asleep among the sedges. The enraged squaw, finding, after several attempts, that she could not get possession of the bottle without waking him, unmoored the canoe, and swimming out of the creek, pushed it before her into the swift tide of the river. She then turned its head toward the Falls and re-gained the shore. The canoe floated down very tranquilly till it struck the first ridge of the rapids. Nearly upset by the shock, she was flung from side to side by the contending waters, and the chief started from his slumbers. The first glance convinced him that effort would be vain; and keeping the canoe up-right with instinctive skill, he drew his bottle from his bosom, and put it to his lips. The draught lasted him till he reached the turn of the cataract; and, as the canoe shot over the glassy curve, he was seen sitting upright, with his head thrown back, and both hands pressed to the bottle.

Not long ago it was advertised that, on a certain day, a large vessel, freighted with two or three menageries of wild beasts, and some domestic animals, would be sent down the Rapids. The announcement drew together an immense concourse of people from every part of the country, and, at the time specified, the vessel was towed into the stream and abandoned, with the animals loose on her deck. She kept her way very gallantly till she got to the Rapids, when, after a tremendous pitching for a few minutes, she stuck fast in the cleft of a rock. The bears and monkeys were seen in the rigging, but the other animals, not being climbers, were invisible from the shore. To the great disappointment of many thousands, she went over the Falls in the night, and of her whole crew the sole survivor was a goose, who was picked up the next day with no damage but a broken wing, and has since been exhibited as a curiosity.

The Rapids are far from being the least interesting feature of Niagara. There is a violence and a power in their foaming career, which is seen in no other phenomenon of the same class. Standing on the bridge which connects Goat Island with the Main, and looking up towards Lake Erie, the leaping crests of the rapids form the horizon, and it seems like a battle-charge of tempestuous waves, animated and infuriated, against the sky. No one who has not seen this spectacle of turbulent grandeur can conceive with what force the swift and overwhelming waters are flung upwards. The rocks, whose soaring points show above the surface, seem tormented with some supernatural agony, and fling off the wild and hurried waters, as if with the force of a giant's arm. Nearer the plunge of the Fall, the Rapids become still more agitated; and it is almost impossible for the spectator to rid himself of the idea, that they are conscious of the abyss to which they are hurrying, and struggle back in the very extremity of horror. This propensity to invest Niagara with a soul and human feelings is a common effect upon the minds of visitors, in every part of its wonderful phenomena. The torture of the Rapids, the clinging curves with which they embrace the small rocky islands that live amid the surge, the sudden calmness at the brow of the cataract, and the infernal writhe and whiteness with which they reappear, powerless from the depths of the abyss, all seem, to the excited imagination of the gazer, like the natural effects of impending ruin, desperate resolution, and fearful agony, on the minds and frames of mortals.

Saratoga Lake

A SINGULAR feature of American scenery is the great number and beauty of its small fresh-water lakes, from one mile to twenty in circumference, fed universally by subjacent and living springs, with outlet rivers which carry off all that is superfluous, and with shores always richly fringed with foliage, and oftenest hilly and picturesque. They lie in the midst of the wild forests, like silver mirrors, tranquil and lovely, mingling a refinement and an elegance with the bold character of the scenery, which contrasts, like Una, with the couchant Lion. Most of them are feeders to the great lakes and rivers. There are counted fifteen which send their waters into Lake Ontario, from the side of New York alone,—a fact which gives a fair idea of their numbers, while it shows the resources, so difficult to conceive, of those vast plains of water.

Saratoga Lake must depend for celebrity on the campaigns of General Burgoyne, and its fish dinners. Of the first, the history has been written and

SARATOGA LAKE

read. Of the last, the traditions are oral; but while appetite returns, and trout venture to the angler's hook, the memory will be renewed. The Springs are distant only three miles; and hither drive the more luxurious visitors of Saratoga, to dine in parties,—those coming early who prefer sympathy with the catastrophe of the fish, and broiling themselves, during the morning, in a flat-bottomed boat among the trout-catchers.

There was a gay party on this lake some six or eight years since, fishing and airing their wit, under the auspices of a belle of some fame and authority. The boat had been pulled into water of five or six feet depth, on the eastern side, and the ladies sat at the ends of their rods, about forty yards from the shore, watching their floats, which lay on the surface of the glassy water like sleeping flies, but, as the old fisherman in the bow could have told them, laughing loud enough to fright even the eels from their appetites. After several hours' bobbing, without bite or nibble, the belle above mentioned discovered that her hook was caught at the bottom. She rose in the stern, to draw it up more easily, and, all the party leaning over at the same time, she lost her balance, and, in falling overboard, upset the boat. For the first minute it was a scene of some terror. The gentlemen were very near drowning the ladies, and the ladies the gentlemen; but the old fisherman, a tall fellow who knew the ground, and was just within his depth, quietly walked about, picking them up one by one, and giving them a hold of the inverted gunwale, and so pushed them safely to shore, suspended round the boat, like herrings on a hoop. Nobody caught cold; other people had caught fish; they dined merrily, and the principal actor in the scene has since been known by the sobriquet of the *diving belle*.

There is an Indian superstition attached to this lake, which probably had its source in its remarkable loneliness and tranquillity. The Mohawks believed that its stillness was sacred to the Great Spirit, and that, if a human voice uttered a sound upon its waters, the canoe of the offender would instantly sink. A story is told of an Englishwoman, in the early days of the first settlers, who had occasion to cross this lake with a party of Indians, who, before embarking, warned her most impressively of the spell. It was a silent, breathless day, and the canoe shot over the smooth surface of the lake like a shadow. About a mile from the shore, near the centre of the lake, the woman, willing to convince the savages of the weakness of their superstition, uttered a loud cry. The countenances of the Indians fell instantly to the deepest gloom. After a moment's pause, however, they redoubled their exertions, and, in frowning silence, drove the light bark like an arrow over the waters. They

[27]

reached the shore in safety, and drew up the canoe, and the woman rallied the chief on his credulity. "The Great Spirit is merciful," answered the scornful Mohawk; "He knows that a white woman cannot hold her tongue."

Saratoga Lake is eight miles in length, and a little over two miles broad. It is about eight miles west of Hudson River, which receives its outlet waters under the name of Fish Creek. The same stream, before its entrance into the lake, is called by the sesquipedalian title of Kayaderosseras River. With its pretty maiden name it loses its beauty, and flows forth from its union with the lake, in a dull and murky stream, and so drops sluggishly into the Hudson. Ah! many an edifying homily has been read from a blinder text.

The Colonnade of Congress Hall
(Saratoga Springs)

CONGRESS HALL has for many years held the palm of fashion among the rival Hotels of Saratoga. It is an immense wooden caravanserai, with no pretensions to architecture beyond what is seen in the drawing, and built with the sole view of affording the average accommodations of packed herrings to an indefinite number of persons. The roominess and liberal proportions of the Colonnade are one of those lies of architecture common to the hotels of this country. The traveller passes from the magnificent promise of the outside, to a chamber ten feet by four, situated in a remote gallery, visited once a day by the "boots" and chambermaid. His bed, chair, and wash-stand, resemble those articles as seen in penitentiaries; and if he chance to be ill at night, he might die like a Pagan, "without bell or candle." The arrangements of the house are, of necessity, entirely gregarious. A bell rings at half-past seven in the morning, at which every body who intends to breakfast, *must* get up; another bell at eight, to the call of which, if he prefers hot omelette to cold, he must be punctual. Dinner and tea exact the same promptitude; and the latter,

COLONNADE OF CONGRESS HALL
(SARATOGA SPRINGS)

which in other countries is a thing of no circumstance or importance, be-comes, where you dine at two, a meal not willingly missed. "Tea" is at six or half past, and consists of cold meats, hot rolls, Indian cakes, all other kinds of cakes, all kinds of berries, pies, sweetmeats, and jellies, coffee and tea. This is not a matter to be slighted after a fast of four hours; and home hurry beaux and belles from their abbreviated drives, with a loss of sentiment and sun-set, and with profit to the keepers of stables, who let their horses "by the afternoon."

After tea, the gentlemen who dressed for dinner and "undressed" for their drive, dress once more for the evening, and the spacious Colonnade is thronged with the five hundred guests of the house, who pace to and fro for an hour, or, if it is a ball night, till the black band have made an orchestra of the tables in the dining-room, and struck up "Hail, Columbia!" A hoop, bound with ever-greens, and stuck full of candles, hangs in the centre of the hall (*ci-devant* dining-room); an audience of all the negroes in the establishment sweetens the breath of heaven as it steals in at the windows; and, as the triumphant music returns a second time to the refrain, the lady Patroness enters on the arm of the gentleman who has the most stock in the Bank, followed in couples by all the gentlemen and ladies who intend to dance or play wall-flower. The black musicians "vex their instruments," and keep time with their heads and heels, as if all their extremities had been hired; the beaux who were inter-rupted in their declarations by the last *chassé*, (if they wish to go on with it,) lead out their partners to take the air and a cold,—perhaps a heart,—on the Colonnade; and at eleven, champagne goes round for the ladies, and the gentlemen take "summat to drink" at "the bar;" after which the candles burn brighter, and every body is much more agreeable.

Congress Hall is built very near the principal Spring, which lies in the westerly edge of a swamp. It was first discovered by the tracks of the deer, who frequented it so much as to wear paths to it from the surrounding woods. The mineral water is highly medicinal, and is not unpleasant to the taste. It formerly rose in the bed of a small brook, but it is now hid under the floor of an open colonnade, and discharges nearly a gallon a minute. The disengaged gas breaks through in limpid globules, giving to the surface the appearance of an active simmer. Here, before breakfast, creep the few who come to Sara-toga for health; and here, before dinner, saunter those who are in need of a walk, or who wish a tonic for the coming meal. A busy varlet, with a capital of a hooked stick and two tin tumblers, drives a thriving trade here, fishing up the sparkling waters at a cent a glass, for all comers. When the gentleman has swallowed his muriate and four carbonates* in proper quantity, a smooth serpentine walk leads to the summit of a prettily wooded hill, where he may either grind himself round a circular rail-road in a self-moving chair, or ramble off to the shade, for a little meditation.

* The analysis of a gallon of Congress water is thus stated:—

Muriate of soda	471.6	grains.
Carbonate of lime	178.474	—
Carbonate of soda	16.5	—
Carbonate of magnesia . .	3.356	—
Carbonate of iron	6.168	—
Total	676.000	—

Albany

ALBANY is the second city in the State of New York, in population, wealth, and commerce. It stands on the west bank of the Hudson, and about one hundred and forty-five miles from New York by the river, and near the head of sloop navigation. It is built just over the pitch of an extensive plain, lying between the Mohawk and the Hudson, and has very much the look of a city sliding down hill.

The history of Albany is not very definite, touching its first settlement. The probability seems, that, in 1614, the Dutch erected a fort and trading-house on an island just below the city; and also, in nine years after, a fort, which they called Fort Orange, on the present site. It would appear to have been canonically christened, and has been called at different periods Auralia, Beverwyck, and Williamstadt. "All this time," says the historian, "it was known also by the name of '*The Fuyck*.'" The Indian appellation in which it rejoiced was Schaunaugh-ta-da, or *Once the pine plains*.

Albany is the residence of several of the oldest and wealthiest families in the State; but except this, it is a mere centre of transit—the channel through which passes the vast tide of commerce and travel to the north and west. The Erie and Champlain canals here meet the Hudson; and that which is passed up by this long arm from the sea, is handed over to the great lakes by the other two,—as if old Enceladus had been turned into a "worky," and stood with his long arms between salt water and fresh.

The association most people have with Albany, is that of having lost a port-

ALBANY

manteau there. The north-river steam-boats land you with from three to seven hundred passengers upon a narrow pier, in the dusk of the evening, where you find from three to seven hundred individuals (more or less), each of whom seems to have no other object in life, than to persuade you, at that particular instant, to go by a certain conveyance, or to stop at a certain hotel. Upon setting your foot on shore, you find yourself among five or six infuriated gentlemen, two or three of whom walk backward before you, and all talking at the pitch which is necessary to drown the deepening hiss of the escape-valve and each other's voices. If you attempt to reason, you have no sooner satisfied the aforesaid six, that your route, your baggage, and your choice of an hotel, are matters in which they cannot be of the slightest assistance to you, than six more take their places, who must be satisfied as well; and so on in the same order. If you resolutely shut your lips, silence is taken for consent; your baggage is seized, and disappears before you have recovered from your amazement; and your only course is to follow the most importunate of your remaining five persecutors to an hotel; advertise in the next morning's paper for your portmanteau; and wait in Albany till it returns from Canada or Lake Erie, or till you are reconciled to its loss.

One of the most amusing scenes in the world, if it were not so distressing, is to see a large family of rather respectable emigrants landed by the steamer in Albany. It is their first step inland; and with all the confidence of those who are accustomed to countries where a man's person and property are outwardly respected, they yield their children and baggage to the persuasive gentlemen who assure them that all is right; and if a passing wonder crosses the mind of the sufferer, that his route should be so immediately comprehended by a perfect stranger, it is chased away the next moment by his surprise at the scene of bustle and confusion. At the end of five minutes the crowd thins a little, and he looks about for his family and effects. A stage coach is dashing off at top-speed in one direction, with his eldest daughter stretching out of the window, and crying in vain that there is some mistake; his two youngest are on board a steam-boat just off from the pier, and bound eight miles further up the river: the respectable part of his baggage has entirely disappeared; and nothing but his decrepit grandmother and the paternal bedstead (both indebted for their escape to being deaf, and not portable,) remain of his family and chattels. For his comfort, the gentry around inform him that his children may be got back in a day or two, and he may find his baggage somewhere on his route to the west—offering, for a consideration not very trifling, to send off an express for either one or the other.

Albany is the seat of government, and has a State House, of which the historian of New York remarks: "In the structure of this edifice, the rules of architecture, Composite, have been violated." Lately, however, a taste for a better style of architecture seems to prevail; and in North Pearl-street we lately noticed a façade (we think, of a new church,) in a very pure and beautiful style. The private houses of Albany are built, many of them, very expensively; and the city is remarkable for its hospitality.

Crow Nest, from Bull Hill, West Point

IT is true of the Hudson, as of all other rivers, that, to be seen to advantage, it should form the middle, not the foreground of the picture. Those who go to Albany by steam have something the same idea of the scenery of West Point, that an inside passenger may have of the effect of the Brighton coach at top-speed. It is astonishing how much foreground goes for in landscape; and there are few passes of scenery where it is more naturally beautiful than those of the Hudson. In the accompanying drawing, the picturesque neighbourhood of Undercliff, the seat of Colonel Morris, lies between the river and the artist, and directly opposite stands the peak of Crow Nest, mentioned in the description of West Point.

Crow Nest is one of the most beautiful mountains of America for shape, verdure, and position; and when the water is unruffled, and the moon sits on his summit, he looks like a monarch crowned with a single pearl. This is the scene of the first piece-work of fancy which has come from the practical brain of America,—the poem of The Culprit Fay. The opening is so descriptive of the spot, that it is quite in place here; and to those who have not seen the poem (as most European readers have not) it will convey an idea of a production which, in my opinion, treads close on the heels of the Midsummer Night's Dream:—

"'Tis the middle watch of a summer's night,—
The earth is dark, but the heavens are bright
Nought is seen in the vault on high,
But the moon, and the stars, and the cloudless sky,
And the flood which rolls its milky hue,—
A river of light on the welkin blue.

CROW NEST FROM BULL HILL, WEST POINT

The moon looks down on old Crow Nest,
She mellows the shades on his shaggy breast

And seems his huge grey form to throw
In a silver cone on the wave below;
His sides are broken by spots of shade,
By the walnut boughs and the cedar made,
And through their clustering branches dark
Glimmers and dies the firefly's spark,—
Like starry twinkles that momently break
Through the rifts of the gathering tempest rack.

The stars are on the moving stream,
And fling, as its ripples gently flow,
A burnish'd length of wavy beam,
In an eel-like, spiral line below.
The winds are whist, and the owl is still,
The bat in the shelvy rock is hid;
And nought is heard on the lonely hill
But the cricket's chirp and the answer shrill
    Of the gauze-wing'd raty-did;
And the plaints of the mourning whip-poor-will,
Who mourns unseen, and ceaseless sings
Ever a note of wail and wo,
Till morning spreads her rosy wings,
And earth and skies in her glances glow.

'Tis the hour of fairy ban and spell:
The wood-tick has kept the minutes well;
He has counted them all with click and stroke
Deep in the heart of the mountain-oak;
And he has awakened the sentry-elve,
Who sleeps with him in the haunted tree,
To bid him ring the hour of twelve,
And call the fays to their revelry.

*   *   *   *   *   *

They come from beds of lichen green,
They creep from the mullen's velvet screen;
Some on the backs of beetles fly
From the silver tops of moon-touch'd trees,
Where they swing in their cob-web hammocks high,
And rock'd about in the evening breeze;
Some from the hum-bird's downy nest,
They had driven him out by elfin power,
And pillow'd on plumes of his rainbow breast,
Had slumber'd there till the charmed hour;
Some had lain in a scarp of the rock,
With glittering ising-stars inlaid,

[36]

And some had open'd the four-o'clock,
And stolen within its purple shade:
And now they throng the moonlight glade,
Above—below—on every side,
Their little minion forms arrayed
In the tricksy pomp of fairy pride."

The general assembly of the fairies is at last complete, and they proceed to the trial of the culprit fay, who has extinguished his elfin lamp and paralyzed his wings by a love for a mortal maid. He is condemned to penances, which are most exquisitely described, and constitute the greater part of the poem; and he finally expiates his sins, and is forgiven. There is a fineness of description, and a knowledge of the peculiarities of American nature, in birds, fishes, flowers, and the phenomena of this particular region, which constitute this little poem a book of valuable information as well as an exquisite work of fancy.

Just under Crow Nest, buried in the heavy leaves of a ravine, springs a waterfall like a Naiad from the depths of the forest, and plunges down into the river. The rambles in and about its neighbourhood are cool and retired; and it is a favourite place for lovers from New York, who run up in the steamer in three hours, and find the honeymoon goes swimmingly off there,—the excellent hotel within half a mile supplying the *real*, without which the *ideal* is found to be very trumpery. The marble tomb of a cadet, who was killed by the bursting of a gun, forms a picturesque object, and gives a story to the spot.

View Below Table Rock

THE interest of the view under this impending cliff is somewhat heightened by the probability that it will fall into the abyss sometime within the next six months. Since the fall of the most projecting part of it, two or three winters since, a large and very deep crack has widened around the remaining area of the platform above, and it is thought that it will scarce survive the next frost. At present, spite of the threat, troops of ladies and gentlemen crowd its broad summit at all hours, walking, drawing, gazing, and philandering, in the fullest confidence that rocks have bases. And so it will go on, probably, till the "one (thunder) too many" hammers through its crack of doom.

The path leading behind the sheet of Horse Shoe Fall, runs close under the cliff of Table Rock; and between the spray and the small rivulets that trickle over the sharp edge, or find their way out of the numerous crevices on the face of the precipice, it is as wet as the lawn blessed with "perpetual rain" by the Witch of Atlas. We were of a considerable party that visited this Naiad's palace in the close of the last summer. A small shanty stands at the head of the staircase, kept by a very civil Englishman, who, with the assistance of his daughter and two sons, keeps a reading-room and registry, vends curious walking-sticks cut at Niagara, minerals, spars, and stuffed scorpions, besides officiating as guide under the Falls, and selling brandy and water to those who survive the expedition.

The ladies of the party were taken into a small apartment to change their dresses preparatory to their descent; and the two smart lads of our conductor soon metamorphosed their cavaliers into as brigand-looking a set of tatter-demallions as could be found in the Abruzzi. Rough duck trowsers, long jackets of green painted cloth, oil-skin hats, and flannel shirts,—the whole turn-out very much like the clothes of the drowned exhibited for recognition at the Morgue in Paris,—constituted our habiliments. The difference of the female costume consisted in the substitution of a coarse petticoat for the trowsers, and a string tied over the broad-brimmed hat;— and, flattery aside, our friends would have looked at home in Billingsgate. Quite the most formidable part of the expedition, to them, was passing in review before some twenty curious persons collected on the way.

The guide went before, and we followed close under the cliff. A cold clammy wind blew strong in our faces from the moment we left the shelter of the staircase; and a few steps brought us into a pelting, fine rain, that penetrated every opening of our dresses, and made our foothold very slippery and difficult. We were not yet near the sheet of water we were to walk through; but one or two of the party gave out and returned, declaring it was impossible to breathe; and the rest, imitating the guide, bent nearly double to keep the beating spray from their nostrils, and pushed on, with enough to do to keep sight of his heels. We arrived near the difficult point of our progress; and in the midst of a confusion of blinding gusts, half deafened, and more than half drowned, the guide stopped to give us a hold of his skirts and a little counsel. All that could be heard amid the thunder of the cataract beside us was an injunction to push on when it got to the worst, as it was shorter to get beyond

VIEW BELOW TABLE ROCK

the sheet than to go back; and with this pleasant statement of our dilemma, we faced about with the longest breath we could draw, and encountered the enemy. It may be supposed that every person who has been dragged through the column of water which obstructs the entrance to the cavern behind this cataract, has a very tolerable idea of the pains of drowning. What is wanting in the density of the element is more than made up by the force of the contending winds, which rush into the mouth, eyes, and nostrils, as if flying from a water-fiend. The "courage of worse behind" alone persuades the gasping sufferer to take one desperate step more.

It is difficult enough to breathe within; but with a little self-control and management, the nostrils may be guarded from the watery particles in the atmosphere, and then an impression is made upon the mind by the extraordinary pavilion above and around, which never loses its vividness. The natural bend of the falling cataract, and the backward shelve of the precipice, form an immense area like the interior of a tent, but so pervaded by discharges of mist and spray, that it is impossible to see far inward. Outward the light struggles brokenly through the crystal wall of the cataract; and when the sun shines directly on its face, it is a scene of unimaginable glory. The footing is rather unsteadfast, a small shelf composed of loose and slippery stones; and the abyss below boils like—it is difficult to find a comparison. On the whole, this undertaking is rather pleasanter to remember than to achieve.

Lake Winnipiseogee

(The Beautiful Lake of the Indians, New Hampshire)

THE Indian fights of the celebrated Captain Lovewell, which took place near the borders of this lake, were not the only feats of courage the early inhabitants of this part of the country were called upon to display. Bears, wolves, and catamounts, were enemies as constantly found in their path as the unfriendly Indian, and were almost as dangerous. The descriptions contained in the grave historical records of the State, of encounters, with bears more particularly, are sometimes sufficiently amusing; and, indeed, whatever the peril to the man, there is a conventional drollery about the bear which throws a

LAKE WINNIPISSEOGEE, FROM RED HILL

spice of fun into all his contests with mankind. This animal, in the early days of New Hampshire, often destroyed the husbandman's hopes by his depredations on the green maize, of the milky ear of which he is especially fond. Sweet fruits, honey, and other simple but "*toothsome*" productions of the orchard and farm, suited bruin equally well, and he had never recourse to animal food while these were to be procured. The kind of bear most mischievous in this way was the small American bear, with a long and pointed nose, remarkable for his alertness in ascending and descending trees. They were often found in hollow trunks, and in clefts of rocks, and were considered delicious meat by the hunters. Among the adventures with this class of their enemies recorded of the first settlers of the State, is an encounter of a Mr. Annis with a bear.

"One day, late in March," says the narrator, "the snow being deep, he mounted his snow-shoes, and in company with Abner Watkins and their dogs, set off towards the Mink Hills for a hunt, armed with an axe and gun. In the neighbourhood of the hills, the dogs were perceived to be very much excited with something in a ledge of rocks. Annis left his companion, Watkins, and ascended a crag twenty or thirty feet to where the dogs were, having no other weapon with him but his staff, which was pointed with iron. After exploring a little, he concluded there was no game there of more consequence than a hedge-hog or some other small animal, and being fatigued laid down in the snow on his back to rest, reclining his head upon the place he had been examining; he had but just laid down when he heard a snuffling under his ear; he started up, and turning round, found an old bear pressing her head up through the old leaves and snow which filled the mouth of her den; he thrust his spear-pointed staff at the bear's briskets, and thus held the bear which was pressing towards him at his staff's length distance, and called to his companion Watkins to come up with the axe and kill the bear, which, after some little time, was effected. After the action was over, Annis complained of Watkins' dilatoriness, but Watkins excused himself by saying he could not get his gun off, that he had snapt, snapt, snapt several times. Where did you take sight? said Annis, knowing that he was directly between him and the bear; *I took sight between your legs*, said Watkins."

Many years ago a cub bear was caught by a stout lad near the borders of Lake Winnipiseogee, carried into town, and after proper drilling, became the playfellow of the boys of the village, and often accompanied them to the school-house. After passing a few months in civilized society, he made his escape to the woods, and after a few years was almost forgotten. The school-house meantime had fallen from the schoolmaster's to the schoolmistress's hands, and in the room of large boys and girls learning to write and cipher, small boys and girls were taught in the same place knitting and spelling. One winter's day, after a mild fall of snow, the door had been left ajar by some urchin going out, when to the unutterable horror of the spectacled dame and her fourscore hopeful abecedarians, an enormous bear walked in, in the most familiar manner in the world, and took a seat by the fire. Huddling over the benches with what expedition they might, the children crowded about their schoolmistress, who had fled to the farthest corner of the room, and stood crying and pushing to escape the horror of being eaten first. The bear sat snuffing and warming himself by the fire, however, exhibiting great signs of satisfaction, but deferring his meal till he had warmed himself thoroughly. The screams of the children continued, but the school-house was far from any other habitation, and the bear did not seem at all embarrassed by the outcry. After sitting and turning himself about for some time, Bruin got up on his hind legs, and shoving to the door, began to take down, one by one, the hats, bonnets, and satchels, that hung on several rows of pegs behind it. His memory had not deceived him, for they contained, as of old, the children's dinners, and he had arrived before the recess. Having satisfied himself with their cheese, bread, pies, dough-nuts, and apples, Bruin smelt a little at the mistress's desk, but finding it locked, gave himself a shake of resignation, opened the door and disappeared. The alarm was given, and the amiable creature was pursued and killed,—very much to the regret of the townspeople, when it was discovered by some marks on his body that it was their old friend and playfellow.

KOSCIUSKO'S MONUMENT

Kosciusko's Monument

A PRETTY marble shaft stands on the edge of the broad highland esplanade of West Point, overlooking the most beautiful scene on the most beautiful river of our country. It commemorates the virtues of Kosciusko, who, during his second sojourn in America, lived at West Point, and cultivated his little garden, near the site of this tribute to his memory. Kosciusko's first laurels were gained in this country under Washington. He was educated in the military school at Warsaw, whence he was sent, as one of four, to complete his education at Paris. On his return to Poland, he had a commission given him, but, being refused promotion, he determined to come to America, and join the colonies in their struggle for independence. With letters from Dr. Franklin to General Washington, he presented himself to the great patriot, and was immediately appointed his aid-de-camp, and later he received the appointment to the engineers, with the rank of colonel. At the close of the war, having distinguished himself by his courage and skill, he returned to Poland, was appointed major-general in the army of the diet, and served as general of division under the younger Poniatowski. Finding, however, his efforts for freedom paralysed by the weakness or treachery of others, he gave in his resignation, and went into retirement at Leipsic. He was still there in 1793, when the Polish army and people gave signs of being in readiness for insurrection. All eyes were turned towards Kosciusko, who was at once chosen for their leader, and messengers were sent to him from Warsaw to acquaint him with the schemes and wishes of his compatriots. In compliance with the invitation, he proceeded towards the frontiers of Poland; but apprehensive of compromising the safety of those with whom he acted, he was about to defer his enterprise, and set off for Italy. He was fortunately persuaded to return, and, arriving at Cracow at the very time when the Polish garrison had expelled the Russian troops, he was chosen generalissimo, with all the power of a Roman dictator. He immediately published an act, authorizing insurrection against the foreign authorities, and proceeded to support Colonel Madalinski, who was pursued by the Russians. Having joined that officer, they gained their first victory, defeating the enemy with inferior numbers. His army now increased to nine thousand men, the insurrection extended to Warsaw, and in a few days the Russians were driven from that palatinate. He obtained some advantage over the enemy in one more contest, but the king of Prussia arriving to the assistance of the Russians, he was exposed to great personal danger, and suffered a defeat. From this period he waged a disadvantageous warfare against superior force, and at last at Maczienice (or Maniejornice), fifty miles from Warsaw, an overwhelming Russian force completely defeated Kosciusko. He fell from his horse wounded, saying *Finis Poloniæ*, and was made prisoner.

Kosciusko was sent to Russia, and confined in a fortress near St. Petersburgh, where he was kept till the accession of Paul I. This monarch, through real or affected admiration for the character of the great man, released him, and presented him with his sword: "*I have no longer occasion for a sword, since I have no longer a country,*" answered Kosciusko.

In 1797 he once more took his departure for the United States, where he was received with honour and warm welcome by the grateful people whose liberty he had aided to achieve. He was granted a pension by the government, and elected to the society of the Cincinnati. He returned to Europe the following year, bought an estate near Fontainebleau, and lived there till 1814. He removed again to Switzerland, and established himself at Soleure, where he died, in consequence of a fall with his horse over a precipice near Vevay. Among the last acts of his life, were the emancipation of the slaves on his own estate in Poland, and a bequest for the emancipation and education of slaves in Virginia.

Kosciusko was never married. His body was removed to Cracow, and deposited with great state in the tomb of the kings beneath the cathedral. The oldest officers were his bearers; two beautiful young girls with wreathes of oak leaves and cypress followed, and then came a long procession of the general staff, senate, clergy, and people. Count Wodsiki delivered a funeral oration on the hill of Wavel, and a prelate delivered an eloquent address in the church. The senate decreed that a lofty mound should be erected on the heights of Bronislawad. For three years men of every age and class toiled gratuitously at this work, and at last the *Mogila Kosziuszki*, the mound of Kosciusko, was raised to the height of 3000 feet! A serpentine path leads to the top, from which there is a noble view of the Vistula, and of the ancient city of the Polish kings. The small monument at West Point has less pretension, but it is the exponent of as deep a debt of gratitude, and of as grateful and universal honour to his memory.

Horse-Shoe Fall, at Niagara
(Seen from Goat Island)

NIAGARA is the outlet of several bodies of water, covering, it is estimated, 150,000 square miles! Dr. Dwight considers the Falls as part of the St. Lawrence, following that river back to the sources near the Mississippi; and, doing away with the intermediate names of St. Marie, Detroit, St. Clair, Iroquois, and Cataraqui, he traces its course through the lakes Superior, Huron, Erie, and Ontario, as the Rhone is followed through the Lake of Geneva, and the Rhine through Lake Constance. In this view the St. Lawrence is doubtless the first river in the world. It meets the tide of the sea four hundred miles from its mouth, which is ninety-five miles broad; and to this height fleets of men of war may ascend and find ample room for an engagement. Merchantmen of all sizes go up to Montreal, which is six hundred miles from the sea; and its navigation for three thousand miles is only interrupted in three places,— Niagara Falls, the rapids of the Iroquois, and the part called the river St. Marie. The St. Marie is navigable for boats, though not for larger vessels; a portage of ten miles (soon to be superseded by a ship canal) conveys merchandise around the Falls of Niagara, and the rapids of the Iroquois present so slight a hinderance, that goods are brought from Montreal to Queenston for nearly the same price as they would pay by unobstructed navigation.

It is necessary to remember the extent of the waters which feed Niagara, to conceive, when standing for an hour only on the projecting rocks, how this almighty wonder can go on so long. Even then,—that these inland seas lie above, tranquil and unexhausted, scarce varying their high-water mark perceptibly, from year to year, yet supplying, for *every* hour, the "ninety millions of tons," which, it is estimated, plunge over the cataract,—it affords you a standard for the extent of those lakes, to which the utmost stretch of the mind seems scarcely competent.

The accompanying view from Goat Island is of course only partial, as the American fall is entirely left out of the picture. The Horse-shoe Fall, as a single object, however, is unquestionably the sublimest thing in nature. To know that the angle of the cataract, from the British shore to the tower, is near half a mile in length; that it falls so many feet with so many tons of water a minute; or even to see it, as here, admirably represented by the pencil; conveys no idea to the reader of the impression produced on the spectator. One of the most remarkable things about Niagara is entirely lost in the drawing—its *motion*. The visitor to Niagara should devote one day exclusively to the observation of

HORSE-SHOE FALL, NIAGARA—WITH THE TOWER

this astonishing feature. The broad flood glides out of Lake Erie with a confiding tranquillity that seems to you, when you know its impending destiny, like that of a human creature advancing irresistibly, but unconsciously, to his death. He embraces the bright islands that part his arms for a caress; takes into his bosom the calm tribute of the Tonewanta and Unnekuqua—small streams that come drowsing through the wilderness—and flows on, till he has left Lake Erie far behind, bathing the curving sides of his green shores with a surface which only the summer wind ruffles. The channel begins to descend; the still unsuspecting waters fall back into curling eddies along the banks, but the current in the centre flows smoothly still. Suddenly the powerful stream is flung with accumulated swiftness among broken rocks; and, as you watch it from below, it seems tossed with the first shock into the very sky. It descends in foam, and from this moment its agony commences. For three miles it tosses and resists, and, racked at every step by sharper rocks and increased rapidity, its unwilling and choked waves fly back, to be again precipitated onward, and at last reach the glossy curve, convulsed with supernatural horror. They touch the emerald arch, and in that instant, like the calm that follows the conviction of inevitable doom, the agitation ceases,—the waters pause,—the foam and resistance subside into a transparent stillness,—and slowly and solemnly the vexed and tormented sufferer drops into the abyss. Every spectator, every child, is struck with the singular deliberation, the unnatural slowness, with which the waters of Niagara take their plunge. The laws of gravitation seem suspended, and the sublimity of the tremendous gulf below seems to check the descending victim on the verge, as if it paused in awe.

THE NARROWS, AT STATEN ISLAND

The Narrows, at Staten Island

ALMOST any land looks beautiful after a long voyage; and it would not be surprising if the Narrows, oftenest seen and described by those who have just come off the passage of the Atlantic, should have this reputation. It does not require an eye long deprived of verdure, however, to relish the bold shores, the bright green banks, the clustering woods, and tasteful villas, which make up the charms of this lovely strait.

Busier waters than the Narrows could scarcely be found; and it is difficult to imagine, amid so much bustle and civilisation, the scene that presented itself to Hendrick Hudson, when the little *Halve-Mane* stole in on her voyage of discovery two hundred years ago. *Hoofden*, or the Highlands, as he then named the hills in this neighbourhood, "were covered with grass and wild-flowers, and the air was filled with fragrance." Groups of friendly natives, clothed in elk skins, stood on the beach, singing, and offering him welcome, and, anchoring his little bark, he explored with his boats the channel and inlets, and penetrated to the mouth of the river which was destined to bear his name. It appears, however, that the Indians on the Long Island side were less friendly; and in one of the excursions into the Bay of Manhattan, his boat was attacked by a party of twenty-nine savages of a ferocious tribe, and an English sailor, named Colman, was killed by an arrow-shot in the shoulder. Other unfriendly demonstrations from the same tribe, induced Hudson to leave his anchorage at Sandy Hook, and he drew in to the Bay of New York, which he found most safe and commodious, and where he still continued his intercourse with the Indians of Staten Island, receiving them on board his vessel, dressing them, to their extravagant delight, in red coats, and purchasing from them fish and fruits in abundance.

At this day there stands a villa on every picturesque point; a thriving town lies on the left shore; hospitals and private sanitary establishments extend their white edifices in the neighbourhood of the quarantine-ground; and between the little fleets of merchantmen, lying with the yellow flag at their peak, fly rapidly and skilfully a constant succession of steam-boats, gaily painted and beautifully modelled, bearing on their airy decks the population of one of the first cities of the world. Yet of Manhattan Island, on which New York is built, Hudson writes, only two hundred years ago, that "it was wild and rough; a thick forest covered the parts where anything would grow; its beach was broken and sandy, and full of inlets; its interior presented hills of stony and sandy alluvion, masses of rock, ponds, swamps, and marshes."

[51]

The gay description which an American would probably give of the Narrows,— the first spot of his native land seen after a tedious voyage,—would probably be in strong contrast with the impression it produces on the emigrant, who sees in it only the scene of his first difficult step in a land of exile. I remember noting this contrast with some emotion, on board the packet-ship in which I was not long ago a passenger from England. Among the crowd of emigrants in the steerage, was the family of a respectable and well-educated man, who had failed as a merchant in some small town in England, and was coming, with the wreck of his fortune, to try the back-woods of America. He had a wife, and eight or ten very fine children, the eldest of whom, a delicate and pretty girl of eighteen, had contributed to sustain the family under their misfortunes at home, by keeping a village school. The confinement had been too much for her, and she was struck with consumption—a disease which is peculiarly fatal in America. Soon after leaving the British Channel, the physician on board reported her to the captain as exceedingly ill, and suffering painfully from the close air of the steerage; and by the general consent of the cabin passengers, a bed was made up for her in the deck-house, where she received the kindest attention from the ladies on board; and with her gentle manners and grateful expressions of pleasure, soon made an interest in all hearts. As we made the land, the air became very close and hot; and our patient, perhaps from sympathy with the general excitement about her, grew feverish and worse, hourly. Her father, and a younger sister, sat by her, holding her hands and fanning her; and when we entered the Narrows with a fair wind, and every one on board, forgetting her in their admiration of the lovely scene, mounted to the upper deck, she was raised to the window, and stood with the bright red spot deepening on her cheek, watching the fresh green land without the slightest expression of pleasure. We dropped anchor, the boats were lowered, and as the steerage passengers were submitted to a quarantine, we attempted to take leave of her before going on shore. A fit of the most passionate tears, the paroxysms of which seemed almost to suffocate her, prevented her replying to us; and we left that poor girl surrounded with her weeping family, trying in vain to comfort her. Hers were feelings, probably, which are often associated with a remembrance of the Narrows.

View of the Capitol at Washington

THERE are many favourable points of view for this fine structure, standing, as it does, higher than the general level of the country. Besides those presented in the different drawings in this work, there are views from the distant eminences, which are particularly fine, in which the broad bosom of the Potomac forms the background. The effect of the building is also remarkably imposing when the snow is on the ground, and the whole structure, rising from a field of snow, with its dazzling whiteness, looks like some admirable creation of the frost. All architecture, however, is very much improved by the presence of a multitude of people, and the Capitol looks its best on the day of inauguration. The following description, written after viewing the ceremony of Mr. Van Buren's induction into office, will give an idea of the effect of this solemnity on the architecture:—

"The sun shone out of heaven without a cloud on the inaugural morning. The air was cold, but clear and life-giving, and the broad avenues of Washington for once seemed not too large for the thronging population. The crowds who had been pouring in from every direction for several days before, ransacking the town for but a shelter from the night, were apparent on the spacious side walks, and the old campaigners of the winter seemed but a thin sprinkling among the thousands of new and strange faces. The sun shone alike on the friends and opponents of the new administration; and, as far as one might observe in a walk to the Capitol, all were made cheerful alike by its brightness. It was another augury, perhaps, and may foretell a more extended fusion under the light of the luminary new-risen. In a whole day, passed in a crowd composed of all classes and parties, I heard no remark that the president would have been unwilling to hear.

"I was at the Capitol a half-hour before the procession arrived, and had leisure to study a scene for which I was not at all prepared. The noble staircase of the east front of the building leaps over three arches; under one of which carriages pass to the basement door; and, as you approach from the gate, the eye cuts the ascent at right angles, and the sky, broken by a small spire at a short distance, is visible beneath. Broad stairs occur at equal distances, with corresponding projections, and from the upper platform rise the outer columns of the portico, with ranges of columns three deep extending back to the pilasters. I had often admired this front, with its many graceful columns and its superb flight of stairs, as one of the finest things I had seen in the world. Like the effect of the assembled population of Rome waiting to re-

VIEW OF THE CAPITOL AT WASHINGTON

ceive the blessing before the front of St. Peter's, however, the assembled crowd on the steps and at the base of the Capitol, heightened inconceivably the grandeur of the design. They were piled up like the people on the temples of Babylon in one of Martin's sublime pictures—every projection covered, and an inexpressible soul and character given by their presence to the architecture. Boys climbed about the bases of the columns, single figures stood on the posts of the surrounding railings in the boldest relief against the sky, and the whole thing was exactly what Paul Veronese would have delighted to draw.

"I was in the crowd thronging the opposite side of the court, and lost sight of the principal actors in this imposing drama till they returned from the Senate Chamber. A temporary platform had been laid and railed in on the broad stair which supports the portico, and, for all preparation for one of the most important and most meaning and solemn ceremonies on earth—for the inauguration of a chief magistrate over a republic of fifteen millions of freemen—the whole addition to the open air and the presence of the people, was a volume of Holy Writ. In comparing the impressive simplicity of this consummation of the wishes of a mighty people, with the ceremonial and hollow show which embarrass a corresponding event in other lands, it was impossible not to feel that the moral sublime was here—that a transaction so important, and of such extended and weighty import, could borrow nothing from drapery or decoration, and that the simple presence of the sacred volume, consecrating the act, spoke more thrillingly to the heart than the trumpets of a thousand heralds.

"The crowd of diplomatists and senators in the rear of the columns made way, and the ex-President and Mr. Van Buren advanced with uncovered heads. A murmur of feeling rose up from the moving mass below, and the infirm old man, emerged from a sick chamber which his physician had thought it impossible he should leave, bowed to the people, and, still uncovered in the cold air, took his seat beneath the portico. Mr. Van Buren then advanced, and with a voice remarkably distinct, and with great dignity, read his address to the people.

"When the address was closed, the Chief Justice advanced and administered the oath. As the book touched the lips of the new President, there arose a general shout, an expression of feeling common enough in other countries, but drawn with difficulty from an American assemblage. The sons and immediate friends of Mr. Van Buren then closed around him, the ex-President and others gave him the hand in congratulation, and the ceremony was over."

VIEW OF THE RUINS OF TICONDEROGA

View of the Ruins of Ticonderoga

THREE weeks before the first battle of the revolution at Lexington, an emissary was sent to Canada by the Committee of Correspondence in Boston, to ascertain the feelings of the people, and to make such reports as his observations might suggest. His first advice was that Ticonderoga should be seized as quickly as possible.

The "Green Mountain Boys" were at this time fresh from their resistance to the *new grants*, and were immediately fixed upon as the best force to achieve this object. The little army, already organized under the famous Ethan Allen, assembled at Castleton, and the main body, consisting of one hundred and forty men, marched directly to the shore of the lake, opposite Ticonderoga. It was important to have a guide who was acquainted with the ground around the fortress and the places of access. Allen made inquiries as to these points of Mr. Beman, a farmer residing near the lake, who answered that he seldom crossed the Ticonderoga, and was little acquainted with the particulars of its situation; but that his son, Nathan, a young lad, passed much of his time there in company with the boys of the garrison.

The boy was called, and appeared by his answers to be familiar with every nook in the fort, and every passage and by-path by which it could be approached. In the eye of Allen, he was the very person to thread out the best avenue; and by the consent of the father, and a little persuasion, he was engaged to be the guide of the party.

The next step was to procure boats, which were very deficient in number. Eighty-three men only had crossed when the day began to dawn; and while the boats were sent back for the rear division, Allen resolved to move immediately against the fort.

He drew up his men in three ranks, addressed them in a short harangue, and, placing himself at the head of the centre file, led them silently, but with a quick step, up the heights of the fortress. Before the sun rose, he had entered the gate, and formed his men on the parade between the barracks. As Allen passed the gate, a sentinel snapped his fusee at him, and then retreated under a covered way. Another sentinel made a thrust at an officer with his bayonet, and slightly wounded him, but Allen cut him over the head with his sword, and he threw down his musket and asked for quarter. Standing on the parade-ground they gave three huzzas and aroused the sleepers. Allen inquired the way to the commandant's apartment, hastily ascended the stairs, and called out with his stentorian voice at the door, ordering the astonished captain instantly to appear. Startled at so strange and unexpected a summons, he sprang from his bed and opened the door, when the first salutation of his boisterous and unseasonable visitor was an order immediately to surrender the fort. Rubbing his eyes, and trying to collect his scattered senses, the Frenchman asked by what authority he presumed to make such a demand. "In the name of the Great Jehovah and the Continental Congress!" replied Allen.

Not accustomed to hear much of the Continental Congress in this remote corner, nor to respect its authority when he did, the commandant began to speak; but Allen cut short the thread of his discourse by lifting his sword over his head, and reiterating the demand for an instant surrender. Having neither permission to argue, nor power to resist, Captain De la Place submitted, ordering his men to parade without arms, and the garrison was given up to the victors.

This surprise was effected about four o'clock in the morning on the 10th of May. The remainder of the troops arrived after the fort was taken, and the prisoners, consisting of a captain, a lieutenant, and forty-eight subalterns and privates, were sent on to Hartford under an escort.

As soon as the bustle was over, Allen sent off a detachment to take Crown Point, a small fortress higher up the lake. Strong head winds drove back the boats, and the party returned the same evening. The attempt was renewed a day or two afterwards, and the garrison, consisting of a serjeant and eleven men, were brought in prisoners.

The principal advantage of these captures, besides the possession of the posts, was the acquisition, at Ticonderoga, of one hundred and twenty pieces of cannon, some swivels, mortars, and small arms; and at Crown Point, of sixty-one cannon and some small stores.

The Green Mountain Boys were at this time under sentence of outlawry from the Provincial Government; but after the good service they had done at Ticonderoga, they were formed into a separate regiment, and permitted to nominate their own officers. Their services to the cause of Independence are well known.

View from Fort Putnam

THIS fort, which commands the military position of West Point, and which was considered so important during the revolutionary war, is now in ruins, and is visited by all travellers for the superb view which it affords of the sublime pass of the Highlands. This was the great key which Arnold's treachery intended to give into the hands of the English; and, associated with the memory of the unfortunate André, and with other painful events of the conspiracy, it possesses an interest which is wanting to other objects of the same description in our country.

Washington's visit of inspection to Fort Putnam, and the other redoubts on this side the river, was made only two or three hours before his discovery of the treason of Arnold, at that moment as he supposed in command at West Point. The commander-in-chief was expected to arrive the evening before, and had he done so, Arnold would probably never have escaped. Having accidentally met the French minister, M. de Lucerne, at Fishkill, however (eight miles above), he was induced to pass the night there for the purpose of some conference, and set off early in the morning on horseback, sending on a messenger to Mrs. Arnold that himself and suite would be with her to breakfast. Arriving opposite West Point, near a small redoubt called Fort Constitution, Washington turned his horse from the road. Lafayette, who was then in his suite, called out, "General, you are going in the wrong direction; you know Mrs. Arnold is waiting breakfast for us." "Ah," answered Washington, "I know you young men are all in love with Mrs. Arnold, and wish to get where she is as soon as possible. Go and take your breakfast with her, and tell her not to wait for me: I must ride down and examine the redoubts on this side the river." Two of the aides rode on, found breakfast waiting, and sat down at once with General Arnold and his family. While they were at table, a messenger came in with a letter for Arnold, which announced the capture of André, and the failure and betrayal, of course, of the whole conspiracy. Showing little or no emotion, though his life hung upon a thread, he merely said to one of his aides that his presence was required at West Point; and, leaving word for General Washington that he was called over the river, but would return immediately, he ordered a horse and sent for Mrs. Arnold to her chamber. He then informed her abruptly that they must part, possibly for ever, and that his life depended on his reaching the enemy's lines without delay. Struck with horror at this intelligence, she swooned and fell senseless. In that state he left her, hurried down stairs, mounted a horse belonging to one of his aides that

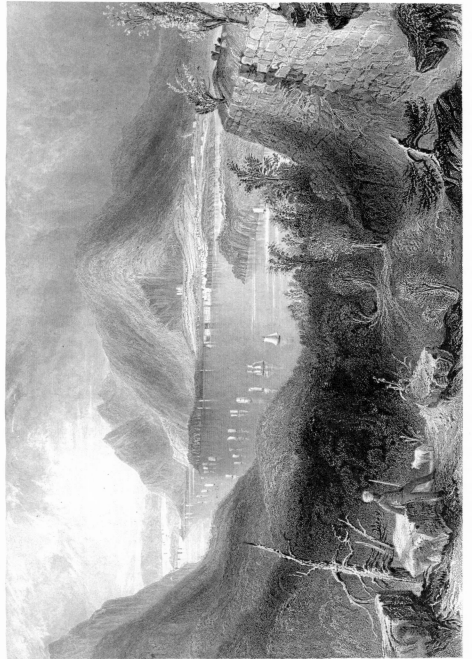

VIEW FROM FORT PUTNAM

(HUDSON RIVER)

stood saddled at the door, and rode with all speed to the bank of the river. A boat with six men was in waiting; and, pretending that he was going with a flag of truce, he pulled down the stream, and arrived safe on board the Vulture sloop of war, lying some miles below.

Having finished his inspection of the redoubt, Washington arrived at Arnold's house, received the message, and concluded to cross immediately and meet Arnold at West Point. As the whole party were seated in the barge moving smoothly over the water, with the majestic scenery of the highlands about them, Washington said, "Well, gentlemen, I am glad, on the whole, that General Arnold has gone before us, for we shall now have a salute; and the roaring of the cannon will have a fine effect among these mountains." The boat drew near to the beach, but no cannon were heard, and there was no appearance of preparation to receive them. "What!" said Washington, "do they not intend to salute us!" At this moment an officer was seen making his way down the hill to meet them, who seemed confused at their arrival, and apologized for not being prepared to receive such distinguished visitors. "How is this, Sir," said Washington, "is not General Arnold here?" "No, Sir," replied the officer, "he has not been here these two days, nor have I heard from him within that time." "This is extraordinary," said Washington; "we were told he had crossed the river, and that we should find him here. However, our visit must not be in vain. Since we have come, we must look round a little, and see in what state things are with you." He then ascended the hill, examined Fort Putnam and the other fortifications, and returned to Arnold's house, where the treason was at once revealed. This had occupied two or three hours, however, and Arnold was beyond pursuit. Washington retained his usual calmness, though Arnold was one of his favourite officers, and had been placed at West Point by his own personal influence with Congress. He called Lafayette and Knox, showed them the proofs, and only said to the former, "Whom can we trust now!"

VIEW OF STATE STREET, BOSTON

View of State Street, Boston

BOSTON is situated at the head of Massachusetts bay, on a peninsula about four miles in circumference, and is about three miles in length, and one mile and twenty-five rods, where widest, in breadth, and is connected with the main land at the south end by a narrow isthmus, called the Neck, leading to Roxbury. The town is built in an irregular circular form round the harbour, which is studded with about forty small islands, many of which afford excellent pasture; and are frequented in summer by numerous parties of pleasure. The harbour is formed by Nahant Point on the north, and Point Alderton on the south, and is so capacious as to allow five hundred vessels to ride at anchor in a good depth of water, while the entrance is so narrow as scarcely to admit two ships abreast. The entrance is defended by Fort Independence, belonging to the United States, on Castle Island, and by Fort Warren, on Governor's Island. There is another fort, called Fort Strong, on Noddle's Island.

Alterations and additions have of late years greatly improved the appearance of Boston. The streets, which were formerly almost without an exception narrow and crooked, have been in a great degree rendered wide and commodious; the old wooden structures have in the greater part of the city been replaced by handsome buildings of stone or brick. In the western part, particularly, there is much neatness and elegance. The splendour of the private buildings here, is not equalled in any other part of the Union.

The literary institutions of this city are of the first order. The public libraries contain 70,000 volumes. The Boston Athenæum is the finest establishment of its kind in the United States; its library contains above 25,000 volumes, and a reading-room, in which the most esteemed periodicals, from all parts of the world, may be found. If we add to these the library of Harvard College, in the neighbourhood, of 40,000 volumes, making the number of books within the reach of the citizens 110,000, it must be allowed that Boston offers to the scholar a more advantageous residence than any other spot in the western world.

State Street, called King Street in the days of Stamp-acts and "the Regulars," is the main artery of the heart of New England. The old State House, which stands at the head of it, was called the Town House, and was first erected in 1660. It is honourably mentioned in a book of travels, written in a pleasant vein, by "John Josselyn, Gent." who visited the colonies in 1663. "There is also a Town House," he says, "built upon pillars, where the merchants may confer. In the chambers above they hold their monthly courts.

Here is the dwelling of the Governor (Bellingham). On the south there is a small but pleasant common, where the gallants, a little before sunset, walk with their marmalet madams, as we do in Moorfields, till the nine o'clock bell rings them home to their respective habitations; when presently, the constables walk the rounds to see good order kept, and to take up loose people." The State House has been twice burnt, and rebuilt. A council chamber, ornamented with full-length portraits of Charles II. and James II. formerly occupied the east end; and it was in this chamber that James Otis declared before a court of admiralty, that "taxation without representation is tyranny," —a phrase which became, before long, a slogan in the mouths of the people. "Then and there," writes President Adams, "was the first scene of the first act of opposition to the arbitrary claims of Great Britain. Then and there, the child Independence was born." It was upon a trial of the question of "Writs for Assistance," a power which was required by the Board of Trade to enforce some new and rigorous Acts of Parliament touching trade; and Otis opposed the Attorney-General. "As soon as he had concluded," says the historian, "Otis burst forth as with a flame of fire, with a promptitude of classical allusion, a depth of research, a rapid summary of historical events, a profusion of legal authorities, a prophetic glance into futurity, and a torrent of impetuous eloquence, which carried all before him." This was the preparation for the resistance to the Stamp Act, and the Revolution soon followed.

State Street has been the scene of most of the events of a very public nature, which are recorded in the annals of Boston. The balcony of the State House is the popular pulpit, and hence was read the Declaration of Independence, and from hence declaimed Colonel David Crockett, who "could lick his weight in wild-cats." In 1770 the "Boston massacre" took place in State Street. For several days preceding the event, there had been disturbances between the king's soldiers and the townspeople, which had put the officers on the alert. The soldiers were collected into the barracks before night, and sentinels were placed around them at all hours to prevent difficulty. One of these sentinels was stationed in a narrow alley, and was striking fire against the walls with his sword, for amusement, when two or three young men attempted to pass him. Having orders to let no one pass, a struggle ensued, and one of the young men received a wound on the head. The noise of the rencontre drew together a considerable crowd, and as but few could enter the narrow scene of action, the remainder listened to an inflammatory speech from "a tall man, with a red cloak, and a white wig," in the adjacent square. At the close of the oration there was a general cry "To the main guard!" and the crowd rushed tumultuously toward its station in State Street. On their way they passed the Custom House, before the door of which stood a single sentinel. Alarmed at their approach, he retreated up the steps, and, the people collecting around, he sent word to the barracks, near by, that he was attacked, and a company in a few moments arrived to his assistance, and formed a half circle round the steps. The captain of the day, named Preston, followed immediately, and the Custom House, which stood at the corner of State and Exchange Streets, was soon thronged by a considerable multitude. The soldiers were soon pressed upon very closely by the mob, who were mostly armed with clubs; and those at a distance soon began to throw snowballs, followed by fragments of ice, stones and sticks, while from every side came the cry, "*Fire, if you dare!*" The soldiers soon heard, or thought they heard, the order, and they fired in quick succession from right to left. Two or three of the guns flashed; but the rest were fatal. Three persons were killed on the spot, two received wounds of which they died next day, and others were more slightly injured. The people immediately dispersed, leaving the dead bodies in the street, but returned in a few minutes; when the soldiers aimed once more at them, but the commanding officer struck up the guns with his sword. The drum was beat to arms, and several of the officers, on their way to join the guard, were knocked down, and their swords taken from them. Order was soon restored, and Captain Preston delivered himself up for trial. The dead were buried with some pomp, and when the excitement had subsided a little, Preston was tried and acquitted.

State Street is at present a street of banks, insurance offices, and similar institutions; and its side walk serves for the merchants' exchange. The buildings are of granite, and some of them, particularly a new bank, lately erected near Kirby Street, present very creditable specimens of city architecture.

Niagara Falls, from Clifton House

THE most comprehensive view of Niagara is, no doubt, that from the galleries of this hotel; but it is, at the same time, for a first view, one of the most unfavourable. Clifton House stands nearly opposite the centre of the irregular crescent formed by the Falls; but it is so far back from the line of the arc, that the height and grandeur of the two cataracts, to an eye unacquainted with the scene, are deceptively diminished. After once making the tour of the points of view, however, the distance and elevation of the hotel are allowed for by the eye, and the situation seems most advantageous. This is the only house at Niagara where a traveller, on his second visit, would be content to live.

Clifton House is kept in the best style of hotels in this country; but the usual routine of such places, going on in the very eye of Niagara, weaves in very whimsically with the eternal presence and power of the cataract. We must eat, drink, and sleep, it is true, at Niagara as elsewhere; and indeed, what with the exhaustion of mind and fatigue of body, we require at the Falls perhaps more than usual of these three "blessed inventions." The leaf that is caught away by the Rapids, however, is not more entirely possessed by this wonder of nature, than is the mind and imagination of the traveller; and the arrest of that leaf by the touch of the overhanging tree, or the point of a rock amid the breakers, is scarce more momentary than the interruption to the traveller's enchantment by the circumstances of daily life. He falls asleep with its surging thunders in his ear, and wakes—to wonder, for an instant, if his yesterday's astonishment was a dream. With the succeeding thought, his mind refills, like a mountain channel, whose torrent has been suspended by the frost, and he is overwhelmed with sensations that are almost painful, from the suddenness of their return. He rises and throws up his window, and there it flashes, and thunders, and agonizes—the same almighty miracle of grandeur for ever going on; and he turns and wonders—What the deuce can have become of his stockings! He slips on his dressing-gown, and commences his toilet. The glass stands in the window, and with his beard half achieved, he gets a glimpse of the foam-cloud rising majestically over the top of the mahogany frame. Almost persuaded, like Queen Christina at the fountains of St. Peter's, that a spectacle of such splendour is not intended to last, he drops his razor, and with the soap drying unheeded on his chin, he leans on his elbows, and watches the yeasty writhe in the abysm, and the solemn pillars of crystal eternally falling, like the fragments of some palace-crested star, descending through interminable space. The white field of the iris forms over

NIAGARA FALLS, FROM CLIFTON HOUSE

the brow of the cataract, exhibits its radiant bow, and sails away in a vanishing cloud of vapour upon the wind; the tortured and convulsed surface of the caldron below shoots out its frothy and seething circles in perpetual torment; the thunders are heaped upon each other, the earth trembles, and—the bell rings for breakfast! A vision of cold rolls, clammy omelettes, and tepid tea, succeeds these sublime images, and the traveller completes his toilet. Breakfast over, he resorts to the colonnade, to contemplate untiringly the scene before him, and in the midst of a calculation of the progress of the Fall towards Lake Erie,—with the perspiration standing on his forehead, while he struggles to conceive the junction of its waters with Lake Ontario,—the rocks rent, the hills swept away, forests prostrated, and the islands uprooted in the mighty conflux,—some one's child escapes from its nurse, and seizing him by the legs, cries out "*Da-da.*"

The *ennui* attendant upon public-houses can never be felt at Clifton House. The most common mind finds the spectacle from its balconies a sufficient and untiring occupation. The loneliness of uninhabited parlours, the discord of baby-thrummed pianos, the dreariness of great staircases, long entries, and bar-rooms filled with strangers, are pains and penalties of travel never felt at Niagara. If there is a vacant half-hour to dinner, or if indisposition to sleep create that sickening yearning for society, which sometimes comes upon a stranger in a strange land, like the calenture of a fever,—the eternal marvel going on without is more engrossing than friend or conversation, more beguiling from sad thought than the Corso in carnival-time. To lean over the balustrade and watch the flying of the ferry-boat below, with its terrified freight of adventurers, one moment gliding swiftly down the stream in the round of an eddy, the next, lifted up by a boiling wave, as if it were tossed up from the scoop of a giant's hand beneath the water; to gaze hour after hour into the face of the cataract, to trace the rainbows, delight like a child in the shooting spray-clouds, and calculate fruitlessly and endlessly by the force, weight, speed, and change of the tremendous waters,—is amusement and occupation enough to draw the mind from any thing,—to cure madness or create it.

View from Hyde Park

THE Hudson at Hyde Park is a broad, tranquil, and noble river, of about the same character as the Bosphorus above Roumeli-bissar, or the Dardanelles at Abydos. The shores are cultivated to the water's edge, and lean up in graceful, rather than bold elevations; the eminences around are crested with the villas of the wealthy inhabitants of the metropolis at the river's mouth; summer-houses, belvideres, and water-steps, give an air of enjoyment and refreshment to the banks, and, without any thing like the degree of the picturesque which makes the river so remarkable thirty or forty miles below, it is, perhaps, a more tempting character of scenery to build and live among.

All along, in this part of the river, occur the "landings," which are either considerable towns in themselves, or indicate a thickly settled country in the rear. The immense steamers that ply on the Hudson leave and receive passengers at all these points, and, to a person making the passage for the first time, the manner and expedition of this operation is rather startling. In the summer time, the principal steam boats average from five to seven hundred passengers, and there is usually a considerable number to go ashore and come off at each place. A mile or two before reaching the spot, a negro makes the tour of the boat, with a large hand-bell, and, in an amusing speech, full of the idioms of his own race, announces the approach, and requests those who are going ashore to select their baggage. This done, the steamer, gliding over the smooth water at the rate of fifteen or twenty miles in the hour, sheers in toward the shore, and the small boat is lowered, with the captain in her at the helm; the passengers are put on board, and away she shoots at the end of a line gradually loosened, but still kept tight enough to send her, like an arrow to her mark. The moment she touches the pier, the loose line is let out from the steamer, which still keeps on her way, and between that moment and the exhaustion of the line, perhaps thirty seconds, the baggage is thrown out, and taken in, passengers jump ashore, and embark, and away shoots the little boat again, her bow rising clear over the crest of her own foam, with the added velocity of the steamer at full speed, and the rapid hauling in of the crew. I never have failed to observe a look of astonishment on the part of the subjects of this hurried transfer, however used to it by frequent repetition; and a long sigh of relief, as they look about on the broad and steady deck, or tread the ground beneath them if they have gone ashore, follows as invariably. As the boat is hauled up again, the negro crier reappears with his bell, and, looking the newly arrived group close in the face, cries out, as if they were a mile off,

VIEW FROM HYDE PARK

(HUDSON RIVER)

"All pas'ng'rs as hasn't paid their passage, please walk to the cap'n's office and settLE-E-E!!"—the whole sentence recited in the most monotonous tone till the last syllable, which rises suddenly to a ludicrous scream, prolonged as long as his breath will continue it.

Many fatal accidents occurred formerly from this practice; but there is now more care and time taken about it, and the accidents, if any, are rather ludicrous than serious. I was going to Albany, some years ago, on board a very crowded boat, and among the passengers were a German and his wife, emigrants of the lower class. They had been down stairs at dinner, and the husband came up in search of his wife, who had preceded him, just as a crowded boatful were going ashore at Poughkeepsie. Either fancying it the end of his journey, or misunderstanding the man who was busy with the baggage, he threw in his bundle, and was peeping through the crowd of ladies on the stern for his wife; when one of the men, impatient of his delay, drew him in, and away he flew to the pier. He sprang ashore with the rest, his bundle was thrown after him, and, as the steamer sped away, we saw him darting about in the crowd to find his *vrouw*, who by this time had missed him, and was running from side to side, in quite as great embarrassment on board. The poor woman's distress was quite pitiable, and when, at last, one of the passengers, who had observed them together, pointed out to her her husband, in his flat cap and foreign *bleuse*, standing on the receding pier, with his hands stretched out after the boat, her agony could no longer be controlled. She was put ashore at the next landing to return by the "down boat;" but as another boat up the river arrived soon after at Poughkeepsie, the probability was, that he would embark again to follow her, and they would thus cross each other by the way; with scarce a word of English, and probably very little money, they may be hunting each other to this day.

Village of Sing-Sing

SING-SING is famous for its marble, of which there is an extensive quarry near by; for its State prison, of which the discipline is of the most salutary character; and for its academy, which has a high reputation. It may be said, altogether, to do the State some service.

[71]

VILLAGE OF SING-SING

(HUDSON RIVER)

The county of West Chester, of which this is the principal village on the Hudson, has been made the scene of, perhaps, the best historical novel of our country, and, more than any other part of the United States, suffered from the evils of war. The character and depredations of the "cow-boys" and "skinners," whose fields of action were on the skirts of this neutral ground, are familiar to all who have read "the Essay" of Mr. Cooper. A distinguished clergyman gives the following very graphic picture of West Chester county in those days: —

"In the autumn of 1777, I resided for some time in this county. The lines of the British were then in the neighbourhood of Kingsbridge, and those of the Americans at Byram river. The unhappy inhabitants were, therefore, exposed to the depredations of both. Often they were actually plundered, and always were liable to this calamity. They feared every body whom they saw, and loved nobody. It was a curious fact to a philosopher, and a melancholy one to hear their conversation. To every question they gave such an answer as would please the inquirer; or, if they despaired of pleasing, such a one as would not provoke him. Fear was, apparently, the only passion by which they were animated. The power of volition seemed to have deserted them. They were not civil, but obsequious; not obliging, but subservient. They yielded with a kind of apathy, and very quietly, what you asked, and what they supposed it impossible for them to retain. If you treated them kindly, they received it coldly; not as a kindness, but as a compensation for injuries done them by others. When you spoke to them, they answered you without either good or ill nature, and without any appearance of reluctance or hesitation; but they subjoined neither question nor remarks of their own; proving to your full conviction that they felt no interest either in the conversation or yourself. Both their countenances and their motions had lost every trace of animation and of feeling. Their features were smoothed, not into serenity, but apathy; and, instead of being settled in the attitude of quiet thinking, strongly indicated, that all thought beyond what was merely instinctive, had fled their minds for ever.

"Their houses, meantime, were, in a great measure, scenes of desolation. Their furniture was extensively plundered, or broken to pieces. The walls, floors, and windows were injured both by violence and decay, and were not repaired, because they had not the means to repair them, and because they were exposed to the repetition of the same injuries. Their cattle were gone. Their enclosures were burnt, where they were capable of becoming fuel; and in many cases thrown down where they were not. Their fields were covered with a rank growth of weeds and wild grass.

[73]

"Amid all this appearance of desolation, nothing struck my eye more forcibly than the sight of the high road. Where I had heretofore seen a continual succession of horses and carriages, life and bustle lending a sprightliness to all the environing objects, not a single, solitary traveller was seen, from week to week, or from month to month. The world was motionless and silent, except when one of these unhappy people ventured upon a rare and lonely excursion to the house of a neighbour no less unhappy, or a scouting party, traversing the country in quest of enemies, alarmed the inhabitants with expectations of new injuries and sufferings. The very tracks of the carriages were grown over, and obliterated; and where they were discernible, resembled the faint impressions of chariot wheels, said to be left on the pavements of Herculaneum. The grass was of full height for the scythe, and strongly realized to my own mind, for the first time, the proper import of that picturesque declaration in the Song of Deborah: 'In the days of Shamgar, the son of Anath, in the days of Jael, the highways were unoccupied, and the travellers walked through by-paths. The inhabitants of the villages ceased: they ceased in Israel.' "

West Chester is a rough county in natural surface, but since the days when the above description was true, its vicinity to New York, and the ready market for produce, have changed its character to a thriving agricultural district. It is better watered with springs, brooks, and mill-streams, than many other parts of New York, and, among other advantages, enjoys, along the Hudson, a succession of brilliant and noble scenery.

View from Ruggle's House, Newburgh, Hudson River

NEWBURGH stands upon a pretty acclivity, rising with a sharp ascent from the west bank of the Hudson; and, in point of trade and consequence, it is one of the first towns on the river. In point of scenery, Newburgh is as felicitously placed, perhaps, as any other spot in the world, having in its immediate neighbourhood every element of natural loveliness; and, just below, the sublime

VIEW FROM RUGGLE'S HOUSE, NEWBURGH, HUDSON RIVER

and promising Pass of the Highlands. From the summit of the acclivity, the view over Wateaman and Fishkill is full of beauty; the deep flow of the Hudson lying between, and the pretty villages just named, sparkling with their white buildings and cheerful steeples, beyond.

Newburgh has a considerable trade with the back country, and supports two or three steam-boats, running daily and exclusively between its pier and New York. If there were wanting an index of the wondrous advance of enterprise and invention in our country, we need not seek farther than this simple fact—a small intermediate town, on one river, supporting such an amount of expensive navigation. Only thirty years ago Fulton made his first experiment in steam on the Hudson, amid the unbelief and derision of the whole country. Let any one stand for one hour on the pier at Newburgh, and see those superb and swift palaces of motion shoot past, one after the other, like gay and chasing meteors; and then read poor Fulton's account of his first experiment—and never again throw discouragement on the kindling fire of genius.

"When I was building my first steam-boat," said he to Judge Story, "the project was viewed by the public at New York either with indifference or contempt, as a visionary scheme. My friends, indeed, were civil, but they were shy. They listened with patience to my explanations, but with a settled cast of incredulity on their countenances. I felt the full force of the lamentation of the Poet:—

'Truths would you teach, to save a sinking land,
All shun, none aid you, and few understand.'

As I had occasion to pass daily to and from the building-yard while my boat was in progress, I have often loitered, unknown, near the idle groups of strangers gathering in little circles, and heard various inquiries as to the object of this new vehicle. The language was uniformly that of scorn, sneer, or ridicule. The loud laugh rose at my expense; the dry jest, the wise calculation of losses and expenditure; the dull but endless repetition of *"the Fulton folly."* Never did a single encouraging remark, a bright hope, or a warm wish, cross my path.

"At length the day arrived when the experiment was to be made. To me it was a most trying and interesting occasion. I wanted many friends to go on board to witness the first successful trip. Many of them did me the favour to attend, as a matter of personal respect; but it was manifest they did it with reluctance, feigning to be partners of my mortification, and not of my triumph. I was well aware that, in my case, there were many reasons to doubt of my own success. The machinery was new, and ill-made; and many parts of it were constructed by mechanics unacquainted with such work; and unexpected difficulties might reasonably be presumed to present themselves from other causes. The moment arrived in which the word was to be given for the vessel to move. My friends were in groups on the deck. There was anxiety mixed with fear among them. They were silent, sad, and weary. I read in their looks nothing but disaster, and almost repented of my efforts. The signal was given, and the boat moved on a short distance, and then stopped, and became immovable. To the silence of the preceding moment, now succeeded murmurs of discontent and agitation, and whispers and shrugs. I could hear distinctly repeated, "I told you so,—it is a foolish scheme.—I wish we were well out of it." I elevated myself on a platform, and stated that I knew not what was the matter; but if they would be quiet, and indulge me for half an hour, I would either go on or abandon the voyage. I went below, and discovered that a slight maladjustment was the cause. It was obviated. The boat went on; we left New York; we passed through the Highlands; we reached Albany!—Yet even then, imagination superseded the force of fact. *It was doubted if it could be done again, or if it could be made, in any case, of any great value.*"

What an affecting picture of the struggles of a great mind, and what a vivid lesson of encouragement to genius, is contained in this simple narration!

Descent into the Valley of Wyoming

In looking down on this lovely scene, made memorable by savage barbarity, and famous by the poet's wand of enchantment, it is natural to indulge in resentful feelings towards the sanguinary race whose atrocities make up its page in story. It is a pity, however, that they too, had not a poet and a partial chronicler. Leaving entirely out of view the ten thousand wrongs done by the white man to the Indian, in the corruption, robbery, and rapid extinction of his race, there are personal atrocities, on our own records, exercised toward that fated people, which, in impartial history hereafter, will redeem them from all charge except that of irresistible retaliation. The brief story of the famous Cornstalk, Sachem of the Shawanees, and King of the Northern Confederacy, is sermon enough on this text.

DESCENT INTO THE VALLEY OF WYOMING

(PENNSYLVANIA)

The north-western corner of Virginia, and that part of Pennsylvania contiguous, on the south, to the valley represented in the drawing, was the scene of some of the bloodiest events of Indian warfare. Distinguished over all the other red men of this region, was Cornstalk. He was equally a terror to the men of his own tribe, (whom he did not hesitate to hew down with his tomahawk if they showed any cowardice in fight,) and a formidable opponent to our troops, from his military talents and personal daring. He was, at the same time, more than all the other chiefs of the confederacy, a friend to the whites; and, energetic as he was when once engaged in battle, never took up arms willingly against them. After the bloody contest at Point Pleasant, in which Cornstalk had displayed his generalship and bravery, to the admiration of his foes, he came in to the camp of Lord Dunmore, to make negotiations for peace. Colonel Wilson, one of the staff, thus describes his oratory:—"When he arose, he was in no wise confused or daunted, but spoke in a distinct and audible voice, without stammering or repetition, and with peculiar emphasis. His looks, while addressing Dunmore, were truly grand and majestic, yet graceful and attractive. I have heard many celebrated orators, but never one whose powers of delivery surpassed those of Cornstalk on this occasion."

In the spring of 1777, it was known that an extensive coalition was forming among the tribes, and that it only waited the consent and powerful aid of the Shawanees, to commence war upon the whites. At this critical time, Cornstalk, accompanied by Red Hawk, came on a friendly visit to the Fort at Point Pleasant, communicated the intentions of the tribes, and expressed his sorrow that the tide set so strongly against the colonists, that he must go with it, in spite of all his endeavours.

Upon receiving this information, given by the noble savage in the spirit of a generous enemy, the commander of the garrison seized upon Cornstalk and his companion as hostages for the peaceful conduct of his nation, and set about availing himself of the advantage he had gained by his suggestions. During his captivity, Cornstalk held frequent conversations with the officers, and took pleasure in describing to them the geography of the west, then little known. One afternoon, while he was engaged in drawing on the floor a map of the Missouri territory, with its water-courses and mountains, a halloo was heard from the forest, which he recognised as the voice of his son Ellinipsico, a young warrior, whose courage and address was almost as celebrated as his own. Ellinipsico entered the fort, and embraced his father most affectionately, having been uneasy at his long absence, and come hither in search of him.

The day after his arrival, a soldier went out from the fort on a hunting excursion, and was shot by Indians. His infuriated companions instantly re-solved to sacrifice Cornstalk and his son. They charged upon Ellinipsico that the offenders were in his company, but he declared that he had come alone, and with the sole object of seeking his father. When the soldiers came within hearing, the young warrior appeared agitated. Cornstalk encouraged him to meet his fate composedly, and said to him, "My son, the Great Spirit has sent you here that we may die together!" He turned to meet his murderers the next instant, and receiving seven bullets in his body, expired without a groan.

When Cornstalk had fallen, Ellinipsico continued still and passive, not even raising himself from his seat. He met death in that position with the ut-most calmness. "The other Indian," says the chronicle, "was murdered piece-meal, and with all those circumstances of cruelty with which the savage wreaks his vengeance on his enemy."

The day before his death, Cornstalk had been present at a council of the officers, and had spoken to them on the subject of the war, with his own pecu-liar eloquence. In the course of his remarks, he expressed something like a presentiment of his fate. "When I was young," he said, "and went out to war, I often thought each would be my last adventure, and I should return no more. I still lived. Now I am in the midst of you, and, if you choose, you may kill me. I can die but once. It is alike to me whether now or hereafter!"

His atrocious murder was dearly expiated. The Shawanees, the most war-like tribe of the West, became thenceforward the most deadly and implacable foes to the white man.

Boston, from Dorchester Heights

THE pretty peninsula of Dorchester Heights, which seems to throw its arm protectingly around the southern bay of Boston, was settled by a company of pilgrims who came out to New England during the administration of Gover-nor Winthrop, in Massachusetts. The party consisted of two Puritan clergy-men, "with many godly families and people" from Devonshire and Somer-setshire, who embarked in the "Mary John," in the spring of 1630. The historian states that they had some difficulty in the passage with the master of the vessel, Captain Squibb, "who, like a merciless man, put them and their goods ashore on Nantasket Point, notwithstanding his engagement was to bring them up Charles river." They obtained a boat, however, and, having laden her with goods, and manned her with able men ("not more than ten, well armed, under Captain Southcot, a brave Low-country soldier,") they followed the river for about ten miles. After landing their goods on a steep bank, they were alarmed by the information that there was encamped near them a body of three hundred savages. Fortunately they had been joined by an old planter, who knew enough of the Indian tongue and disposition to persuade the chiefs not to attack the party till morning. At day-break, some of the savages made their appearance, but stood awhile at a distance. At last one of them held out a bass, and the pilgrims sent a man with a biscuit to exchange for it, and thus a friendly intercourse was established. Not liking the neighbourhood, however, they descended the river again, and an exploring party having discovered some good pasture at Mattapau (present Dorchester) they settled there.

The neighbouring peninsula of Shawmut (now Boston) was destined to be the principal settlement, and Dorchester is at this day a rural suburb of the capital of New England. The fort which crowns its summit (from which this view is taken) is the scene of an important chapter in the history of the Revolution.

Boston had been occupied for some time by the British army under General Gage, who sailed for England in October 1776, leaving General Howe in command. After the battle of Bunker's Hill, both armies remained quiet for several months; General Washington occupying both sides of the Charles river with about fourteen thousand men; and the English, besieged in their quarters within the town, amusing themselves with private theatricals in Faneuiel Hall, varied occasionally with feats of horsemanship from a squadron of cavalry, who had turned the old South Church into a circus. As the cold became severe, the North "meeting-house," an immense wooden building, was torn down and consumed for fuel, and the soldiers had made a holiday of felling a gigantic Liberty-tree for the same purpose.

Washington became impatient of this inactive situation; and as soon as the ice in the bay and river became firm enough to allow the passage of troops, he called a council of war, and proposed an attack on Boston. The opinion against the measure was unanimous, and he reluctantly abandoned it. He soon after determined to take possession of Dorchester Heights, which command both harbour and town,—a step which he knew must bring on a general

[81]

BOSTON, FROM DORCHESTER HEIGHTS

action, during which he intended to cross over to Cambridge with a few chosen men, and force an entrance into the town. During the two or three preceding nights, he bombarded the town heavily from his camp, to divert the attention of the garrison; and on the night of the 4th of March, a large detachment took possession of Dorchester Heights, and immediately commenced throwing up an intrenchment. The night was mild, but the ground was frozen almost impenetrably hard; and it was with excessive labour that a sufficient bulwark was presented by day-light, to cover them from the shot of the enemy.

The morning broke,—and a thin haze, which magnified the size of the works, overspread the landscape. The astonishment of General Howe, at discerning this phantom fortification looming up through the mist, upon heights which had been bare and desolate at sunset, was without bounds. The position was so commanding that the town could not be held unless the Americans were disloged; but this seemed, from the advantages of the ground in favour of the Provincials, next to impossible. The British commander undertook it with great spirit, and two thousand troops were embarked on the same day to cross the harbour to the attack. The transports fell down to the Castle, a small island just below the town; but a tremendous storm suspended their operations. The next day a council of war was held, and it was thought advisable to evacuate the town immediately. The provincials went on completing their fortifications, undisturbed; and in a few days General Howe embarked with all his forces, accompanied by those Americans who adhered to the royal cause. The embarkation commenced at four in the morning of the 17th of March, and at ten in the forenoon General Washington entered the city at the head of his army. The English fleet sailed for Halifax. They were ten thousand strong, including the marines; and left stores to the value of 30,000*l.* with several pieces of cannon, mortars, &c. &c.

The view of Boston from these heights is very commanding. The bay, with its fortified islands, stretches away to the right, beautiful from its shape and from the brightness of its water; the city, clustering upon its heights, rises in graceful lines to the pinnacled State House; and the country to the left is all that is lovely in cultivation, sprinkled here and there with gay and thrifty-looking villages. The calenture of speculation is just now at its height in America; and Dorchester, like other places, is laid out in lots, and busy with the builders of fancy cottages and hotels. If calculation has not overreached itself, the suburbs of Boston will soon sparkle with villas on every hill side within the horizon.

[83]

View of Faneuiel Hall, and Adjacent Buildings, Boston

THERE are very few remaining of the many covered, gable-ended, top-heavy, old houses which constituted the compact centre of Boston in the days of English governors. The finest specimens long stood in the neighbourhood of Faneuiel Hall; but, with one exception, we believe, their picturesque heaps of triangles have dropped beneath the merciless hand of speculation and improvement. Boston has not grown so thriftily, or rather so miraculously, as the capitols of other States, through which the flood of emigration rolls more directly; but it is certainly the handsomest town in the United States, and probably its prosperity is more permanent and solid. Its granite houses and fine public buildings are in strong contrast with the description given of it by John Josselyn, Gent. who visited it in 1638, and afterwards favoured the world with his observations under the title of "New England Rarities." "Having refreshed myself for a day or two on an island in the bay," he says, "I crossed the harbour in a small boat to Boston, which was then rather a village than a town, there not being more than above twenty or thirty houses: and presented my respects to Mr. Muthrop the governor, and to Mr. Cotton the teacher of Boston Church, to whom I delivered from Mr. Francis Quarles, the poet, the translation of several Psalms in English metre for his approbation."

A facetious bookseller, John Dunton, visited Boston some fifty years afterwards; and, in a book upon his "Life and Errors," gives a humorous account of its inhabitants in his time. The passage, which is now commonly made in from sixteen to twenty-five or thirty days, occupied the unfortunate bibliopole four months; and he was reduced, at the latter part of it, to one bottle of water for four days.

"When we came within view of Boston," he writes, "we were all overjoyed, being just upon the point of starving; we put off to land in the long boat, and came ashore near the Castle, which stands about a mile from Boston. The country appeared at first a barren waste, but we found humanity enough when we came among the inhabitants. We lodged the first night at the Castle, and next morning we found our way to Boston Bay over the ice, which was but cold comfort to us after we had been stowed up so many months in a cabin. The air of New England was sharper than at London; which, with the temptation of fresh provisions, made me eat like a second Mariot of Gray's Inn. The first person that welcomed me to Boston was Mr. Burroughs. He heaped

FANEUIEL HALL, BOSTON

upon me more civilities than I can reckon up, offered to lend me moneys, and made me his bedfellow till I had provided lodgings."

Dunton's book would have sold merrily in our scandal-loving days. Its personalities are delightful. The following list of his acquaintance is as good as a portrait gallery.

"Mr. Phillips, my old correspondent.—He treated me with a noble dinner, and (if I may trust my eyes) is blest with a pretty, obliging wife. I'll say that for Sam (after dealing with him for some hundred pounds), he is very just, and (as an effect of that) very thriving. I shall add to his character, that he is young and witty, and the most beautiful man in the town of Boston.

"The next was Mr. King.—Love was the cause of this gentleman's long ramble hither. Sure his mistress was made of stone, for King had a voice would have charmed the spheres; he sang "*All hail to the Myrtle Shades*" with a matchless grace.

"Another acquaintance was Mr. York. He had his soft minutes as well as other men; and when he unbent his bow, (for he was very industrious,) he treated the fair sex with so much courtship and address, as if loving had been all his trade.

"I pass to my good friend Dr. Bullivant—both a gentleman and a physician. As a gentleman, he came of noble family, but his good qualities exceed his birth. He never practises new experiments on his patients, except in danger-ous cases, where death must be expelled by death. This is also praiseworthy in him, that to the poor he always prescribes cheap medicines; *not curing them of a consumption in their bodies and sending it into their purses*, nor yet direct-ing them to the East Indies for drugs, when they may have better out of their own gardens.

"I proceed in the next place to Mr. Gouge, a linen-draper from London. He is owner of a deal of wit; his brain is a quiver of smart jests. He pretends to live a bachelor, but is no enemy to a pretty woman."

Dunton winds up his list with an apostrophe to Mrs. Comfort, the married daughter of his landlady. "You may well take it amiss," he says, "if I should forget your favours to me in your father's house, your pleasant company to Ipswich, your assistance when I was ill, and the noble looking-glass you sent my dear, and all with a world of innocence."

> "Kind Boston, adieu! part we must, though 'tis pity,
> But I'm made for mankind: the world is my city.
> Look how on the shore they whoop and they holloa,
> Not for joy I am gone, *but for grief they can't follow*."

View from the Telegraph Signal, New York Bay

THE first visitor to the Bay of New York, and the writer of the first description on record, was John de Verrazzano, a Florentine, in the service of Francis the First. This bold navigator had been for some time in command of four ships, cruising against the Spaniards. But his little fleet being separated in a storm, Verrazzano determined, with one of them, the Dauphin, to take a voyage in search of new countries. He arrived on the American coast, somewhere near North Carolina, and first proceeded south as far as "the region of palm-trees," probably Florida. He then turned, and proceeded north till he entered a harbour, which he describes thus, in a passage of a letter addressed by him to his Royal master:—

"This land is situated in the paralele of Rome, in forty-one degrees and two terces; but somewhat more colde by accidentall causes. The mouth of the haven lieth open to the south, half a league broad; and being entred within it, between the east and the north, it stretcheth twelve leagues, where it wareth broader and broader, and maketh a gulfe about twenty leagues in compass, wherein are five small islands, very fruitfull and pleasant, full of hie and broad trees, among the which islands any great navie may ride safe without any feare of tempest or other danger."

In this harbour Verrazzano appears to have remained about fifteen days. He and his men frequently went on shore to obtain supplies and see the country. He says in another part of his letter—"Sometimes our men stayed two or three daies on a little island neere the ship for divers necessaries. We were oftentimes within the land five or six leagues, which we found as pleasant as is possible to declare, very apt for any kind of husbandry, of corne, wine, and ayle. We entered afterwards into the woods, which we found so thicke that any army, were it never so great, might have hid itself therein; the trees whereof are okes, cypresse-trees, and other sortes unknown in Europe."

These were probably the first European feet that ever trod on any part of the territory now included in the State of New York. Verrazzano and his crew seem to have had considerable intercourse with the natives, and generally to have been treated well, though by his own account he did not always deserve it. Speaking of an excursion made by his men somewhere on the coast, he says:—"They saw only one old woman, with a young maid of eighteen or twenty yeeres old, which, seeing our companie, hid themselves in the grasse

VIEW FROM THE TELEGRAPH SIGNAL, NEW YORK BAY

for feare. The old woman carried two infants on her shoulders, and the young woman was laden with as many. As soone as they saw us, to quiet them and win their favours, our men gave them victuals to eate, which the old woman received thankfully, but the young woman threw them disdainfully on the ground. *They took a child from the old woman to bring into France; and going about to take the young woman, which was very beautiful, and of tall stature*, they could not possibly, for the great outcries that she made, bring her to the sea; and especially having great woods to pass thorow, and being far from the ship, we proposed to leave her behind, *bearing away the child only*."

In a subsequent part of his narrative, Verrazzano presents a very favourable picture, not only of the amenity, but of the discretion of the aborigines. "They came in great companies of their small boats unto the ship, with their faces all bepainted with divers colours, and bringing their wives with them, whereof they were very jealous; they themselves entring aboard the ship, and staying there a good space, but causing their wives to stay in their boats; and for all the entreatie that we could make, offering to give them divers things, we could never obtaine that they would suffer them to come aboard the ship. And oftentimes one of the two Kings comming with his Queene, and *many gentlemen* for their pleasure to see us, they all stayed on shore 200 paces from us, sending us a small boat to give us intelligence of their comming; and as soon as they had answere from us they came immediately, and wondered at hearing the cries and noyses of the mariners. The Queene and her maids staied in a very light boat at an island a quarter of a league off, while the King abode a long space in our ship, uttering divers conceits with gestures, viewing with great admiration the furniture of the shippe. And sometimes our men staying one or two days on a little island near the ship, he returned with seven or eight of *his gentlemen* to see what we did; then the King drawing his bow, and running up and down with *his gentlemen*, made much sport to gratify our men."

The sail-studded bay of New York at this day presents another scene; and one of these same "*gentlemen*" is now almost as much a curiosity here as was John de Verrazzano, only three centuries ago, to the rightful lords of this fair land and water.

Peekskill Landing

LIKE most of the *landings* on the Hudson, Peekskill is a sort of outstretched hand from the interior of the country. It is about eighty miles from New York, and the produce from the country behind is here handed over to the trading sloops, who return, into the waiting palm, the equivalent in goods from the city. A sort of town naturally springs up at such a spot, and, as a river-side is a great provocative of idleness, all the Dolph Heyligers of the country about seem to be collected at the landing.

The neighbourhood of this spot is interesting from its association with the history of the Revolution. The head-quarters of General Washington were just below, at Verplank's Point; and the town of Peekskill, half a mile back from the river, was the depôt of military stores, which were burnt by General Home in 1777. "On my return southward in 1782," says the translator of Chastellux, who has not given his name, "I spent a day or two at the American camp at Verplank's Point, where I had the honour of dining with General Washington. I had suffered severely from an ague, which I could not get quit of, though I had taken the exercise of a hard-trotting horse, and got thus far to the north in the month of October. The General observing it, told me he was sure I had not met with a good glass of wine for some time,—an article then very rare,—but that my disorder must be frightened away. He made me drink three or four of his silver camp cups of excellent Madeira at noon, and recommended to me to take a generous glass of claret after dinner; a prescription by no means repugnant to my feelings, and which I most religiously followed. I mounted my horse the next morning, and continued my journey to Massachusetts, without ever experiencing the slightest return of my disorder.

"The American camp here presented the most beautiful and picturesque appearance. It extended along the plain, on the neck of land formed by the winding of the Hudson, and had a view of this river to the south. Behind it, the lofty mountains, covered with wood, formed the most sublime back-ground that painting could express. In the front of the tents was a regular continued portico, formed by the boughs of the trees in full verdure, decorated with much taste and fancy. Opposite the camp, and on distinct eminences, stood the tents of some of the general officers, over which towered predominant that of Washington. I had seen all the camps in England, from many of which drawings and engravings have been taken; but this was truly a subject worthy the pencil of the first artist. The French camp, during their stay in Baltimore, was

PEEKSKILL LANDING

(HUDSON RIVER)

decorated in the same manner. At the camp at Verplank's Point we distinctly heard the morning and evening gun of the British at Knightsbridge."

The curiosity seizes with avidity upon any accidental information which fills up the bare outline of history. The personal history of Washington more particularly, wherever it has been traced by those who were in contact with him, is full of interest. Some of the sketches given by the Marquis of Chastellux, who passed this point of the Hudson on his way to Washington's headquarters below, are very graphic.

"The weather being fair on the 26th," he says, "I got on horseback, after breakfasting with the General. He was so attentive as to give me the horse I rode on the day of my arrival. I found him as good as he is handsome; but, above all, perfectly well broke and well trained, having a good mouth, easy in hand, and stopping short in a gallop without bearing the bit. I mention these minute particulars, because it is the General himself who breaks all his own horses. He is an excellent and bold horseman, leaping the highest fences, and going extremely quick without standing upon his stirrups, bearing on the bridle, or letting his horse run wild; circumstances which our young men look upon as so essential a part of English horsemanship, that they would rather break a leg or an arm than renounce them."

After passing some days at head-quarters, this young nobleman thus admirably sums up his observations on Washington: —

"The strongest characteristic of this great man is the perfect union which reigns between his physical and moral qualities. Brave without temerity, laborious without ambition, generous without prodigality, noble without pride, virtuous without severity; he seems always to have confined himself within those limits beyond which the virtues, by clothing themselves in more lively but more changeable colours, may be mistaken for faults. It will be said of him hereafter, that *at the end of a long civil war he had nothing with which he could reproach himself*. His stature is noble and lofty, he is well made and exactly proportioned; his physiognomy mild and agreeable, but such as to render it impossible to speak particularly of any of his features; so that on quitting him, you have only the recollection of a fine face. He has neither a grave nor a familiar air; his brow is sometimes marked with thought, but never with inquietude; in inspiring respect he inspires confidence, and his smile is always the smile of benevolence."

Lighthouse Near Caldwell's Landing

THIS picturesque object is seen to great effect by the passenger in the evening boat from New York to Newburgh. Leaving the city at five in the summer afternoon, she makes the intervening forty miles between that hour and twilight; and while the last tints of the sunset are still in the sky, the stars just beginning to twinkle through the glow of the west, the bright light of this lofty beacon rises up over the prow of the boat, shining apparently on the very face of the new-starred heaven. As he approaches, across the smooth and still purpled mirror of the silent river is drawn a long and slender line of light, broken at the foot of the beacon by the mild shrubbery of the rock on which it stands; and as he rounds the point, and passes it, the light brightens and looks clearer against the darker sky of the east, while the same cheering line of reflection follows him on his way, and is lost to sight as he disappears among the mountains.

The waters of the river at this point were the scene of the brief and tragic drama enacted so fatally by poor André. Four or five miles below stands Smith's house, where he had his principal interview with Arnold, and where the latter communicated to him his plans for the delivery of West Point into the hands of the English, and gave him the fatal papers which proved his ruin.

At Smith's house Mrs. Arnold passed a night, on her way to join her husband at West Point, soon after he had taken command. The sufferings of this lady have excited the sympathy of the world, as the first paroxysms of her distress moved the kind but firm heart of Washington. There seems to have arisen a doubt, however, whether her long and well-known correspondence with André had not so far undermined her patriotism, that she was rather inclined to further than impede the treason of Arnold; and consequently could have suffered but little after Washington generously made every arrangement for her to follow him. In the "Life of Aaron Burr," lately published, are some statements which seem authentic on the subject. It is well known that Washington found Mrs. Arnold apparently frantic with distress at the communication her husband had made to her the moment before his flight. Lafayette, and the other officers in the suite of the commander-in-chief, were alive with the most poignant sympathy; and a passport was given her by Washington, with which she immediately left West Point to join Arnold in New York. On her way she stopped at the house of Mrs. Prevost, the wife of a British officer, who subsequently married Colonel Burr. Here "the frantic scenes of West Point were renewed," says the narrative of Burr's biographer, "and continued so

[93]

LIGHTHOUSE NEAR CALDWELL'S LANDING

(HUDSON RIVER)

long as strangers were present. As soon as she and Mrs. Prevost were left alone, however, Mrs. Arnold became tranquillized, and assured Mrs. Prevost that she was heartily sick of the theatrics she was exhibiting. She stated that she had corresponded with the British commander; that she was disgusted with the American cause, and those who had the management of public affairs; and that, through great persuasion and unceasing perseverance, she had ultimately brought the General into an arrangement to surrender West Point to the British. Mrs. Arnold was a gay, accomplished, artful, and extravagant woman. There is no doubt, therefore, that, for the purpose of acquiring the means of gratifying her vanity, she contributed greatly to the utter ruin of her husband, and thus doomed to everlasting infamy and disgrace all the fame he had acquired as a gallant soldier, at the sacrifice of his blood."

It is not easy to pass and repass the now peaceful and beautiful waters of this part of the Hudson, without recalling to mind the scenes and actors in the great drama of the revolution, which they not long ago bore on their bosom. The busy mind fancies the armed guard-boats, slowing pulling along the shore; the light pinnace of the Vulture plying to and fro on its errands of conspiracy; and not the least vivid picture to the imagination, is the boat containing the accomplished, the gallant André and his guard, on his way to his death. It is probable that he first admitted to his own mind the possibility of a fatal result, while passing the very spot presented in the drawing. A late biographer of Arnold gives the particulars of a conversation between André and Major Tallmadge, the officer who had him in custody, and who brought him from West Point down the river to Tuppau, the place of his subsequent execution.

"Before we reached the Clove" (a landing just below the beacon represented in the drawing,) "Major André became very inquisitive to know my opinion as to the result of his capture. When I could no longer evade his importunity, I remarked to him as follows:—'I had a much-loved classmate in Yale College, by the name of Hale, who entered the army in 1775. Immediately after the battle of Long Island, Washington wanted information respecting the strength of the enemy. Hale tendered his services, went over to Brooklyn, and was taken, just as he was passing the outposts of the enemy on his return.' Said I, with emphasis, 'Do you remember the sequel of this story?' 'Yes,' said André, 'he was hanged as a spy. But you surely do not consider his case and mine alike?' I replied, 'Yes, precisely similar, and similar will be your fate.' He endeavoured to answer my remarks, but it was manifest he was more troubled in spirit than I had ever seen him before."

[95]

Harper's Ferry, from the Potomac Side

PERHAPS it will not be uninteresting to the reader, to vary a little the monotony of description which is entailed upon us by the character of the work, and give some account of the varieties of sporting on the Potomac.

This noble river abounds in fish, of which the principal are the white shad, the herring, and the sturgeon. The latter is taken in a way that, as far as we know, is entirely peculiar to this part of the country. The sturgeon is a noble denizen of the waters, weighing from seventy-five to one hundred and fifty pounds. His enormous leaps out of the water, and his alacrity at mounting a cascade, are accomplishments for which he is, as the advertisements phrase it, favourably known." He has a habit, however, of scratching himself against any stationary object he finds in the river, which has been detected by the Potomac fishers, and employed, very successfully, to his detriment. A stout line, with a weight attached to it, is lowered from a boat, and a large hook, of peculiar contrivance, but without a bait, fastened to the extremity. The rubbing of the sturgeon against the line informs the fisherman of his neighbourhood, and, with a little skill, he succeeds in hooking him under the belly. The fish makes off with prodigious speed; the fisherman pays out line, and casts loose his painter; and away flies the boat with a speed and suddenness that seems like magic. A mile or so of this hard work is enough for the sturgeon, who gives out exhausted, and is easily drawn in. Some years ago, a negro, celebrated for his skill in this fishery, incautiously tied the line to his leg. The sudden jerk of the hooked fish pulled him overboard, and away he went down the stream, sometimes above, and sometimes under water, to the extreme astonishment of some people accidentally passing on the shore. He was an expert swimmer, however, and a heavy-limbed athletic fellow, and by remarkable coolness and courage he succeeded in bringing the sturgeon ashore. It is a singular fact, that this fish is only good in certain rivers: those of the Delaware, for example, being considered unfit to eat; and those of the rivers on either side of it, the Hudson and the Potomac, considered a great delicacy. It is recorded, by the way, that one of these enormous fish descended from an aerial leap into a ferry-boat, during the revolutionary war, and falling into the lap of an officer, seated on the gunwale, broke his thigh. Every passenger up this fine river has seen the sturgeon leaps; and an ascent of eight or ten feet above the water is not uncommon.

The shad and herring are taken by thousands, in nets, very much in the usual way.

The wild birds that frequent the bosom and shores of the Potomac, are very numerous. Among them are the swan, the wild goose, the red-head shoveler, the black-head shoveler, the duck and mallard, the black duck, the blue-winged teal, the green-winged teal, the widgeon, and, last not least, the far-celebrated *canvass-back*. This duck, which we believe is unrivalled in the world for richness of flavour, is one of a class called *drift fowl*, from their habit of floating in the middle of the river when at rest. The two species of shoveler have the same habit, and are scarcely inferior in flavour. The canvass-back breeds, it is supposed, on the borders of the northern lakes, or on the shores of Hudson's Bay; and in their migrations confine their pasture almost exclusively to the Chesapeake and Potomac. They feed, it is well ascertained, on the bulbous root of a grass which grows on the flats in these rivers, and which is commonly known as wild celery. It is said, that during a hard winter, some forty years ago, a strong wind blew so much of the water off the flats of James river, that the remainder froze to the bottom, enclosing the long tops of this grass so closely in the ice, that when it broke up, and was floated off in the spring, it tore whole fields of it up by the roots, and destroyed the pasture. Since that time, the canvass-back has never been seen on the river.

The bald duck feeds very frequently among these water-fowl; and not having the power to dive entirely under water in search of food, he watches for the rising of the canvass-back, and, by his superior quickness on the wing, seizes on the celery the moment it appears above the surface, and escapes with it to the shore.

The canvass-back is often shot from behind blinds of brush, which conceal the sportsman, in the midst of their feeding ground. There is a practice, however, of *tolling them in*, as it is called, by shaking a coloured handkerchief tied to the branch of a decayed tree. On what propensity of the bird the success of this manœuvre is founded, it would be difficult to say. There is no doubt of the fact, however, that they are thus decoyed within gun-shot; and it is related of an old sportsman on the Potomac, that a long queue of red hair, which he wore in a brush, and shook over his shoulder, served the purpose admirably well. Perhaps we have yet to discover that birds have *curiosity*.

Among the many varieties of wild fowl found on the Potomac, below Harper's Ferry, is the wild swan. The young bird is considered a great delicacy; while the old one is hard and without flavour. In a book on the District of Columbia, by Mr. Elliott, there are some curious particulars respecting their habits, and the manner of taking them.

"This noble bird," says the author, "is seen floating near the shores, in

HARPERS FERRY, FROM THE POTOMAC SIDE

flocks of some two or three hundred, white as the driven snow, and from time to time emitting fine sonorous, and occasionally melodious songs; so loud, that they might be heard, on a still evening, two or three miles. There are two kinds, so called from their respective notes—the one the trumpeter, and the other the hooper; the trumpeter is the largest, and when at full size will measure from five to six feet from the bill to the point of the toe, and from seven to eight feet from the tip of one wing to the tip of the other, when stretched and expanded. They are sagacious and wary, and depend more on the sight than on the sense of smell. On a neck nearly three feet in length, they are enabled to elevate their heads so as to see and distinguish, with a quick and penetrating eye, objects at a great distance; and by means of this same length of neck they feed in slack tides, by immersing, as is their habit, nearly all of the body, and throwing only their feet and tails out in three or four feet water, and on the flatty shores they frequent, generally beyond gun-shot; the sportsman availing himself, however, of a peculiar propensity (of which we shall presently speak more particularly) prevailing with them, and some of the other water fowl, often *toll* them within reach of their fire. The swans remain here the whole winter, only shifting their ground in severe weather, from the frozen to the open part of the river, and dropping down into the salts, where it is rarely frozen. They get into good condition soon after their arrival in autumn, and remain fat until toward spring, when, a few weeks before their departure (about the first of March), they gradually become thinner in flesh; and in the latter part of their sojourn here, are found so poor and light, that when shot the gunner gets nothing fit for use but the feathers. Whether this circumstance be owing to their having exhausted the means of subsistence at their feeding-places, or that they are taught by Him who rules the universe, in small as well as great things, thus by abstaining, to prepare themselves for the long aerial voyages they are about to undertake, we pretend not to determine with certainty; there is nothing more wonderful in this, than in the fact, which is notorious, that they, by exercise, regularly and assiduously fit themselves for this continuous effort, to bear themselves through the air to the distance of perhaps a thousand miles or leagues. Large flocks are seen every day rising from the river, and taking a high position, flying out of sight, and apparently moving in a circuit to a considerable distance, again returning to or near the same place, during the last two or three weeks of their stay.

"The swan is tolled by a dog, that is taught to play about within easy call of his master, at the edge of the water; the hunter contrives to place himself behind a log, or some other cover well concealed, before he begins his operations, taking care to observe that the direction of the wind is not unfavourable to him, and that the flock he means to toll is near enough to distinguish such objects on the shore, and under no alarm at the time. By what motive these fowls are influenced, we have not heard satisfactorily explained; but certain it is, they are very commonly brought in from some hundreds of yards' distance, in this way, to within point-blank shot. It is said, and perhaps truly, in the case of the dog, that they fancy themselves in pursuit of some animal, as the fag, or mink, by which their young are annoyed at their breeding-places.

"The wild goose is yet more wary and vigilant to keep out of harm's way than the swan. He too is sharp-sighted, but depends much on his sense of smell for protection: this is so well known to the huntsman, that he never attempts, however he may be concealed from this bird, to approach it from the direction of the wind; since he would assuredly be scented before he could get within gun-shot, and left to lament his error, by the sudden flight of the whole flock. These geese, towards spring, often alight on the land, and feed on the herbage in fields; and sometimes in such numbers as to do great injury to the wheat fields on the borders of the river. When so employed they are difficult of approach, always taking a position at a distance from cover of any kind, and marching in a single and extended rank, flanked by a watch goose at each extremity; which, while all the others are busily feeding, and advancing with their heads down among the herbage, moves erect, keeping pace with his comrades,—his eyes and nose in a position so as to give him the earliest intelligence of the presence of an enemy, though at a great distance; and the moment such is perceived, it is communicated to the whole company by certain tones used for alarm; and immediately is responded to by a halt, and the lifting of heads; and an instant flight, or a deliberate return to feeding, takes place, according as the nature of the danger, after the examination, may be considered."

Caldwell, Lake George

IN the future poetry of America, Lake George will hold the place of Loch Katrine in Scotland. The best idea that can be given of it, indeed, to a person who has seen Loch Katrine, is to say, that it is the Trosachs on a little larger scale. There is the same remarkably clear water in both,—the same jutting and bold shores, small green islands, and bright vegetation; and the same profusion of nooks and bays. It struck me at Loch Katrine, that the waters seemed to have overflowed the dells of an undulating country, and left nothing visible but the small green hill-tops loaded with vegetation. The impression was owing, no doubt, to the reach of the shrubs and grass to the very edge of the water; and the same thing produces the same effect at Lake George. When the bosom of the lake is tranquil, the small islands, with their reflections below, look like globes of heaped-up leaves suspended in the air.

The extraordinary purity of the waters of Lake George procured for it the name of Lake Sacrament; and every stranger is struck with their singular transparency. It is singular, that the waters on every side of it,—those of Lake Champlain, for example, of the Hudson, and of the whole region between the Green Mountains and the Mississippi,—are more or less impregnated with lime, while Lake George alone is pellucid and pure. It receives its waters, probably, from subjacent springs.

The surface of this lake is said to be one hundred feet higher than Lake Champlain. Another, and probably a more correct estimate, makes the difference three hundred. There are three steps to the falls, which form the outlet into the latter lake; and the lower one, when the snow is melting in spring, is a cataract of uncommon beauty. Lake George is frozen over from three to four months; and it is remarked of it, that the ice does not sink, as in Lake Champlain, but gradually dissolves.

Before it became a part of the fashionable tour, this lake was a solitude, appropriated more particularly by the deer and the eagle. Both have nearly disappeared. The echo of the steam-boat, that has now taken the place of the noiseless canoe,—and the peppering of fancy sportsmen, that have followed the far-between but more effectual shots of the borderer's rifle,—have drawn from its shores these and other circumstances of romance. The only poetry of scene which can take the place of that of nature, is historical and legendary; and ages must lapse, and generations pass away, and many changes come over the land, before that time. We are in the interregnum, now, least favourable for poetry.

CALDWELL, LAKE GEORGE

Caldwell is a flourishing town, built at the end of the lake, and remarkable for nothing, in itself, but a famous hotel, where scenery-hunters dine. We turn from this too succulent theme, to give an extract from the works of a grave and eminent divine; proving, by its glowing enthusiasm, the effect of this lovely scenery even on minds of the most serious bent.

"The whole scenery of this lake is greatly enhanced in beauty and splendour, by the progressive change which the traveller sailing on its bosom perpetually finds in his position, and by the unceasing variegations of light and shade which attend his progress. The gradual and the sudden openings of scoops and basins, of islands and points, of promontories and summits—the continual change of their forms, and their equally gradual and sudden disappearance,—impart to every object a brilliancy, life, and motion, scarcely inferior to that which is seen in the images formed by the camera-obscura, and in strength and distinctness greatly superior. Light and shade are here not only far more diversified, but are much more obvious, intense, and flowing, than in smooth, open countries. Every thing, whether on the land or water, was here affected by the changes of the day; and the eye, without forecast, found itself, however disposed on ordinary occasions to inattention, instinctively engaged, and fastened with emotions approximating to rapture. The shadows of the mountains, particularly on the west, floating slowly over the bosom of the lake, and then softly ascending that of the mountains on the east, presented to us, in a wide expanse, the uncommon and most pleasing image of one vast range of mountains slowly moving up the ascent of another.

"On the evening of Friday, the 1st of October, while we were returning from Ticonderoga, we were presented with a prospect superior to any which I ever beheld. An opening lay before us, between the mountains on the west and those on the east, gilded by the departing sunbeams. The lake, alternately glassy and gently rippled, of a light and exquisite sapphire, gay and brilliant with the tremulous lustre already mentioned floating upon its surface, stretched in prospect to a vast distance, through a great variety of larger and smaller apertures. In the chasm, formed by the mountains, lay a multitude of islands, differing in size, shape, and umbrage, and clothed in deeply-shaded green. Beyond them, and often partly hidden behind the tall and variously-figured trees with which they were tufted, rose, in the west and south-west, a long range of distant mountains, tinged with a deep misty azure, and crowned with an immense succession of lofty pines. Above the mountains, and above each other, were extended in great numbers long streaming clouds, of the happiest forms, and painted with red and orange light, in all their diversities of tincture.

"To complete the scenery of this lake, the efforts of cultivation are obviously wanting. The hand of the husbandman has already begun to clear these grounds, and will, at no great distance of time, adorn them with all the smiling scenes of agriculture. It does not demand the gift of prophecy to foresee, that the villas of opulence and refinement will, within half a century, add here all the elegances of art to the beauty and majesty of nature."

Centre Harbour, Lake Winnipiseogee

THERE are several considerable promontories which intrude into Lake Winnipiseogee, and on one of them is built the town of Centre Harbour. The lake is near the middle of the state of New Hampshire, of a very irregular form, and at the western end is divided into three large bays. There are nine townships on its borders, of which Centre Harbour, the largest, is on the northwest side. The waters of the lake in some places are unfathomable, but abound with fish. It will still be some years, probably, before the navigation of this body of water will become of much importance.

Beside the beauty of nature, which is prodigal on the borders of this lovely lake, there is little of interest beyond what is found in the recollections of the Indian wars. Penhallow's History, which till lately has been a rare book, has rescued New Hampshire from the obscurity in which some of the other states remain, on these curious and interesting subjects. One wonders, in reading of the critical adventures of the early settlers, what offset the country could give them against such a frail tenure of life. "At one time," says the journal, "the people of Dunstable were advised of a party of two hundred and seventy Indians that were coming upon them. Their first descent was on the 3d of July, when they fell on a garrison that had twenty troopers in it, who, by their negligence, keeping no watch, suffered them to enter, which tended to the destruction of half their number. After that, a small party attacked Daniel Galusha's house, who held them in play for some time, till the old man's courage failed; when, on surrendering himself, he informed them of the state of

CENTRE HARBOUR, LAKE WINNIPISSEOGEE

the garrison; how that one man was killed, and only two men and a boy left; which caused them to rally anew, and with greater courage than before. Upon which, one with the boy got out on the back side, leaving only Jacob to fight the battle, who, for some time, defended himself with much bravery; but overpowered with force, and finding none to assist him, was obliged to quit it, and make his escape as well as he could: but before he got far, the enemy laid hold of him once and again; and yet, by much struggling, he rescued himself. Upon this, they burnt the house; and next day about forty more fell on Amesbury, where they killed eight: two, at the same time, who were at work in a field, hearing an outcry, hastened to their relief, but being pursued, ran to a deserted house, in which were two flankers, where each of them found an old gun, but neither of them fit for service; and if they were, had neither powder nor shot to load with: however, each took a flanker, and made the best appearance they could, by thrusting the muzzles of their guns outside the port-holes, crying aloud, 'Here they are, but do not fire till they come nearer;' which put the enemy into such a fright, that they instantly drew off."—
Penhallow.

"From thence they went to Kingstown, where they killed and wounded several cattle. About the same time, Joseph English, who was a friend Indian, going from Dunstable to Chelmsford, with a man and his wife on horseback, was shot dead; the woman taken, but the man made his escape. On the 8th of July, five Indians, a little before night, fell on an out-house in Reading, where they surprised a woman with eight children: the former, with the three youngest, were instantly despatched, and the others they carried captive; but one of the children, unable to travel, they knocked on the head, and left in the swamp, concluding it was dead; but awhile after, it was found alive. The neighbourhood being alarmed, got ready by the morning, and coming on their track, pursued them so near that they recovered three of the children, and put the enemy in such a terror, that they not only quitted their plunder and blankets, but the other captive also: several strokes were afterwards made on Chelmsford, Sudbury, and Groton, where three soldiers, as they were going to public worship, were waylaid by a small party, who killed two, and made the other prisoner.

"At Exeter, a company of French Mohawks, who some time kept lurking about Captain Hilton's garrison, took a view of all that went in and out; and observing some to go with their scythes to mow, lay in ambush till they laid by their arms, and while at work, rushed on at once, and by intercepting them from their arms, killed four, wounded one, and carried three captive; so that out of ten, two only escaped. A while after, two of those that were taken, viz. Mr. Edward Hall and Samuel Myals, made their escape; but the fatigue and difficulty that they went through (besides the terror and fear they were under of being taken) were almost incredible; for in three weeks together, they had nothing to subsist on except a few lily roots, and the rinds of trees.

"It would be an endless task to enumerate the various sufferings that many groaned under, by long marching with heavy burdens through heat and cold; and when ready to faint for want of food, they were frequently knocked on the head: teeming women, in cold blood, have been ript open; others fastened to stakes and burnt alive; and yet the finger of God did eminently appear in several instances, of which I shall mention the following:—

"Of Rebekah Taylor, who after her return from captivity, gave me the following account:—That when she was going to Canada, on the back of Montreal river, she was violently insulted by Sampson, her bloody master, who without any provocation was resolved to hang her; and for want of a rope, made use of his girdle, which when he had fastened about her neck, he attempted to hoist her up on the limb of a tree (that hung in the nature of a gibbet), but in hoisting her, the weight of her body broke it asunder; which so exasperated the cruel tyrant that he made a second attempt, resolving if he failed in that, to knock her on the head; but before he had power to effect it, Bomaseen came along, and seeing the tragedy on foot, prevented the fatal stroke."

Yale College at New Haven

YALE COLLEGE was founded in the year 1700, sixty-five years after the erection of the first house in the Colony of Connecticut. Ten of the principal ministers, nominated by general consent of the clergy, met at New Haven, and formed themselves into a society, the object of which was to found a college in the colony. At their next meeting each brought a number of books, and presented them for the library, and the following year the Legislature granted them a charter, constituting them "Trustees of a Collegiate School in his Majesty's Colony of Connecticut."

YALE COLLEGE AT NEW HAVEN

The principal benefactor of the infant institution was the Hon. Elihu Yale, of London, Governor of the East India Company. This gentleman was descended from a family in Wales, which for many generations held the manor of Plas Grannow, near Rexon. His father, Thomas Yale, Esq., came from England with the first colonists of New Haven. In this town, Elihu, the subsequent benefactor of the College, was born, and at ten years of age he was sent to England. Thence he went to Hindostan, and after twenty years' residence, was made Governor of Madras. He returned to London with an immense fortune, was chosen Governor of the East India Company, and died at Rexon in 1721. "This gentleman," says the College historian, "sent, in several donations, to the Collegiate School, five hundred pounds sterling; and a little before his death, ordered goods to be sent out to the value of five hundred pounds more; but they were never received. In gratitude for this munificence, the Trustees, by a solemn act, named their seminary Yale College; a name which, it is believed, will convey the memory of his good works to distant generations."

Among other benefactors to this institution was the Rev. Dr. Berkeley, Dean of Derry, in Ireland, and afterwards Bishop of Cloyne. This distinguished divine came to America in 1732, for the purpose of establishing a college in the island of Bermuda; a purpose to which he sacrificed considerable time, property and labour. He had been promised twenty thousand pounds by the ministry for the completion of this work, but the sum was never paid, and the project failed. Dr. Berkeley then bought a farm in Newport, Rhode Island, and while residing there, became acquainted with the circumstances of Yale College, and ultimately made the institution a present of his farm, and sent the Trustees from England "the finest collection of books that ever came at one time to America."

Since this period Yale College has continued to thrive in means and usefulness, and it is now, in the numbers of its students, and in its practical advantages, we believe, the first College in the United States. That of Harvard, (founded sixty or seventy years earlier,) is better endowed, but more expensive and less frequented. It is a curious fact, in the early history of nations, by the way, that the Act to incorporate Harvard College was passed, and the College in operation, *ten years after the first settlement of the Colony.*

The whole amount of fees of tuition at Yale College is about thirty-five dollars a year, near seven pounds sterling. Board and every expense included, it is thought in New England that three hundred dollars (60*l.*) a year is a sufficient allowance for the education of a boy at this institution. The course of study embraces four years, and the discipline is impartial and severe. Instances occur annually of degrees refused, and degradations of standing in consequence of failures in examination; and over the morals of the students, particularly, the vigilance of the faculty is untiring and effective.

Perhaps one of the best, and certainly one of the peculiar advantages of Yale College, is the extent and excellence of the society in New Haven, and its accessibility to the students. The town contains near ten thousand inhabitants, most of them people of education, connected in some way with the College; or opulent families drawn thither by the extreme beauty of the town, and its air of refinement and repose. The upper classes of students mingle freely in this simple and pure society, which, it is not too much to say, is one of the most elegant and highly cultivated in the world. Polished manners and the usages of social life are thus insensibly gained with improvement of mind; and in a country like this, where those advantages are not attainable by all in early life, the privilege is inestimable.

The college buildings of New Haven are more remarkable for their utility than for the beauty of their architecture; but, buried in trees, and standing on the ridge of a sloping green, they have altogether a beautiful effect, and an air of elegant and studious repose. Few strangers ever pass through New Haven without expressing a wish to take up their abode, and pass their days, among its picturesque avenues and gardens.

The Willey House—White Mountains

THE particulars of what is called the *Willey Tragedy* are well known to all readers of newspapers. This family lived in the Notch of the White Mountains, under the western range, and consisted of nine persons. They had retired at night, when a very unusual noise in the mountains aroused them from their beds, and, in terror at its increasing thunders, they unfortunately abandoned the house, and sought refuge in flight. A vast mass of earth and rocks, disengaged from the precipices above them, suddenly rushed down the side of the mountain, and sweeping every thing before it, divided in the rear of the house, reunited again, leaving it unharmed, and thundered down to the val-

THE WILLEY HOUSE

ley, overwhelming the fugitive family in its career. The manuscript journal of a friend, who had made two excursions to the spot, gives us an account of its present aspect.

"In a short time we came to the well-known house of the Willey family, which of course we paused to examine. Nothing can be conceived more lonely than this wild place. The mountains tower on both sides of the valley to the height of four or five hundred feet, with deep channels worn into their sides by the winter torrents; and in many places the rocks are left bare for acres by the slides of avalanches that have rushed into the valley. The house in which the unfortunate family dwelt stands under the western range of mountains, and the avalanche came down nearly from the summit. We remained gazing on the scene for some time. The sky above was clear, and spanned the interval between the mountains, seeming to rest on their summits, while a swift breeze drove over the hills below, in swift succession, a few thin and fleecy clouds. The wind entered the outer door of the desolate dwelling, which had been left open, with a broken chair set against it; and as it surged back and forth, violently shut and opened the inner doors, with a noise that seemed the voice of the very spirit of desolation. The effect was startling and dismal."

This is, we believe, the most disastrous avalanche on record in this country, and the only one of any importance, which was merely a descent of earth and rocks. What is called a *cloud-burst* is not uncommon in the mountainous regions of the north; and there are several striking examples recorded.

In the autumn of 1784, in the latter part of the night, a deluge of water descended from Saddle Mountain, in Massachusetts. A family, which lived in a house at some distance from the foot of the mountain, not far from a brook, were suddenly awakened out of their sleep by the united roaring of the wind and the torrent. In their flight they hastily dressed themselves, and escaped from the house, the ground-floor of which was by this time six inches under water. When they returned in the morning, they found the house so completely swept away, that no part of it was left. The brook, through the channel of which this flood discharged itself, had never before, even in the highest freshets, approached the house by a considerable distance.

Subsequent examination of the mountain disclosed that the descent of water commenced not far from the summit; for two or three rods above the spot where the ground first began to be broken, the trees and shrubs appear to have been swept away by the violence of the deluge. The broken ground is, at first, not more than six feet wide, but rapidly becomes wider as it descends; so that within one hundred and fifty feet it is about three rods in breadth, and in the widest place five or six. Towards the lower limit its breadth gradually diminishes, until it terminates in a gutter, which in some places is five or six feet deep; this continues several rods, and then branches into other channels, which, though covered with leaves and moss, are discernible quite down to the brook at the foot of the mountain. The whole length of the broken ground is about one hundred and thirty rods. Towards the bottom there were standing the stumps of large trees, whose tops were broken off by the deluge; and above they were entirely swept away, not leaving a trace. By what means a mass of water, sufficient for these phenomena, is collected and suspended over the mountains, or what occasioned the disruption of the mass of earth and rock which overwhelmed the family in the White Mountains, are points not easily settled.

Battle Monument, Baltimore

THIS monument stands on the summit of a rising ground, in the centre of one of the best built squares of Baltimore, and is a very considerable ornament to the town. It is intended to commemorate the name and fame of those citizens of Baltimore who fell in its defence in 1814. An Egyptian base, raised to the height of about four feet from the pavement of the street, is surmounted by a column, representing fasces, upon the bands of which are placed in bronze letters the names of the thirty-nine citizens. On each angle of the base are griffins, and the lower part of the column is ornamented with *bassi relievi*, representing scenes of the contest. The whole is crowned by a statue personifying the city, with the eagle at her side, holding a laurel wreath. The entire height of the monument is fifty-two feet.

The defence of Baltimore was one of the most spirited of the many gallant actions on our sea-board and frontier during the late war; and it occurred more opportunely, as it followed so closely upon the defeat at Bladensburgh, which, though inevitable from the superior numbers of the enemy, was still accompanied with the mortification inseparable from such disaster.

After the embarkation of the troops under General Ross, (who had bought his victory at Bladensburgh with the loss of nearly a thousand men,) Admiral

BATTLE MONUMENT, BALTIMORE

Cochrane concentrated his fleet, and made preparations for the attack on Baltimore. The whole squadron, amounting to forty vessels, sailed soon after for the Patapsco, and arriving near North Point, twelve miles from the city, the ships of the line anchored across the channel, and commenced the debarkation of troops. By the morning of the 12th of September about 8,000 soldiers, sailors, and marines, were in readiness to march upon the town, and sixteen bomb vessels and frigates proceeded up the river, and anchored within two miles and a half of Fort M'Henry.

This garrison, which was mainly relied on for the protection of the city, was defended by about 5,000 men, and a detachment of about 3,000 was sent on by the North Point road to annoy or engage the enemy at his approach. Intelligence soon came in, that a light corps was advancing; and two companies of infantry, with a few riflemen, and ten artillerists with a single four-pounder, proceeded half a mile, and met and engaged the main body. The situation of the ground would not admit of the cooperation of the artillery and cavalry; and the infantry and riflemen sustained the whole action with great gallantry. The advance of the enemy was checked, and Major-General Ross and several other British officers killed.

The detachment now fell back upon the main line of the American force, and after some skirmishing with rockets and artillery at a distance, the whole force of the enemy pushed forward, and attacked the two regiments on the left with great impetuosity. These being thrown into confusion, a general fire was opened upon the British line, and a vigorous action followed, which lasted till four o'clock. At that hour the American force amounting to but about 1,400, and the British to about 7,000, General Stucker fell back upon the reserve regiment, and was joined by some other companies, who took position with him within half a mile of the entrenchments.

Early the following morning the Admiral made signals to the British officer in command on shore, that the frigates, bomb-ships, and flotilla of barges, would take their stations to bombard the town and fort in the course of the morning. The land forces accordingly moved forward, and took up a position two miles eastward of the entrenchments. The day was chiefly passed in manœuvring; but Colonel Brooke, after a vain attempt to make a detour through the country, concentrated the English force directly in front of the American line, drove in the out-posts, and made preparations for an attack in the night.

The night was stormy; and in the morning it was discovered that the enemy had abandoned his position. The troops were re-embarked, and a bombardment commenced, which lasted till the following morning, during which a fleet of barges attempted to storm Fort Covington, but were repulsed with great loss. With the failure of this attempt the undertaking was abandoned altogether, and the fleet stood down the river.

When the bombardment commenced, the fort opened its batteries upon the ships; but, the shot falling short, the little garrison were compelled to keep their post without retaliation. There were four killed and twenty-four wounded in the entrenchments, and among the former were two very gallant young men, Lieutenants Clagett and Clem, volunteer officers.

The entire loss of the British could not be ascertained. That of the Americans on the field was about 150, which, added to those in the fort, makes a total of 178.

A Forest, on Lake Ontario

THE view over this immense forest was taken in the Tuscarora reservation, from an Indian cabin, which serves as a sort of halting-place for travellers to Niagara. We arrived here about noon, emerging from a tract of deep woods which had darkened the road for several miles, and glancing off to the right, discovered that we were following a high ridge, from which extended, with a radius of forty miles, one unbroken sea of foliage. A thin silver line on the very rim of the horizon looked brighter than the sky, and we found on inquiry that it was Lake Ontario, which, with its thread of bright light, forms a limit to what, else, were an object as boundless as the sea.

An Indian woman of about forty, dressed very neatly, came out to offer for sale specimens of Indian workmanship, such as moccosins, pouches, &c.; and, among other things, a beautiful little model of a bark canoe. De Kalm, who travelled in this country in 1749, gives a very detailed account of the making of a canoe. He was going to Canada under the escort of a party of Indians, who, on coming to a portage of forty miles, between the Hudson and Lake Champlain, (now superseded by a canal,) were compelled to leave their canoe and build another.

"The making of the canoe," he says, "took up half yesterday and all this

A FOREST, ON LAKE ONTARIO

day. To make such a boat, they pick out a thick, tall birch, with a smooth bark, and with as few branches as possible. This tree is cut down, and great care is taken to prevent the bark from being hurt by falling against other trees, or against the ground. With this view some do not fell the trees, but climb to the top of them, split the bark, and strip it off; which was the method our boat-builder took. The bark is split on one side, in a straight line along the tree, as long as the boat is intended to be; at the same time the bark is carefully cut from the stem a little way on both sides of the slit, that it may more easily separate. The bark is then peeled off very carefully, and particular care is taken not to make any holes in it; this is easy when the sap is in the trees; and at other seasons the tree is heated by the fire for that purpose.

"The bark thus stripped off is spread on the ground, in a smooth place, turning the inside downwards, and the rough outside upwards; and to stretch it better, some logs of wood or stones are carefully put on it, which press it down. Then the sides of the bark are gently bent upwards, in order to form the sides of the boat. Some sticks are then fixed into the ground at the distance of three or four feet from each other, in the curve line in which the sides of the boat are intended to be, supporting the bark intended for the sides. The sides of the bark are then bent in the form which the boat is to have, and according to that, the sticks are either put near or further off.

"The ribs of the canoe are made of thick branches of hickory, they being tough and pliable. They are cut into several flat pieces, about an inch thick, and bent into the form which the ribs require, according to their places in the broader or narrower part of the boat. The upper edge on each side is made of two thin poles, of the length of the boat, which are put close together on the side, being flat where they are joined. The edge of the bark is put between these two poles, and sewed up with threads of the mouse-wood, or other tough bark, or with roots.

"After this is done, the poles are sewed together, and being bent properly, both ends join at each end of the boat, where they are tied togther with ropes. To prevent the widening of the boat at the top, three or four transverse bands are put across it, from one edge to the other, at the distance of thirty or forty inches from each other, made of hickory.

"As the bark at the two ends of the boat cannot be put so close together as to keep out the water, the crevices are stopped up with the crushed or pounded bark of the red elm, which in that state looks like oakum. Some pieces of bark are put on the ribs of the boat, without which the foot would easily pierce the thin and weak bottom. The side of the bark which runs next the wood thus becomes the outside of the boat, because it is smooth and slippery, and cuts the water with less difficulty than the other.

"The building of these boats is not always quick; for sometimes it happens that after peeling the bark off an elm, and carefully examining it, it is found pierced with holes and slits, or is too thin to venture one's life in. That which we made was big enough to bear four persons, with our baggage, which weighed somewhat more than a man.

"All possible precautions must be taken in rowing on rivers with bark canoes; for when rowing fast, a broken branch under water would carry half the boat away. To get into it also requires great care, for the heels may very easily pierce through the bottom."

Viaduct on the Baltimore and Washington Railroad

The Patuxent, which is leaped over so lightly at this place by the arches of the Viaduct, becomes, ere long, a stream which is not only respectable in size, but most respectable in story. It will ever be associated with the name and fame of the gallant Barney, who, though his exertions could not prevent ultimate defeat, did much to sustain his country's honour, and has made his own imperishable.

While the British squadron was blockading the eastern coast during the summer of 1814, Commodore Barney sailed from Baltimore in command of a flotilla consisting of a cutter, two gun-boats, a galley, and nine large barges, for the protection of the inlets and harbours in the several parts of the bay. On the 1st of June, being at the mouth of the Patuxent, he discovered two schooners, one of which carried eighteen guns; and immediately gave chase. The schooners were joined, however, by a large ship, which despatched a number of barges to their assistance; and the commodore sailed up the Patuxent to avoid being cut off from the Potomac. The schooners and barges following him, he engaged and drove them back, and then anchored within three miles of the seventy-four. In the course of a few days, the enemy was reinforced by a rasee and a sloop of war; and joining the barges of these vessels, they followed

VIADUCT ON THE BALTIMORE AND WASHINGTON RAILROAD

the flotilla into St. Leonard's Creek, across which Commodore Barney formed his boats in line of battle. A sharp engagement ensued, the enemy gave way, and the flotilla pursued them to within a short distance of their shipping. In the afternoon, the enemy made another attempt with twenty barges and two schooners. After a warm action, the barges were driven back upon the eighteen-gun schooner, which, in attempting to beat out, was so severely handled, that her crew ran her aground and abandoned her. On the 26th, a corps of artillery arrived from Washington to the commodore's assistance, and a combined attack was made on the whole squadron. The action continued two hours; at the end of which the enemy's ships were driven from their anchorage, and stood down the river.

The cessation of hostilities in Europe, enabled the British government to send out powerful reinforcements to their fleets and armies in America; and Sir Alexander Cochrane soon arrived with thirty sail, having on board several thousand men, under command of Major General Ross. This force entered the Chesapeake, and a plan of attack on Washington, Alexandria, and Baltimore, was adopted. Admiral Cochrane very honourably informed the Secretary of State that he had orders to lay waste all the accessible towns on the coast; and the fleet, in two divisions, soon after approached the capital by the Potomac and the Patuxent.

In obedience to orders, Commodore Barney blew up his flotilla in the Patuxent, and with his seamen and marines, joined the army under General Winder. General Ross landed six thousand men at the head of frigate navigation, and, with five thousand, General Winder met him at Bladensburgh. The action commenced at mid-day. Commodore Barney had been placed with his battery in the main road by which the enemy advanced; and after two or three vain attempts were made to pass him, the main column fell back in disorder, and it was found necessary to flank his right. The British were gaining ground, however, in every other part of the line; and Commodore Barney was soon left with his small force standing alone.

General Ross had now nearly complete command of the field; the ammunition waggons had been driven off in the disorder, and the commodore was reduced to a single round of cartridge. He had besides received a severe wound in the thigh. Thus situated, he gave reluctant orders for retreat; and after being carried a short distance, he fell, exhausted with loss of blood. He was soon after taken prisoner, and removed to the enemy's hospital, where he was treated, by the orders of General Ross, with the greatest kindness; and, on his recovery, released on his parole.

After his victory at Bladensburgh, General Ross marched directly to the capital, and proceeded immediately to burn all the public buildings, library, &c. Then, as now, Washington was merely a diplomatic capital, very thinly populated; and the few inhabitants were unable to make any show of resistance. No comment is necessary on an act which the English nation itself was the first to condemn.

The division of the enemy's fleet which sailed up the Potomac, consisting of eight sail, was directed to attack Alexandria. That small town surrendered, and obtained a stipulation, upon very ungenerous conditions, that their houses should not be entered or destroyed. Captain Gordon, who was in command, sailed soon after down the river with a fleet of prize vessels taken from the town, and a great amount of property. He received some damage from the batteries lower down, but joined the rest of the squadron in the Chesapeake, and accompanied them in their less successful attacks on Baltimore.

We think the "City of Monuments," as the last-mentioned town is called, should erect a monument to the memory of Barney.

"A TRIBUTE TO THE BRAVE

"Though furled be the banner of blood on the plain,
　And rusted the sabre once crimsoned with gore;
　Though hushed be the ravens that croaked o'er the slain,
　And calmed into silence the battle's loud roar;
　Though Peace with her rosy smile gladden the vales,
　And Commerce unshackled dance over the wave;
　Though Music and Song may enliven the gales,
　And Joy crown with roses and myrtle the brave;
　Like spirits that start from the sleep of the dead,
　Our heroes shall rouse when the 'larum shall blow;
　Then Freedom's broad flag on the wind shall be spread,
　And Valour's sword flash in the face of the foe.
　Our Eagle shall rise 'mid the whirlwinds of war,
　And dart through the dun cloud of battle his eye—
　Shall spread his wide wings on the tempest afar,
　O'er spirits of valour that conquer or die.
　And ne'er shall the rage of the conflict be o'er,
　And ne'er shall the warm blood of life cease to flow,
　And still 'mid the smoke of the battle shall roam
　Our Eagle—till scattered and fled be the foe.
　When Peace shall disarm War's dark brow of its frown,
　And roses shall bloom on the soldier's rude grave—
　Then Honour shall weave of the laurel a crown,
　That Beauty shall bind on the brow of the brave."—Percival.

Indian Fall, Opposite West Point

THIS is a secluded and delicious bit of nature, hidden amid rocks and woods, on the shore of the Hudson, but possessing a refinement and an elegance in its wildness which would almost give one the idea that it was an object of beauty in some royal park. One of the most secret streams that feed this finest of our rivers, finds its way down through a winding and almost trackless channel; and after fretting over rocks, and loitering in dark and limpid pools for several miles, suddenly bursts out over a precipice of fifty feet, and fills with its clear waters the sheltered basin seen in the drawing. Immense trees overhang it on every side, and follow the stream still on in its course; and, in the depth of summer, the foaming current scarcely catches a ray of the sun from its source to its outlet. The floor of the basin below the Fall is pebbly, the water is clear and cool, the spot secluded, and, in all respects, Nature has formed it for a bath. A fair and famous lady, residing a summer or two since at West Point, was its first known Musidora, and the limpid and bright basin is already called after her name.

A large party visiting at a hospitable house, where the artist and his travelling companion were entertained during the heat of the last summer, proposed to accompany him on his visit to the Indian Fall. Excursions on the banks of the Hudson are usually made in boats; but it was necessary to see some points of view from the hills between, and we walked out to the stables to see what could be done for vehicles and cattle. A farm waggon, with its tail up in the air, built after an old Dutch fashion, which still prevails in New York,— a sort of loosely jointed, long, lumbering vehicle, which was meant to go over any rock smaller than a beer-barrel without upsetting—was the only "consarn," as the "help" called it, which would hold the party. With straw in the bottom, and straps put across from peg to peg, it would carry eleven, and the driver.

Horses were the next consideration; and here we were rather staggered. A vicious old mare, that kept a wheelwright and a surgeon in constant employ, —and a powerful young colt, half broken,—were the only steeds in stable. However either might be made to go alone, they had never been tried together; and the double waggon harness was the worse for service. The "help" suggested very sensibly that the load would be too heavy to run away with, and that if the mare kicked, or the colt bolted—or, in short, if any thing happened, except backing over a precipice, we had only to sit still and let them do their "darndest."

THE INDIAN FALLS, OPPOSITE WEST POINT

We cobbled the harness in its weak spots, shook down the straw for the ladies, nailed up the tail-board, which had lost its rods, got the cattle in, and brought up quietly to the door. The ladies and the champagne were put in, and the colt was led off by the bit, shaking his head, and catching up his hind leg; while the demure old mare drew off tamely and steadily, "never wicked," as the ploughman said, "till you got her dander up with a tough hill." The driver had a chain with a list bottom, and, having had some practice in Charing Cross and Fleet Street, fingered his reins and flourished his maple whip through the village, evidently not thinking himself or his driving *de la petite bière*.

The road, which followed the ridges of the superb hills skirting the river opposite West Point, was, in some places, scarce fit even for a bridle-path; and, at every few paces, came a rock, which we believed passable when we had surged over it—not before. The two ill-matched animals drew to a wonder; and the ladies and the champagne had escaped all damage, till, as the enemy of mankind would have it, our ambitious whip saw stretching out before him a fair quarter of a mile of more even road. A slight touch of the whip sent off the colt in a jump, carrying away the off trace with the first spring; the old mare struck into a gallop, and, with the broken trace striking against the colt's heels, and the whippletree parallel with the pole, away they went as nearly in a tandem as the remaining part of the harness would allow. The tail-board soon flew off, and let out two unsuspecting gentlemen, who had placed their backs and their reliance upon it; and the screams of the ladies added what was wanting to raise the "dander" of the old mare to its most unpleasant climax. The straps gave way, the ladies rolled together in the straw, the driver tossed about on his list-bottomed chain, the champagne corks flew, —and presently, as if we were driven by a battering-ram against a wall, we brought up with a tremendous crash, and stood still. We had come to a sharp turn in the road; and the horses, unable to turn, had leaped a low stone wall, and breaking clear of every thing, left us on one side, while they thrashed the ripe wheat with the whippletrees on the other.

The ladies were undamaged, fortunately; and, with one champagne bottle saved from the wreck, we completed the excursion to the Fall on foot, and were too happy to return by water.

COLUMBIA BRIDGE, OVER THE SUSQUEHANNA

Columbia Bridge, Over the Susquehanna

THIS fine bridge is a mile and a half in length, and forms a beautiful span over the broad waters of the river at this place. The many windings of the Susquehanna makes its shallowness and incapacity for navigation less a disadvantage than would have been felt on a more direct water-course; and the ingenuity and enterprise of the country in the construction of canals, bridges, and rail-roads, have left nothing to desire in the matter of facilities for travel. It is always a reasonable query to any, except a business traveller, whether the saving of time and fatigue in the wonderful improvements in locomotion is an equivalent for the loss of rough adventure and knowledge of the detail of a country acquired by hardship and delay. Contrast the journey over a rail-road at a pace of fifteen miles in the hour, through the rough, the picturesque valley of the Susquehanna, with a journey over the same ground ninety years ago, as presented in the travels of Peter Kalm. He was on horseback, with Indian guides.

"About sun-set it cleared up, and we encamped on the east branch of the Susquehanna. In the night it thundered and rained very fast, and took us at a disadvantage; for we had made no shelter to keep off the rain, neither could we see it till just over our heads, and it began to fall.

"One of our Indians cut four sticks, five feet long, and stuck both ends in the ground, at two feet distance one from another; over these he spread his watch-coat, and crept through them, and then fell to singing. In the mean time, we were setting poles slantwise in the ground, tying others across them; over which we spread our blanket, and crept close under it, with a fire before us, and fell fast asleep. I waked a little after midnight and found our fire almost out; so I got the hatchet and felled a few saplings, which I laid on, and made a rousing fire, though it rained stoutly; and lying down once more, I slept sound all night.

"In the morning, when we had dried our blankets, we kept along the side of a hill, and looked about us, not having had such an opportunity for two days, on account of the forest. The valley differed from all I had ever seen before, in its easy and fruitful ascent and descent,—in its great width, everywhere crowned with noble and lofty woods,—but above all, in being entirely free from naked rocks and sharp precipices."

A night or two after, our traveller fell in with a variety of Indian character I never have seen noticed elsewhere: —

"Soon after we were laid down to sleep, and our fire almost burnt out, we

[127]

were entertained by a comical fellow, disguised in as odd a dress as Indian folly could invent. He had on a clumsy vizard of wood, coloured black, with a nose four or five inches long, a grinning mouth set awry, and furnished with long teeth; round the eyes were circles of bright brass, surrounded by a larger circle of white paint. From his forehead hung long tresses of buffalo's hair; and from the catch part of his head (his tuft) hung ropes, made of the plaited husks of Indian corn.

"I cannot recollect the whole of his dress, but that it was equally uncouth. He carried in one hand a large staff, in the other a calabash, with small stones in it for a rattle; and this he rubbed up and down with his staff. He came in at the further end of the wigwam, and, holding up his head, made a noise like the braying of an ass. I asked Weisar, who, as well as myself, lay next the alley, what noise that was. Shickalamy, the chief, who thought I was scared, called out, 'Lie still, John!' I never heard him speak so much English before.

"The jack-pudding presently came up to us, and an Indian boy came with him and kindled our fire, that we might see his glittering eyes and antic postures, as he hobbled round the fire. Sometimes he would turn the buffalo's hair on one side, that we might take a better view of his ill-favoured phiz. When he had tired himself, (which was some time after he had well tired us,) the boy that attended him struck two or three smart blows on the floor, at which the hobgoblin seemed surprised; and, on repeating them, he jumped fairly out of doors and disappeared.

"I suppose this was to divert us, and get some tobacco; for, as he danced about, he would hold out his hand to receive this gratification, for which, as often as he received it, he would return an awkward compliment. After this farce, we endeavoured to compose ourselves to sleep, but towards morning were again disturbed by a drunken squaw coming into the cabin, frequently complimenting us and singing."

We doubt if any traveller's journal on the Mauch Chunk rail-road can show as diverting a page. There are no incidents now-a-days short of a boiler bursting.

Genessee Falls, Rochester

IN the three thousand miles between the Atlantic and the Rocky Mountains, there may be said to be three water-steps formed by the different levels of Lake Ontario, Lake Erie, and Lake Superior. Niagara and the Genessee river fall over the middle step, the edge of which is formed by the brow of a bed of limestone, computed to be four hundred and ten feet above the level of Lake Ontario. Saint Lawrence may thus be said to take but three leaps from the Rocky Mountains to the ocean—an agility which, one would suppose, might have saved the holy martyr from his gridiron.

The ledge over which these two celebrated falls are precipitated, comes out of Canada from an immense distance, and keeps its course along the shore of Lake Ontario, in a direction nearly due east. At the Genessee Falls, as at Niagara, the descent to the lake is between the walls of a tremendous ravine, the grandeur of which seems to have had no terror for the souls of manufacturers. The thriving village of Rochester stands round the lip of the fall; and if you talk to the inhabitants of the beauty of the cascade, they stop your mouth, and strike calculation dumb, with the number of sledge-hammers, nail-cutters, mill-stones, and cotton-jennies, it carries; the product *per diem;* the corresponding increase of population, *et cetera et cetera*—the only instance in the known world of a cataract turned, without the loss of a drop, through the pockets of speculators.

The Genessee river rises in the Alleghany Mountains, and it is not for want of poetical names on its banks that it is not a poetical river. Its source is ten miles below *Nunda*, between the head waters of the *Owago* and the *Cawanisque* rivers; and it runs one hundred and fifty miles, receiving tribute from the *Canassaraga* and *Angelica* creeks, and the *Canesus* and *Honcoye* outlets. It has a great reputation for fertility; and along its valley lies the celebrated farm of Mr. Wadsworth, the agriculturist, who holds in this country the place occupied in England by Mr. Coke of Holkham—now Earl of Leicester.

The Rapids of the Genessee commence a mile above the Fall at Rochester, and descend, when there is much water, with great swiftness and beauty. The first pitch of the stream is ninety-seven perpendicular feet; after which it goes sullenly on down the ravine—black, where it is not covered with foam—till, forty rods below, it takes another leap of one hundred and six feet, at a place called Carthage. We suggested to the landlord that the fall at Carthage should be called after Marius, but he did not see the propriety of it very clearly.

[129]

GENESEE FALLS, ROCHESTER

The Genessee Fall, like Niagara, is gradually *backing up*. It is computed that the latter wears back a rood every three years—the former much less, of course. There is little doubt among the geologists, that the Genessee at one time ran directly into Lake Ontario without much of a cascade, but that, on the retreat of the lake, the surface of which has perceptibly lowered, the stream began to wear back with the attrition of the fall, and they are now three miles asunder. An aqueduct of the great Erie canal runs close across the head of the Fall at Rochester, and is built in full confidence that the cascade will continue the sobriety and order it has hitherto preserved in its retreat. If it were to take a long step up stream of a sudden, that great vein of the west would breathe more freely than is provided for by the "weirs and feeders." This aqueduct at Rochester is a work of some pretension. It is seven hundred and fifty feet in length, and has twelve piers and eleven arches, two of which are over Mill-races. A path is railed off on the side of the canal, and it forms a picturesque promenade across the bed of the river.

The country about the Falls of the Genessee was a wilderness in 1812. Now it contains nearly twenty thousand inhabitants, and is one of the most flourishing towns in the world. In 1830, it supported one daily, two semi-weekly, and three weekly newspapers; and in the single year of 1826, (an age ago, by the Rochester reckoning,) it exported two hundred and two thousand nine hundred barrels of flour. It seems to grow visibly before your eyes; the eternal hammering and clipping of bricks, and heaps of rubbish, remind the traveller so pertinaciously that it is in a state of transition only. The hotels are excellent, and the inhabitants famed for their public spirit, hospitality, and enterprise—the latter, of course.

VIEW OF THE FERRY AT BROOKLYN, NEW YORK

View of the Ferry at Brooklyn, New York

BROOKLYN is as much a part of New York, for all purposes of residence and communication, as "the Borough" is of London. The steam ferry-boats cross the half-mile between it and the city every five minutes; and in less time than it usually takes to thread the press of vehicles on London Bridge, the elegant equipages of the wealthy cross to Long Island for the afternoon drive; morning visits are interchanged between the residents in both places—and, indeed, the east river is hardly more of a separation than the same distance in a street.

Brooklyn is the shire-town of King's County, and by this time, probably, is second in population only to New York. Land there, has risen in value to an enormous extent within the last few years; and it has become the fashion for business-men of New York to build and live on the fine and healthy heights above the river, where they are nearer their business, and much better situated than in the outskirts of the city itself. The town of Brooklyn is built on the summit and sides of an elevation springing directly from the bank of the river, and commanding some of the finest views in America. The prospect embraces a large part of East River, crowded with shipping, and tracked by an endless variety of steamers, flying through the channel in quick succession; of the city of New York, extending, as far as the eye can see, in closely piled masses of architecture; of the Hudson, and the shore of Jersey, beyond; of the bay and its bright islands, and of a considerable part of Long and Staten Islands, and the Highlands of Neversink. A more comprehensive, lively, and interesting view is nowhere to be found.

Historically, Brooklyn will long be remembered for the battle fought in its neighbourhood between the British and Hessians under the command of General Howe, and the Americans under the immediate command of Generals Putnam and Sullivan. It was a contest of a body of ill-disciplined militia against twice their number of regular troops, and ended in defeat; but the retreat conducted by General Washington saved the army, and relieved a little the dark fortunes of the day.

The American forces were composed of militia and raw recruits, and without even dragoons to serve as videts. They were stationed on a chain of eminences running from Yellow Hook towards Hempstead; and the British, from the Ferry between Staten and Long Islands, through the level country to the village of Flatland. From the last-mentioned place, a strong column, led by General Clinton and Lord Percy, marched into the Jamaica Road, through an unoccupied pass in this chain of hills on the right, and turned the left of the

American army. General Grant at the same time attacked the right of the Americans under the command of Lord Sterling, posted near the Ferry; while the fleet commenced a powerful cannonade upon a battery at Red Hook, to draw off the attention of the Americans from the main attack directed by Sir Henry Clinton.

As soon as the Americans perceived that the enemy had gained the rear, they were thrown into confusion, and attacks were made on the centre, commanded by General Sullivan, and the right, commanded by Lord Stirling, and both divisions completely routed. A gallant attempt was made by the latter officer, which, though unavailing, facilitated the retreat of part of the troops under his command. He was himself taken prisoner, as were also Generals Sullivan and Woodhull. The number of Americans killed is estimated at four hundred, and the wounded and prisoners at a thousand.

General Washington, who had passed over from New York to Brooklyn during the heat of the action, perceived that nothing could be done to turn the fortune of the day, and that the only thing to be accomplished was a retreat. The British were only waiting for a wind to move their shipping into the East River, and the next morning might find the ferry in their possession. The British were encamped within six hundred yards of him; and the wind, until eleven o'clock, was unfavourable. At that hour it lulled, and a thick fog covered the bosom of the river. The army commenced their embarkation under this fortunate protection; and the whole of the forces, with their ammunition, provision, horses, waggons, &c. crossed undisturbed. The retreat was discovered by the British half an hour after the evacuation. The sound of their pickaxes was distinctly heard within the American lines during the embarkation.

View of the Railroad to Utica

(Taken at Little Falls)

BEFORE the completion of the Railroad, when travellers to the West were contented with the philosophic pace of the canal-boat, one might take up a novel at Little Falls, and come fairly to the sequel by the time the steersman cried out "Bridge!" at Utica. There were fifteen miles between them in those days; but now (to a man of indistinct ideas of geography, at least, and a traveller on the Railroad) they are as nearly run together as two drops on the window-pane. The intermediate distance is, by all the usual measurements of wear and time, annihilated.

All this is very pleasant to people in a hurry; and as most people in our busy country come under that category, it is a very pleasant thing for the white man altogether. There is a class of inhabitants of the long valley of the Mohawk, however, of whose sufferings, by the advance of the white man's enterprise, this is not the first, though it may be the least, and last. The poor half-naked Oneida, who ran by the side of the once crowded canal-boat for charity, has not time, while the rail-car passes, even to hold out his hand!

The Oneidas have not long been beggars by the road side. They were one of the five tribes confederated under the name of the Iroquois, who gloried in having fought their way into the country of the Mohawks, and kept their place and possessions in the midst of them; the latter tribe enjoying the undisputed honour of being an original people on the soil. Though merged in a confederacy, however, the Oneidas had their own chiefs; and a mythology of their own, which is not a little curious. It will not be *mal-apropos*, accompanying drawings of the towns that have usurped their ancient seat, to give some account of their ideas upon the origin of the earth and the human race.

According to the Oneida, an unlimited expanse of water once filled the space now occupied by the world which we inhabit. At this time the human family dwelt in a country situated in the upper regions of the air, abounding in every thing conducive to the comfort and pleasure of life. The inhabitants were strangers to death, and its harbingers, pain and disease; whilst their minds were free from the corroding passions of jealousy, hatred, and revenge.

At length, however, an event occurred which interrupted their tranquillity, and introduced care and anxiety, until then unknown. A certain youth was noticed to withdraw himself from the circle of their social amusements: the solitary recesses of the grove became his favourite walks. Care and chagrin

[135]

VIEW OF THE RAILROAD TO UTICA

(TAKEN AT LITTLE FALLS)

were depicted in his countenance, and his body, from long abstinence, presented to the view of his friends the mere skeleton of a man. Anxious solicitude in vain explored the cause of his grief; until, at length, debilitated both in body and mind, he yielded to the importunity of his associates, and promised to disclose the cause of his trouble on condition that they would dig up by the roots a certain white pine-tree, lay him in his blanket by the margin of the hole, and seat his wife by his side. In a moment all hands were ready. The fatal tree was taken up by the roots; in doing which, the earth was perforated, and a passage opened into the abyss below. The blanket was spread by the hole, the youth laid upon it, and his wife, then in a state of pregnancy, took her seat by his side. The multitude, eager to learn the cause of such strange and unusual conduct, pressed around; when, on a sudden, to their horror and astonishment, he seized upon the woman, and precipitated her headlong into the regions of darkness below; then, rising from the ground, he informed the assembly, that he had for some time suspected the chastity of his wife, and that, having now disposed of the cause of his trouble, he should soon recover his usual health and vivacity.

All those amphibious animals which now inhabit this world then roamed through the watery waste to which the woman, in her fall, was hastening. The LOON first discovered her coming, and called a council in haste to prepare for her reception; observing, that the animal which approached was a human being, and that earth was indispensably necessary for its accommodation. The first subject of deliberation was, who should support the burden.

The sea-bear first presented himself for a trial of his strength. Instantly the other animals gathered round and scrambled on his back; while the bear, unable to support the weight, sank beneath the surface of the water, and was, by the whole assembly, judged unequal to the task of supporting the earth. Several others in succession presented themselves as candidates for the honour, with similar success. Last of all the turtle modestly advanced, tendering his broad shell as the basis of the earth now about to be formed. The beasts then made a trial of his strength to bear, heaping themselves on his back; and finding their united pressure unable to sink him below the surface, adjudged to him the honour of supporting the world.

A foundation being thus provided, the next subject of deliberation was, how to procure earth. Several of the most expert divers plunged to the bottom of the sea, and came up dead; but the *mink*, at last, though he shared the fate of the others, brought up in his claws a small quantity of earth. This was placed on the back of the turtle.

[137]

In the mean time, the woman continued falling, and, at length, alighted on the turtle's back. The earth had already grown to the size of a man's foot, where she stood, with one foot covering the other. Shortly, she had room for both feet, and was soon able to sit down. The earth continued to expand; and when its plain was covered with verdure, and traced with streams, which poured into the ocean, she erected her habitation on the sea-shore.

Not long after, she was delivered of a daughter, and was supported by the spontaneous productions of the earth, till the child arrived to womanhood. She was then solicited in marriage by several animals, changed into the forms of young men; but they were rejected successively by the mother, until the turtle offered himself as a suitor, and was received. After she had laid herself down to sleep, the turtle placed two arrows on her body, in the form of a cross—one headed with flint, the other with the rough bark of a tree. In due time she was delivered of two sons, but died in child-birth.

The grandmother, enraged at her daughter's death, resolved to destroy them, and threw them into the sea. Scarcely had she reached her wigwam, when the children overtook her at the door. She then concluded to let them live; and, dividing the corpse of her daughter in two parts, she threw them up towards the heavens, where one became the sun, the other the moon. Then first began the succession of day and night. The children speedily became men, and expert archers. The elder had the arrow of the turtle which was pointed with flint; the younger had the arrow headed with bark. The former was, by his malignant disposition, and his skill and success in hunting, a favourite with his grandmother. They lived in the midst of plenty, but would not permit the younger brother, whose arrow was insufficient to kill any thing larger than birds, to share in their abundance.

As this young man was wandering one day along the shore, he saw a bird perched on a bough, projecting over the water. He attempted to kill it; but his arrow, till that time unerring, flew wide of the mark, and sank in the sea. He determined to recover it, and plunged to the bottom. Here, to his astonishment, he found himself in a small cottage. A venerable old man, sitting there, received him with a smile, and thus addressed him:—"My son, I welcome you to the habitation of your father! To obtain this interview, I directed all the circumstances which have conspired to bring you hither. Here is your arrow, and here is an ear of corn. I have watched the unkindness of your brother, and command you to take his life. When you return home, collect all the flints you can find, and hang up all the bucks'-horns. These are the only things which will make an impression on his body, which is made of flint."

Having received these instructions, the young man took his leave, and, in a quarrel with his brother, drove him to a distant region, far beyond the Savannahs, in the south-west, where he killed him, and left his huge form of flint on the earth. The great enemy to the race of the turtle being thus destroyed, they sprang from the ground in human form, and multiplied in peace.

The grandmother, roused to furious resentment for the loss of her favourite son, resolved to be revenged. For many days successively she caused the rain to descend from the clouds in torrents, until the whole surface of the earth, and even the highest mountains, were covered. The inhabitants escaped by fleeing to their canoes. She then covered the earth with snow; but they betook themselves to their snow-shoes. She then gave up the hope of destroying them at once, and has ever since employed herself in inflicting lesser evils on the world, while her younger son displays his benevolence by showering blessings on his race.

The reader will have traced the analogy between this and the Scripture account of the deluge, &c.

UTICA

This long tradition has left us little room for Utica, which truly is among those spots (said to be the happiest in the world) with no striking events in its history. It is a pretty and thriving town, half way between Lake Ontario and the Susquehannah, and on the great routes by canal, road, and railroad, to the west; and in the centre of these radii of communication is fast becoming a focus of wealth and refinement. A high reputation for the latter, however, its society has long and deservedly enjoyed.

UTICA

The Landing on the American Side, Falls of Niagara

THE cliff and staircase at this Landing would be considered highly pictur-esque any where but at the side of Niagara. The hundred stairs clinging to the rock, the wild vines overgrowing the temporary shed under which travellers take shelter from the spray, the descending and ascending figures, and the athletic boatmen, whose occupation of pulling across this troubled ferry re-quires herculean strength and proportions, all form a subject for the painter, which could only be disregarded amid the engrossing scenes of Niagara.

There is another staircase extending down the precipitous front of Goat Island, between the two cataracts, which is less picturesque in itself, but much more daring in its position. One marvels at first how it ever was constructed; but a story told in an old book of travels, published in London in 1750, shows that human feet have stood on the isolated and quaking cliff below, and re-turned again to the summit without the aid of mechanical science. The narrator is a Mr. Peter Kalm, a Swedish gentleman, then on his travels in America:—

"It was formerly thought impossible for any body living to come at the is-land that is in the middle of the Fall; but an accident that happened twelve years ago made it appear otherwise. The history is this:—Two Indians of the Six Nations went out from Niagara Fort to hunt upon an island that is in the middle of the river, or strait, some miles above the great Fall, on which there used to be abundance of deer. They took some French brandy with them from the fort, which they tasted several times as they were carrying their canoe around the Fall; and when they were in the canoe, they now and then took a dram, and so went along up the strait toward the island where they proposed to hunt; but growing sleepy, they laid themselves down in the canoe, which getting loose, drove back with the stream farther and farther down, till it came nigh that island that is in the middle of the Fall. Here, one of them, awakened by the noise, cries out to the other that they were gone!—yet they tried if possible to save life. This island between the Falls was nighest, and with much working they got there. At first, they were glad; but when they had considered every thing, they thought themselves hardly in a better state than if they had gone down the Fall, since they had now no other choice than either to throw themselves down the same, or to perish with hunger: but hard necessity put them on invention. At the lower end of the island the rock is

THE LANDING ON THE AMERICAN SIDE, FALLS OF NIAGARA

perpendicular, and there is a break in the fall. The island having plenty of wood, they went to work directly and made a ladder, or shrouds, of the bark of linden tree, which is very tough and strong, so long, that it would reach to the edge of the water below. One end of this bark ladder they tied fast to a great tree that grew at the side of the rock above the Fall, and let the other end down to the water.

"So they went down their new-invented stairs; and when they came to the bottom in the middle of the Fall, they rested a little; and as the water next below the Fall is not rapid, they threw themselves out into it, thinking to swim on shore. Hardly had the Indians began to swim, before the waves of the eddy threw them with violence against the rock from whence they started. They tried it several times, but at last were weary, and being often thrown against the rock they were much bruised, and the skin of their bodies torn in many places. So they were obliged to climb up their stairs again to the island, not knowing what to do. After some time they perceived Indians on the opposite shore, to whom they cried out. These two pitied them, but gave them little help; yet they made haste down to the fort, and told the French commander where two of their brethren were. He persuaded them to try all possible means of relieving the two poor Indians; and it was done in this manner. The water that runs on the east side of the island is shallow, and breaks in rapids over the rocks. The commandant caused poles to be made and pointed with iron: two Indians determined to walk to this island by the help of these poles to save the others, or perish. They took leave of their friends as if they were going to death. Each had two such poles in his hands to set against the bottom of the stream to keep them steady: so they went and got to the island, and having given poles to the poor Indians there, they all returned safely to the main. The unfortunate creatures had been nine days on the island, and were almost starved to death."

A bridge is now thrown across where these adventurous Indians made their passage. If the story be true, it is one of the most gallant feats on record.

VIEW FROM MOUNT WASHINGTON

View from Mount Washington

OF two attempts to obtain a view from the summit of Mount Washington, the MS. Journal from which we have already made extracts, gives an interesting account of one which the weather rendered unsuccessful.

"The morning opened with every symptom of a fine day for the ascent. We had an early breakfast, and started a little before six, with the intention of first ascending Mount Clinton, and afterwards Mount Washington. Before we came to the peak of Clinton, however, a thick mist had swept over the mountains, which grew heavier and heavier. At the beginning of the granite pile that caps Mount Washington, a heavy wind with violent rain came on, and, as we climbed upwards, the storm increased, and the cold became every moment more intense. In four hours we reached the summit, thoroughly drenched, and stiff as icicles. The rain beat across the peak with tremendous force, and it was with difficulty we could stand. Below us was a sea of mist, around us a howling tempest, and our only resource was to seek the shelter of a rock, and seek consolation in the guide's knapsack. Though my hands were so benumbed with cold, and my limbs so heavy with the water which had been driven into every thread of my dress that I could hardly raise the food to my lips, I contrived to cut the cork of a bottle of champagne, and its sparkling contents sent a momentary and grateful thrill through my veins: when it had passed, however, I was colder than ever.

"We found so few attractions on the mountain that we soon began our descent towards Ethan Crawford's, but were so blinded by the tempest that the guide could not at once discover the way. Half an hour we wandered about in absolute uncertainty whether we should get down the mountain, or bide the peltings of the storm through the night. We hit at last upon the path, and after some sharp scrambling reached the wood, the friendly shelter of which afforded us a most welcome protection from the rain. The path was execrable, owing to the heavy rain, and the trampling of the horses of another party who had gone up before us; but at four we arrived at our destination, tired, cold, wet, and hungry. A change of dress, a roaring fire, and a substantial dinner, soon put us in better condition and humour."

From a more successful attempt by the same gentleman, we take the following description of the view from Mount Washington.

"The light streamed down through breaks in the clouds on the scenery below in such masses, and in such a manner, as to bring out fully and distinctly all the leading points in the immeasurable panorama. In our immediate neigh-

[145]

bourhood, but far below us, lay on one side, Mounts Clinton, Pleasant, Munroe, and Franklin; on the other, Jefferson, Adams, and Madeson. On the east and west, openings were visible, through which several rivers, taking their rise in the mountains, wound their way and widened their valleys toward the lowlands. Far in the distance, chains of hills and mountains, distinct in outline and beautiful in form, arose on all sides; and these were still overtopped by others beyond, whose blue summits mingled with the sky, and shut in the overpowering scene. Far to the south, the bright sheet of Lake Winipiseogee met the eye, and with its calm and gem-like beauty, set, as it were, in a framework of distant hills, relieved and contrasted the bewildering and boundless majesty which encircled the mountain. On the west the green mountains of Vermont, and on the east the mountains of Maine, skirted the horizon, and seemed to support the heavens. Occasionally, a cloud would rest for a few moments on some distant or neighbouring summit, but during the whole of our visit the awful head of Mount Washington was surrounded by a pure atmosphere and the clearest light."

Mount Washington was ascended by several scientific gentlemen in July, 1784. The historian of the expedition records that one of the company had taken a thermometer from his bosom, when it stood at fever heat, and it fell to 44°; and that, during the time he was adjusting a barometer and thermometer, the cold nearly deprived him of the use of his fingers.

Mount Washington and the White Hills
(From Near Crawford's)

THE White Hills have a double claim to their title—one founded upon the fact, that, for nine, ten, and sometimes eleven months in the year, they are covered with snow; and the other, that, in all clear days, (the only times in which they can be distinctly seen,) white fleecy clouds resting upon them, give them a white aspect. When viewed from a neighbouring position, they are always, except where snow lies, or the rocks are naked, shrouded in misty azure.

The height of these mountains has been a subject of much dispute. A scien-

MOUNT WASHINGTON AND THE WHITE HILLS

(FROM NEAR CRAWFORD'S)

tific gentleman, whose remarks on physical subjects merit consideration and respect, supposes the summit of Mount Washington to be about seven thousand eight hundred feet above the level of the ocean; seventy-two feet below the point, which, in the latitude of 44° 15′ (that of these mountains) is the estimated point of perpetual congelation on the eastern continent. This point, he says, from the greater coldness of the American climate, cannot exceed, but must rather fall short, of what it is in the European climate. The climates of America are indeed colder than those of Europe in the same latitude during the winter, but in the summer they are generally much hotter. Nor are the mountains in any part of New England of sufficient height and extent to lessen materially the degree of heat generally prevailing. The air on the summit of Mount Washington, therefore, must continually be rendered less cold by the ascent of the intensely heated atmosphere from the subjacent regions. As the whole country partakes of this heat, the ascending volume, whencesoever derived, must be heated to nearly the same temperature. It seems scarcely credible, therefore, that the temperature of the atmosphere around the single point of Mount Washington should not, during the summer, be sensibly raised by the general heat of the country: for we are to remember that this is the only height in the United States which approximates near to the region of perpetual frost.

The following observations of Dr. Cutler exhibit the state of vegetation on these mountains:—

"At the base of the summit of Mount Washington, the limits of vegetation may with propriety be fixed. There are indeed, on some of the rocks, even to their apices, scattered specks of a mossy appearance; but I conceive them to be extraneous substances accidentally adhering to the rocks, for I could not discover, with my botanical microscope, any part of that plant regularly formed. The limits of vegetation at the base of this summit are as well defined as that between the woods and the bald and mossy part. So striking is the appearance, that, at a considerable distance, the mind is impressed with the idea that vegetation extends no farther than a line, as well defined as the penumbra and shadow in a lunar eclipse. The stones that I have by me from the summit have not the smallest appearance of moss upon them.

"There is evidently the appearance of three zones—the woods, the bald, mossy part, and the part above vegetation. The same appearance has been observed on the Alps, and all other high mountains.

"I recollect no grass on the plain. The spaces between the rocks in the second zone and on the plain are filled with spruce and fir, which, perhaps, have been growing ever since the deluge; and yet many of them have not attained a greater height than three or four inches; but their spreading tops are so thick and strong as to support the weight of a man without yielding in the slightest degree. In many places on the sides we could get glades of this growth some rods in extent, when we could, by sitting down on our feet, slide the whole length. The tops of the growth of wood were so thick and firm as to bear us currently a considerable distance before we arrived at the utmost boundaries, which were almost as well defined as the water on the shore of a pond. The tops of the wood had the appearance of having been shorn off, exhibiting a smooth surface from their upper limits to a great distance down the mountains."

On the summit of Mount Washington there is usually little or no snow. That which is so long visible in the regions below is blown from the summit, and the north-western side, and lies only on the southern and south-eastern, where it is defended from every cold wind by the precipice above, and exposed through June, July, and sometimes a part of August, to the full strength of the sun.

The Park and City Hall, New York

THE first *Stadt Huys* in this city was constructed of stone, and stood originally at the head of Coenties Slip, facing on Pearl Street, towards the East river. It was built as early in the Dutch dynasty as 1642, and became so weakened and impaired in half a century afterwards, that the court sitting there recommended it to be sold, and another to be constructed. In 1699, they sold the old building for nine hundred and twenty pounds, "reserving only the bell, the king's arms, and iron works (fetters) belonging to the prison." By the agreement, leave was granted "that the cage, pillory, and stocks, before the same, be removed any time within one year, and prisoners in the city hall to remain one month." "In front of all these, on the river, was placed the *Rondeal*, or Half-Moon Fort, where it probably assisted the party sheltered in the City Hall, while the civil war prevailed."

The new building must have been finished in 1700. It stood at the head of

THE PARK AND CITY HALL, NEW YORK

Broad Street, fronting on Wall Street; and its lower story formed an open arcade over the foot pavement. It was also the proper prison of the city, and had before it, on Broad Street, a whipping-post, pillory, &c. There were also held the sessions of the Provincial Assembly, the Supreme Court, and the Mayor and Admiralty Courts. It was finally altered to suit the Congress; and at that time the prisoners were moved to the new jail in the park; but the Congress removing to Philadelphia, it was again altered to receive the courts and the State Assembly.

"It was in the gallery of the old City Hall, on Wall Street," says Watson in his Annals, "that General Washington was inaugurated the first President of the United States. The oath of office was taken in the open gallery in front of the Senate Chamber, in the view of an immense concourse of citizens. There this nobleman of nature, with his noble height and port, in a suit of dark silk velvet of the old cut, steel-hilted small sword by his side, hair in bag and full powdered, in black silk hose, and shoes with silver buckles, made his pledge on a quarto Bible, still preserved in St. John's Lodge. How uprightly, intelligently, and disinterestedly, he executed his task, history will never cease to tell to his fame and glory."

The present City Hall was erected in 1803, at an expense of half a million of dollars. The front and sides are constructed of white marble, and the remainder of red sandstone. It is a beautiful edifice, and only wants elevation. When the trees of the park are in full leaf, it is difficult to get an entire view of it.

The park is the centre of New York, and its two most thronged and finest avenues form the two sides of it. Broadway, the much crowded and much praised Broadway, the Corso, the Toledo, the Regent Street, of New York, pours its tide of population past the western side of the verdant triangle, and, just at the park, its crowd and its bustle are thickest. Broadway is a noble street, and on its broad side-walks may be seen every thing that walks the world in the shape of a foreigner, or a fashion—beauties by the score, and men of business by the thousand; but, besides every possible ingredient of continental crowds, there are to be seen in Broadway two additional classes of peripatetics seen never on foreign *pavés* but in rare specimens—coloured dandies, and belligerent pigs. The former take the wall of you, and the latter, when the question of passing on one side or the other becomes embarrassing, escape with great dexterity between your legs.

It would be difficult in one day to describe the prevailing style of dress in Broadway, for fashions have become unfashionable, and each man and woman dresses as Fortune pleases. But here is a picture of dresses in Broadway a century ago: —

"Men wore three-square, or cocked hats, and wigs; coats with large cuffs, and big skirts lined and stiffened with buckram. The coat of a beau had three or four large plaits in the skirts, and wadding, like a coverlet, to keep them smooth. The cuffs were very large, up to the elbows, open below, and loaded with lead to keep them down. The cape was thin and low, so as readily to expose the close-plaited neck-stock of fine linen cambric, and the large silver stock-buckle on the back of the neck. The shirts were worn with hand-ruffles, and sleeve-buttons were worn at the wrist, of precious stones, or gold. The little boys wore wigs, like their elders, and their dresses generally were similar to those of the men. Coats of red plush were very fashionable, and the breeches were commonly made of this material."

We refer the reader to Watson's Annals for many curious particulars touching the apparel and habits of the New Yorkers in the early part of the last century.

The Two Lakes and the Mountain House on the Catskills

AT this elevation, you may wear woollen and sleep under blankets in midsummer; and that is a pleasant temperature where much hard work is to be done in the way of pleasure-hunting. No place so agreeable as Catskill, after one has been parboiled in the city. New York is at the other end of that long thread of a river, running away south from the base of the mountain; and you may change your climate in so brief a transit, that the most enslaved broker in Wall Street may have half his home on Catskill. The cool woods, the small silver lakes, the falls, the mountain-tops, are all delicious haunts for the idler-away of the hot months; and, to the credit of our taste, it may be said they are fully improved—Catskill is a "resort."

From the Mountain-House, the busy and all-glorious Hudson is seen winding half its silver length—towns, villas, and white spires, sparkling on the

THE TWO LAKES AND THE MOUNTAIN HOUSE ON THE CATSKILLS

shores, and snowy sails and gaily-painted steamers, specking its bosom. It is a constant diorama of the most lively beauty; and the traveller, as he looks down upon it, sighs to make it a home. Yet a smaller and less-frequented stream would best fulfil desires born of a sigh. There is either no seclusion on the Hudson, or there is so much that the conveniences of life are difficult to obtain. Where the steamers come to shore, (twenty a day, with each from one to seven hundred passengers,) it is certainly far from secluded enough; yet, away from the landing-places, servants find your house too lonely, and your table, without unreasonable expense and trouble, is precarious and poor. These mean and *menus plaisirs* reach, after all, the very citadel of philosophy. Who can live without a cook or a chambermaid, and dine seven days in the week on veal, consoling himself with the beauties of a river-side?

On the smaller rivers these evils are somewhat ameliorated; for in the rural and uncorrupt villages of the interior, you may find servants born on the spot, and content to live in the neighbourhood. The market is better, too, and the society less exposed to the evils that result from too easy an access to the metropolis. No place can be rural, in all the *virtues* of the phrase, where a steamer will take the villager to the city between noon and night, and bring him back between midnight and morning. There is a suburban look and character about all the villages on the Hudson which seems out of place among such scenery. They are suburbs; in fact, steam has destroyed the distance between them and the city.

The Mountain-House on the Catskill, it should be remarked, is a luxurious hotel. How the proprietor can have dragged up, and keeps dragging up, so many superfluities from the river level to that eagle's nest, excites your wonder. It is the more strange, because in climbing a mountain the feeling is natural that you leave such enervating indulgences below. The mountain-top is too near heaven. It should be a monastery to lodge in so high—a St. Gothard, or a Vallambrosa. But here you may choose between Hermitages, "white" or "red," Burgundies, Madeiras, French dishes, and French dances, as if you had descended upon Capua.

Trenton High Falls

THOSE who visit these Falls in the pleasantest season for travelling, (the time at which the drawing was taken by Mr. Bartlett,) see them when there is the least water; consequently, when they are (as falls) at their lesser phase of grandeur. It is like seeing a race-horse in the stall, or a line-of-battle-ship in port, with sails furled. It is possible that after one of the tremendous thunderstorms which burst upon this climate sometimes in summer, the glory of the cataract may, for a few hours, renew, and so unite the splendour of full foliage with the flashing of mighty waters: but this is a chance which the traveller for pleasure will scarce hit or wait for. It should be remembered, however, in looking on the drawing, that it is one of a sleeping lion. The frowning walls on either side, driven asunder by the plunges of the torrent in more "yeasty moods," present a sufficient scale by which to measure its slumbering power. Those who live in climes where snow seldom falls, and more seldom lies through one sunny day unmelted, can have but a faint idea of a spring *freshet* in America. After the first heavy snow in December, each successive fall adds solidity to the heap upon the earth's bosom, and the alternate thawing and freezing consolidates the bottom into ice, and cuts off the heat of the soil from the flakes added almost daily to the surface. Till the middle of March, perhaps, or later, the sleighing (*Anglicè* sledging) is hard and crisp. Then the sun draws towards the line, and with the equinox come soft southern winds, with sharp changes to the north, pouring sleet and rain upon the crusty covering of nature; and, first of all, the small streams begin to trickle under the ice, smothered and faint; the roads across the hard-frozen rivers crack and grow treacherous; and the horse, as they phrase it here, *slumps through* in travelling on the highway. As the days grow longer, the snow gets clammy and heavy, and drops to the ground, (undermined by the water,) an acre at a time, clicking like a troop of morris-dancers. If you "sit upon a rail" at noon-day, and send a dog to run over an untrodden field, his weight will break it down in large tablets, like the giving way of a marble floor. Then comes the spring thaw. Instead of one rivulet to half a mile, every hill-side sends down a hundred streams, every road is a brook, every hollow in the fields an overflowing pond. The benevolent societies which thrive more by the "widows' mites" than the rich man's gift, have learned the secret of these "small contributions." Down they pour, in troops of legions, to the beds of the larger watercourses, "drowning the springs," over-flowing the banks, and laying every low plain under water. The ice crashes and loosens in the large rivers, and

TRENTON HIGH FALLS

with the loosening of their frost-bound chains, the merry dance is led off to the ocean. If you would see waterfalls, it should be then; though the foliage is not around them, nor the sky or the moon-light so genial above. Niagara alone, of all the cataracts, remains unchanged. He rolls on in his calm sublimity, spring and autumn, summer and winter, the same. His floods seem never to increase by the melting of snow, nor to be drunk up by the fervour of the sun. If changes he has, they are imperceptible, or seen only in the crumbling of rock beneath him, mountains at a convulsion, and at intervals of years.

Trenton is in a wild and not very accessible part of the country, else it were worth the while of the traveller to see these fine Falls during the spring. I am very sure that a series of sketches upon the same ground—the same scenes by the same artist, done when the waters are at the flood, would not be recognised as at all resembling. The attempt would be curious to the artist, at least.

Valley of the Shenandoah, from Jefferson's Rock

THIS is one of the most harmonious combinations of mountain, vale, and river, to be found in America; we know not whether to call it more beautiful or grand. Fine as is all the scenery of this neighbourhood, however, it is not till very lately that the current of travel has turned thither, and but partially yet. Harper's Ferry will soon be a resort for admirers of nature from all nations, and it may well share the honours of pilgrimage with Trenton Falls and Niagara. Steam navigation across the Atlantic will make our New World *lions* as tame as the Pyramids.

It is difficult, at least for me, to stand on any eminence commanding a landscape, wild, yet formed for a blest human residence, without seeing in it the forfeited inheritance of the red man. The unpicturesque new village of the white man, his mill, or his factory, does not convey to my imagination an image of happiness; and I regret the primitive rover of the wild, who neither blackened nature with smoke, nor violated her harmony with brick and shin-

[157]

VALLEY OF THE SHENANDOAH, FROM JEFFERSON'S ROCK

(HARPER'S FERRY)

gle. The tide of sympathy seems turning of late against these oppressed tribes, and it is not amiss sometimes to remember our own atrocities as well as theirs. What will be thought hereafter of the massacre of the poor Conestogoes, as related in the history of these middle regions of our territory!

"On the first arrival of the English," says the chronicler, "messengers from this tribe entered into a treaty of friendship with the first proprietary, William Penn, which was to last as long as the sun should shine, or the waters run in the rivers.

"This treaty has been since frequently renewed, and the chain brightened, as they express it, from time to time. It has never been violated on their part, or ours, till now. As their lands by degrees were mostly purchased, and the settlement of the white people began to surround them, the proprietor assigned them lands on the manor of Conestogoe, which they might not part with; there they have lived many years in friendship with their white neighbours, who loved them for their peaceable inoffensive behaviour.

"It has always been observed, that Indians, settled in the neighbourhood of white people, do not increase, but diminish continually. This tribe accordingly went on diminishing, till there remained in their town on the manor but twenty persons, namely, seven men, five women, and eight children, boys and girls.

"Of these, Shehaes was a very old man, having assisted at the second treaty held with them by Mr. Penn, in 1701, and ever since continued a faithful friend to the English; he is said to have been an exceeding good man, considering his education, being naturally of a kind, benevolent temper.

"This little society continued the custom they had begun, when more numerous, of addressing every new governor, and every descendant of the first proprietary, welcoming him to the province, assuring him of their fidelity, and praying a continuance of that favour and protection which they had hitherto experienced. They had accordingly sent up an address of this kind to our present governor (John Penn, Esq.) on his arrival; but the same was scarcely delivered, when the unfortunate catastrophe happened which we are about to relate. On Wednesday, the 14th December, 1763, fifty-seven men from some of our frontier townships, who had projected the destruction of this little commonwealth, came all well mounted, and armed with firelocks, hangers, and hatchets, having travelled through the country in the night to Conestogoe manor. There they surrounded the small village of Indian huts, and just at break of day broke in upon them all at once. Only three men, two women, and a young boy, were found at home; the rest being out among the neighbouring white people—some to sell the baskets, brooms, and bowls, they manufactured, and others on other occasions. These poor defenceless creatures were immediately fired upon, stabbed, and hatcheted to death! the good Shahaes among the rest cut to pieces in his bed!—all of them were scalped, and otherwise horribly mangled. Then their huts were set on fire, and most of them burned down. The magistrates of Lancaster sent out to collect the remaining Indians, brought them into the town for their better security against any further attempt, and, it is said, condoled with them on the misfortune that had happened, took them by the hand, and promised them protection. They were put into the workhouse, a strong building, as the place of greatest safety. These cruel men again assembled themselves; and hearing that the remaining fourteen Indians were in the workhouse at Lancaster, they suddenly appeared before that town on the 27th December. Fifty of them, armed as before, dismounting, went directly to the workhouse, and, by violence, broke open the door, and entered with the utmost fury in their countenances. When the poor wretches saw they had no protection nigh, nor could possibly escape, and being without the least weapon of defence, they divided their little families, the children clinging to their parents; they fell on their faces, protested their innocence, declared their love to the English, and that, in their whole lives, they had never done them injury; and in this posture they all received the hatchet! Men, women, and children, were every one inhumanly murdered in cold blood!"

Lockport—Erie Canal

THIS town, so suddenly sprung into existence, is about thirty miles from Lake Erie, and exhibits one of those wonders of enterprise which astonish calculation. The waters of Lake Erie, which have come thus far without much descent, are here let down sixty feet by five double locks and thence pursue a perfectly level course, sixty-five miles, to Rochester. The remarkable thing at Lockport, however, is a deep cut from here to the Torenanta Creek, seven miles in length, and partly through solid rock, at an average depth of twenty feet. The canal boat glides through this flinty bed, with jagged precipices on each side; and the whole route has very much the effect of passing through an immense cavern.

This tract of country is very interesting to the antiquarian, from the remains of fortifications, and other probable traces of a race who existed, and whose arts perished before the occupation of the country by the tribes who lately possessed it. On Seneca river, on the south side of Lake Erie, in many different parts of the State of New York, and in a long chain extending west through the valley of the Ohio, down that of the Mississippi, and so westward through Mexico, are traces of a people who were settled in towns defended by forts, and altogether far more advanced in civilization than the Iroquois found here by Europeans. The region in the neighbourhood of Lockport and Torenanta was visited with reference to these remains by the Rev. Mr. Kirkland, missionary to the Iroquois confederacy, in 1778. His account is very curious. At a deserted Indian village, near the old Indian town of Kanawageas, he discovered an ancient fort. It enclosed about six acres, and had six gates. The ditch appeared to be eight feet wide, and in some places six feet deep, and drawn in a circular form on three sides. The fourth side was defended by nature with a high bank, at the foot of which is a fine stream of water. The bank had probably been secured by a stockade, as there appeared to have been a deep covered way in the middle of it down to the water. Some of the trees on the bank and in the ditch appeared to Mr. Kirkland to have been at the age of two hundred years. About half a mile south of this, and upon a greater eminence, he traced the ruins of another old fortified town, of less dimensions than the other, but with a deeper ditch, and in a situation more lofty and defensible. Having examined these fortifications, Mr. Kirkland returned to *Kanawageas*, and thence renewed his tour westward, until he encamped for the night at a place called *Joàika*, (i.e. Racoon,) on the river *Tanawànde*, about twenty-six miles from *Kanawangeas*. Six miles from this place of encampment, he rode to the open fields, and arrived at a place called by the Senecas *Tegatàineàaghgwe*, which imports a *double-fortified* town, or a town with a fort at each end. Here he walked about half a mile with one of the Seneca chiefs, to view one of the vestiges of this double-fortified town: they were the remains of two forts. The first which he visited, as above, contained about four acres of ground: the other to which he proceeded, distant from this about two miles, and situated at the other extremity of the ancient town, enclosed twice that quantity of ground. The ditch around the former, which he particularly examined, was about five or six feet deep. A small stream of water and a high bank circumscribed nearly one-third of the enclosed ground.

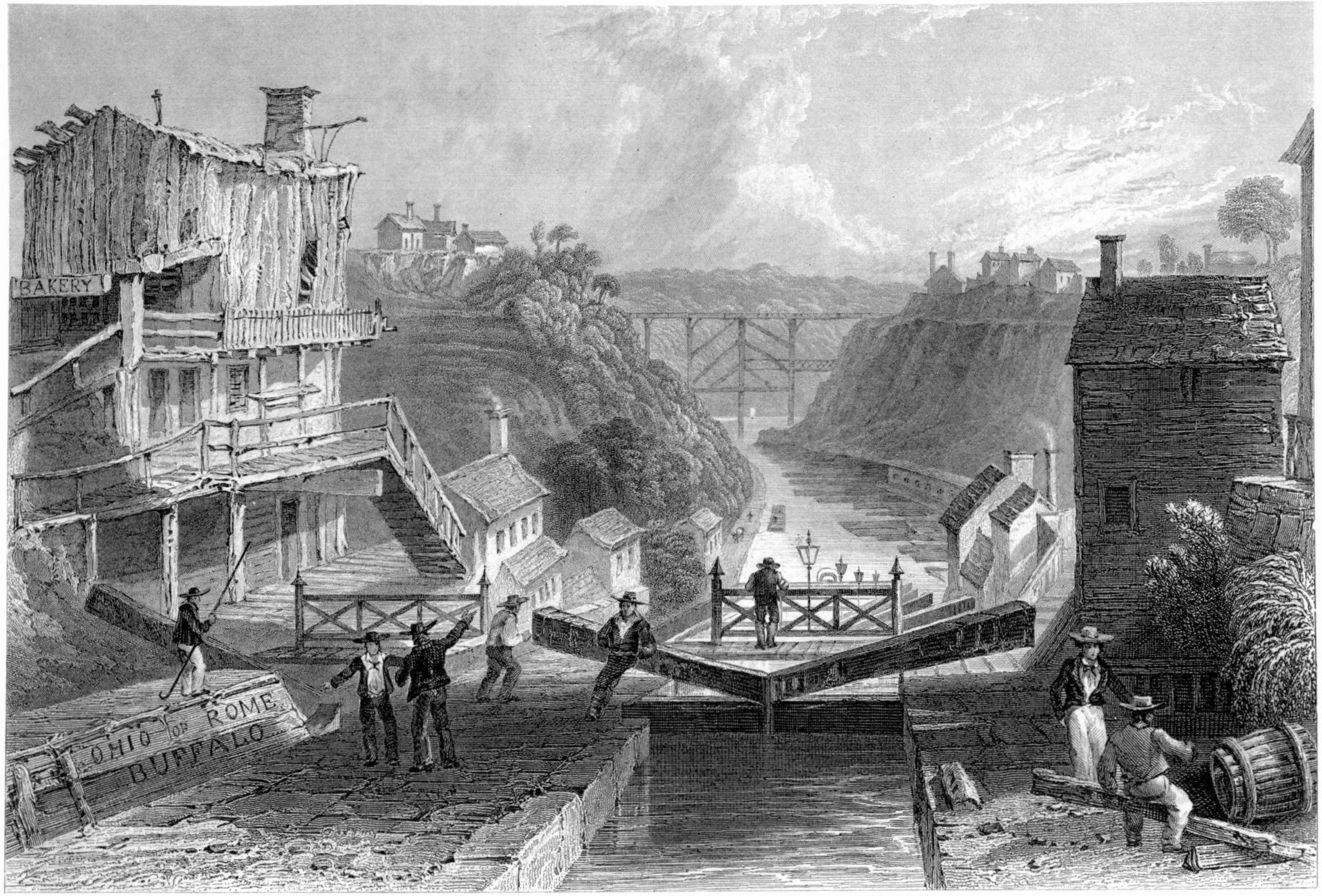

LOCKPORT—ERIE CANAL

There were the traces of six gates, or avenues, round the ditch; and near the centre a way was dug to the water. The ground on the opposite side of the water was in some places nearly as high as that on which the fort was built, which might render this covered way to the water necessary. A considerable number of large thrifty oaks had grown up within the enclosed ground, both in and upon the ditch; some of them appeared to be at least two hundred years old, or more. The ground is of a hard gravelly kind, intermixed with loam, and more plentifully at the brow of the hill. In some places, at the bottom of the ditch, Mr. Kirkland ran his cane a foot or more into the ground, from which circumstance he concluded that the ditch was much deeper in its original state than it then appeared to him. Near the northern fortification, which was situated on high ground, he found the remains of a funeral pile, where the slain were buried, in a great battle, which will be spoken of hereafter. The earth was raised about six feet above the common surface, and betwixt twenty and thirty feet diameter. The bones appeared on the whole surface of the raised earth, and struck out in many places on the sides. Pursuing his course towards Buffalo Creek, (his ultimate destination,) Mr. Kirkland discovered the vestiges of another ancient fortified town. He does not in his manuscript delineate them, but, from the course he described, they might be easily ascertained. "Upon these heights, near the ancient fortified town, the roads part; we left the path leading to Niagara on our right, and went a course nearly south-west for Buffalo Creek. After leaving these heights, which afforded an extensive prospect, we travelled over a fine tract of land for about six or seven miles; then came to a barren white oak-shrub plain, and one very remarkable spot of near two hundred acres, and passed a steep hill on our right, in some places near fifty feet perpendicular, at the bottom of which is a small lake, affording another instance of pagan superstition. The old Indians affirm that, formerly, a demon, in the form of a dragon, resided in this lake, and had frequently been seen to disgorge balls of liquid fire; and that, to appease his wrath, many a sacrifice of tobacco had been made at that lake by the fathers. The barren spot above mentioned is covered with small white stone, that appears like lime and clay; in some spots, for a considerable distance, there is no appearance of earth. Notwithstanding its extreme poverty, there are many trees of moderate size. At the extremity of this barren plain, we came again to the Tanawande river, and forded it about two miles above the Indian town called by that name. This village contains fourteen houses, or huts; their chief is called Gashagaàle, nicknamed the *black chief*. On the south side of the Tanawande Creek, at a small distance, are to be seen

the vestiges of another ancient fortified town." Mr. Kirkland further remarks, that there are vestiges of ancient fortified towns in various parts
throughout the extensive territory of the Six Nations, and, by Indian report,
in various other parts; particularly one on a branch of the Delaware river,
which, from the size and age of some of the trees that have grown upon the
banks and in the ditches, appears to have existed nearly one thousand years.

The Tomb of Washington

THE current of life seems to be too rapid in America to allow time for reflection upon any thing which can possibly be deferred. The monuments are left
unfinished on our battle-fields; the tombs of great men become indistinguishable before marked with a stone; and the sacred places where patriotism has
dwelt, are rated by the value of their material, and left to decay. It is difficult
to visit Mount Vernon, and feel, from any mark of care or respect visible
about it, that America owes any thing to the sacred ashes it entombs.

The family tomb at Mount Vernon has once been robbed by a sacrilegious
ruffian, whose ignorance alone preserved for us the remains of Washington.
It has been proposed to Congress to buy Mount Vernon, and establish a guard
over relics so hallowed. Why should not this be done, and a sufficient sum be
appropriated to enclose and keep in order the whole estate, improve the execrable road leading to it from Alexandria, and employ persons to conduct
strangers over the place?

The vault in which the ashes of Washington repose, is at the distance of,
perhaps, thirty rods from the house, immediately upon the bank of the river.
A more romantic and picturesque site for a tomb can scarcely be imagined.
Between it and the Potomac is a curtain of forest-trees, covering the steep
declivity to the water's edge, breaking the glare of the prospect, and yet affording glimpses of the river, where the foliage is thickest. The tomb is surrounded by several large native oaks, which are venerable by their years, and
which annually strew the sepulchre with autumnal leaves, furnishing the
most appropriate drapery for the place, and giving a still deeper impression to
the *memento mori*. Interspersed among the oaks, and overhanging the tomb,

THE TOMB OF WASHINGTON, MOUNT VERNON

is a copse of red cedar, whose evergreen boughs present a fine contrast to the hoary and leafless branches of the oak; and while the deciduous foliage of the latter indicates the decay of the body, the eternal verdure of the former furnishes a fitting emblem of the immortal spirit. The sacred and symbolic *cassia* was familiar to Washington, and, perhaps, led to the selection of a spot where the evergreen flourished.

One of the most interesting associations with the tomb of Washington, is La Fayette's visit to it, as related by Levasseur: —

"After a voyage of two hours, the guns of Fort Washington announced that we were approaching the last abode of the father of his country. At this solemn signal, to which the military band accompanying us responded by plaintive strains, we went on deck, and the venerable soil of Mount Vernon was before us. At this view, an involuntary and spontaneous movement made us kneel. We landed in boats, and trod upon the ground so often trod by the feet of Washington. A carriage received General Lafayette; and the other visitors silently ascended the precipitous path which conducted to the solitary habitation of Mount Vernon. In re-entering beneath this hospitable roof, which had sheltered him when the reign of terror tore him violently from his country and family, George Lafayette felt his heart sink within him, at no more finding him whose paternal care had softened his misfortunes; while his father sought with emotion for every thing which reminded him of the companion of his glorious toils.

"Three nephews of General Washington took Lafayette, his son, and myself, to conduct us to the tomb of their uncle: our numerous companions remained in the house. In a few minutes the cannon, thundering anew, announced that Lafayette rendered homage to the ashes of Washington. Simple and modest as he was during life, the tomb of the citizen hero is scarcely perceived among the sombre cypresses by which it is surrounded. A vault, slightly elevated and dodded over—a wooden door without inscriptions—some withered and green garlands, indicate to the traveller who visits the spot, where rest in peace the puissant arms which broke the chains of his country. As we approached, the door was opened. Lafayette descended alone into the vault, and a few minutes after re-appeared, with his eyes overflowing with tears. He took his son and me by the hand, and led us into the tomb, where, by a sign, he indicated the coffin. We knelt reverentially, and rising, threw ourselves into the arms of Lafayette, and mingled our tears with his."

Black Mountain—Lake George

THE mountains on the shore of this exquisite lake consist of two great ranges, bordering it from north to south. The western range passes westward of the north-west bay, at the head of which a vast spar, shooting towards the southeast, forms the whole of the peninsula between that bay and the lake. Both these ranges alternately approach the lake, so as to constitute a considerable part of its shores, and recede from it again to the distance sometimes of two or three miles.

The summits of these mountains are of almost every figure, from the arch, to the bold, bluff, and sharp cone. In some instances, the loftier ones are bald, solemn, and forbidding; in others, they are clothed and crowned with verdure. It is the peculiarity of Lake George, that, while all the world agrees to speak only of its loveliness, it is surrounded by features of the highest grandeur and sublimity. The Black Mountain is one of these; and there is every variety of chasm, crag, promontory, and peak, which a painter would require for the noblest composition of mountain scenery. The atmospheric changes here, too, are almost always violent; and storms are so frequent, that there is scarce a traveller to Lake George in the summer who has not seen it in a thunder-storm.

It was remarked to me on this lake by a foreigner, that, with all the luxuriance of the vegetation, the trees seemed small; and it is a remark that is frequently made by Englishmen, who compare the common trees in the woods on the roadside with the oaks left to flourish for centuries in venerating and venerable England. The best answer to this remark is contained in a letter, addressed to a friend in England, by an able writer of this country: —

"The soil of New England is naturally quite as rich and productive as that of England: of this the thrifty growth and ultimate size of our forest-trees is ample proof. *Few of them, indeed, can now be found of this size: almost all the original forests of this country having been long since cut down.* I have seen many of these trees, and have compared them with the accounts given of forests in many parts of the globe, and am assured that they will very rarely suffer by such comparison. It may seem strange to you, accustomed as you are to see forest-trees planted in great numbers, and preserved with great care, that the inhabitants of this country should, so soon after its colonization, have cut down their forests in this extensive manner. This is one of the ten thousand subjects, presented to the mind by the existing state of things here, about which a foreigner must necessarily misconceive. Should he travel

[167]

BLACK MOUNTAIN—LAKE GEORGE

through New England he would naturally conclude that the forest-trees failed of arriving at the size which they attain in Europe. He would, indeed, see that they were tall, and apparently very thrifty, but small in the girth. I do not mean that they are universally so; but that this is extensively the fact throughout the southern division. For the reason of it he would be at a loss, and most probably would attribute it, notwithstanding the thrifty appearance of the trees, to sterility of soil, or, in the mystic language of Buffon, to 'a deficiency of matter.' Should he be informed that the real cause was the age of the trees, almost all of which are young, his perplexity would be increased. On the one hand he would be astonished at the folly of destroying forests in this wanton manner, without any apparent reason; and, on the other, would be unable to comprehend how these forests renewed themselves without the aid of planting. All this is, however, easily explicable. The wood of this country is its fuel. An Englishman who sees the various fires of his own country sustained by peat and coal only, cannot easily form a conception of the quantity of wood, or, if you please, of forest which is necessary for this purpose. To this quantity must be added the timber for the uses of building, in a country where almost all buildings are formed merely of timber; of fencing, furniture, and commerce; and a prodigious mass annually destroyed in the recent settlements for the mere purpose of clearing the ground. With these facts before him, he will cease to wonder that forests are very extensively felled in New England. All these forests renew themselves. The seeds of the forest-trees spring more readily and successfully when left on the surface than when buried in the ground, even at a very small depth. They will not, however, germinate upon a sward: they demand a soil loose and light. In this state the soil is always kept in forested ground by the leaves deposited on the earth. These also supply the necessary moisture for germination, and effectually shelter the seeds, particularly the nuts and acorns, from the ravages of animals. In this manner, and by a process totally superior to any contrived by the human mind, forests are furnished by the Author of nature with the means of perpetual self-restoration.

"But this is not the only mode, nor the most expeditious, nor that which is principally relied on in this country. When a field of wood is, in the language of our farmers, *cut clean*—i.e. when every tree is cut down, so far as any progress is made, vigorous shoots sprout from every stump; and having their nourishment supplied by the roots of the former tree, grow with a thrift and rapidity never seen in stems derived from the seed. Good grounds will thus yield a growth amply sufficient for fuel, once in fourteen years. A multitude of farmers, therefore, cut their wood in this manner; although, it must be confessed, there are different opinions and practices concerning the subject. In these two modes the forests in New England become, in a sense, ever-living, and supply plentifully the wants of the inhabitants."

Connecticut Valley, from Mount Holyoke

THE broad open lands, or *intervals*, as they are called in this country, which border upon the Connecticut, contain some of the most sunny and fertile pictures of cultivation to be found on our continent. From the mouth of the river up to its rise beyond the White Mountains, it is gemmed with beautiful rural towns, many of them among the first in our country for prosperity, neatness, and cultivated society.

The history of these towns presents some of the bloodiest traits marked on the early settlements of New England. The event which gave the name to Bloody Brook, a small village near the southern extremity of Deerfield, is among many sanguinary records of the difficulties and dangers of the first settlers in this valley.

For a considerable number of years the inhabitants of the valley had lived in as perfect harmony with the Indians among whom they had settled, as was possible, with the great difference between their characters, principles, and pursuits. They had purchased their lands at an equitable price, and in all their transactions with them had observed the strictest equity and humanity. This state of tranquillity was only disturbed by the wide-spreading intrigues of the bold sachem, Philip, whose discernment, comprehensiveness of views, and admirable address, entitle him to the first rank of superiority among the aborigines known in our history. By means of emissaries, and personal solicitation, and eloquence, this renowned warrior succeeded in uniting all the numerous tribes of Indians within the territories colonized by the whites, in one extensive conspiracy of extermination. Though divided into many tribes, hostile to each other and perpetually at war, they joined in this common cause, and a general war broke out at once in every part of the country.

The first symptom in the Valley of the Connecticut, was an abandonment

CONNECTICUT VALLEY, FROM MOUNT HOLYOKE.

by the Indians of their fortresses and houses. They were pursued by a party of settlers, and overtaken about eight miles above Hatfield; where a skirmish ensued, in which nine or ten whites were killed, and about twenty-six Indians.

Several attacks upon the settlements in the valley immediately followed, repelled always with loss of life; and on the 30th of May, 1676, a body of six or seven hundred attacked Hatfield again. The men were abroad in the fields, but, reinforced by a small band from Hadley, they broke through the Indians, and joined the families who had fled to the fortified houses for protection. After a prolonged contest, they succeeded in driving the Indians from the settlement, which was never again attacked.

The village of Deerfield was among those which had suffered most from the first incursions of the Indians, the houses having been burnt, and the town evacuated in consequence. Their harvest had been cut about two months before, and having been stacked in the fields, escaped the conflagration. About eighty men from the settlements below came up to protect the harvesters in carting it in, and about three thousand bushels of wheat were thrashed, loaded upon the waggons, and had been drawn as far as the brook before mentioned without molestation. The settlers stopped here to gather grasses, and while thus occupied, were suddenly and furiously attacked by a body of eight hundred Indians. Captain Lathrop, the leader of the party, ordered his men to fight the Indians in their own manner, availing themselves of the protection of the trees; but the natives, trained to run from tree to tree, and to conceal themselves in this sort of warfare with unexampled address and caution, fought at great advantage, and soon decided the battle in their own favour. Lathrop was killed at the commencement of the attack; and of the whole number of reapers and armed men, ninety were killed on the spot.

Captain Mosely, who was at Deerfield when the enterprise was undertaken, marched immediately with a small band to the relief of Lathrop; but, when he arrived, the contest was over, and the savages, flushed with success, were pillaging the dead. Forming his men into a close column, and commanding them to keep their ranks, he charged the Indians with the greatest intrepidity. Spite of their numbers, he drove them into a swamp, and forced his way through the whole body. They then attempted to hang upon his rear, but with great presence of mind he wheeled and broke through them again. In this manner the fight was continued for five hours. He drove them several miles, and, with only two men killed, and five or six wounded, succeeded in killing ninety-six of their number, and returned, unmolested, on his way to Deerfield.

The next morning, the little band went out to bury the dead, and found the savages again stripping the bodies on the field of battle. Mosely drove them once more before him, and then, having performed his melancholy task, heaped a monument of loose stones over the victims, and returned. The name of the stream, Bloody Brook, is, at present, the only memorial of the catastrophe.

View on the Erie Canal, Near Little Falls

THE passage of the Canal, under the lofty bluff which springs at this place from the edge of the Mohawk, is one of the most beautiful of the many beautiful features disclosed to the voyager on this great outlet of the West. No traveller sees a greater variety of fine objects within the same distance than the follower of the Canal from Schenectady to Buffalo; and certainly none sees them with more ease and comfort to himself. The packet-boats are long drawing-rooms, where he dines, sleeps, reads, lolls, or looks out of the window; and if in want of exercise, he may at any time get a quick walk on the tow-path, and all this without perceptible motion, jar, or smell of steam. Of all the modes of travelling in America, the least popular and the most delightful, to our thinking, is travelling on the Canal.

One of the descriptions of scenery through which the Canal passes, and one which is, we believe, peculiar to our country, is what are called *openings*. When one of these plains is seen at a little distance, a traveller emerging from the forest naturally concludes that it is the commencement of a settled country; and as he advances towards it, is instinctively led to cast his eye forward to find the town or village of which it is the outskirt. From this impression he will be unable to free himself; for though given up, the thought will recur again, spite of his conviction, that he is in the heart of a wilderness. At the same time a sense of stillness and solitude, a feeling of absolute retirement from the world, deeper and more affecting than any he has ever felt before, will be forced upon him while roving in these sequestered regions. No passage out of them is presented to his eye. Yet, though the tract around him is seemingly bounded every where, the boundary is every where obscure, being formed of trees, thinly dispersed, and retired beyond each other at such dis-

VIEW ON THE ERIE CANAL, NEAR LITTLE FALLS

tances, that, while they actually limit the view, they appear rather to border dim, indistinct openings into other tracts of country. Thus he always feels the limit to be uncertain, and until he is actually leaving one of these plains, will continually expect to find a part of the expansion still spreading beyond the reach of his eye. On every side, a multitude of chasms conduct his eye beyond the labyrinth by which he is surrounded, and present an imaginary passage back into the world from which he is withdrawn, bewildering him with expectation continually awakened to be continually disappointed. Thus, in a kind of romantic rapture, he wanders over these plains with emotions similar to those with which, when a child, he roamed through the wildernesses created in Arabian tales.

The origin of the peculiar appearance of these grounds, Dr. Dwight supposes, is probably this. The Indians annually, and sometimes oftener, burned such parts of the North American forests as they found sufficiently dry. In every such case, the fuel consists chiefly of the fallen leaves, which are rarely dry enough for an extensive combustion, except on uplands; and on these only when covered with a dry soil. Of this nature were always the oak and yellow pine grounds, which were therefore usually subjected to an annual conflagration. The beech and maple grounds were commonly too wet to be burned. Hence, on these grounds, the vegetable mould is from six inches to a foot in depth, having been rarely or never consumed by fire; while on the oak and pine grounds, it often does not exceed an inch. That this is the effect of fire only, and not of any diversity in the nature of the trees, is evident from the fact, that, in moist soils, where the fire cannot penetrate, the mould is as deep on the oak as on the maple grounds. This mould is combustible, and by an intense fire is wholly consumed.

The object of these conflagrations was to produce fresh and sweet pasture, for the purpose of alluring the deer to the spots on which they had been kindled. Immediately after the fires, a species of grass springs up, sometimes called *fire-grass*, because it usually succeeds a conflagration. Either from its nature, or from the efficacy of the fire, it is remarkably sweet, and eagerly sought by the deer. All the underwood is at the same time consumed, so that these animals are easily discovered at considerable distances—a thing impracticable where the forests have not been burned. To supply himself with timber for a wigwam, and with wood for fuel, was the only use the Indian could make of the forest; and the earth furnished him with nothing but a place for his residence, his garden, and his game. While, therefore, he destroyed both the forest and the soil, he converted them to uses most profitable for himself.

[175]

When these grounds had been often burned, the seeds and nuts whence future trees would have germinated, were, of course, destroyed by fire. The small number scattered over these plains, or *openings*, grew on spots which were less ravaged by fire, because they were moist, or because they were less covered with leaves.

Hudson Highlands, from Bull-Hill

THIS view out from the gorge of the highlands presents a foreground of cliff and shadow, with their reflections almost folded across in the bosom of the river, and a middle ground of the village of Newburgh and the gently-undulating country in the rear. The blue and far-off line of the Catskills shuts in the horizon.

There is some very romantic scenery hidden among the undulations just mentioned, embracing several small rivers, and a romantic stream, called Murderer's Creek, a tributary of the Hudson. Mr. Poulding, in his "New Mirror for Travellers," gives the following interesting legend in explanation of the name:—

"Little more than a century ago, the beautiful region watered by this stream was possessed by a small tribe of Indians, which has long since become extinct, or been incorporated with some other savage nation of the West. Three or four hundred yards from where the stream discharges itself into the Hudson, a white family, of the name of Stacey, had established itself in a log-house, by tacit permission of the tribe, to whom Stacey had made himself useful by his skill in a variety of little arts highly estimated by the savages. In particular, a friendship existed between him and an old Indian, called Naoman, who often came to his house and partook of his hospitality. The Indians never forgive injuries or forget benefits. The family consisted of Stacey, his wife, and two children, a boy and girl, the former five, the latter three years old."

The legend goes on to say, that Naoman, in grateful friendship, gave the wife of Stacey a secret warning, that a massacre of the whites was resolved

HUDSON HIGHLANDS, FROM BULL-HILL

on, exacting from her a solemn pledge of secrecy, and advising instant escape across the river.

"The daily visits of old Naoman, and his more than ordinary gravity, had excited suspicion in some of the tribe, who had accordingly paid particular attention to the movements of Stacey. One of the young Indians, who had kept on the watch, seeing the whole family about to take their boat, ran to the little Indian village, about a mile off, and gave the alarm. Five Indians collected, ran down to the river side, where their canoes were moored, jumped in, and paddled after Stacey, who by this time had got some distance out into the stream. They gained on him so fast, that twice he dropped his paddle, and took up his gun. But his wife prevented his shooting, by telling him, that if he fired, and they were afterwards overtaken, they would meet no mercy from the Indians. He accordingly refrained, and plied his paddle, till the sweat rolled in big drops down his forehead. All would not do; they were overtaken within a hundred yards of the shore, and carried back with shouts of yelling triumph.

"When they got ashore, the Indians set fire to Stacey's house, and dragged himself, his wife, and children, to their village. Here the principal old men, and Naoman among the rest, assembled to deliberate on the affair. The chief among them stated that some one of the tribe had undoubtedly been guilty of treason, in apprising Stacey, the white man, of the designs of the tribe, whereby they took the alarm, and had well nigh escaped. He proposed to examine the prisoners as to who gave the information. The old man assented to this, and Naoman among the rest. Stacey was first interrogated by one of the old men, who spoke English, and interpreted to the others. Stacey refused to betray his informant. His wife was then questioned, while at the same moment two Indians stood threatening the two children with tomahawks in case she did not confess. She attempted to evade the truth, by declaring she had a dream the night before which had alarmed her, and that she had persuaded her husband to fly. 'The Great Spirit never deigns to talk in dreams to a white face,' said the old Indian: 'woman! thou hast two tongues and two faces: speak the truth, or thy children shall surely die.' The little boy and girl were then brought close to her, and the two savages stood over them, ready to execute their bloody orders.

"'Wilt thou name,' said the old Indian, 'the red man who betrayed his tribe? I will ask thee three times.' The mother answered not. 'Wilt thou name the traitor? This is the second time.' The poor mother looked at her husband, and then at her children, and stole a glance at Naoman, who sat smoking his pipe with invincible gravity. She wrung her hands and wept, but remained silent. 'Wilt thou name the traitor? 'Tis the third and last time.' The agony of the mother waxed more bitter; again she sought the eye of Naoman, but it was cold and motionless. A pause of a moment awaited her reply, and the next moment the tomahawks were raised over the heads of the children, who besought their mother not to let them be murdered.

"'Stop!' cried Naoman. All eyes were turned upon him. 'Stop!' repeated he in a tone of authority. 'White woman, thou hast kept thy word with me to the last moment. I am the traitor. I have eaten of the salt, warmed myself at the fire, shared the kindness of these christian white people, and it was I that told them of their danger. I am a withered, leafless, branchless trunk; cut me down if you will. I am ready.' A yell of indignation sounded on all sides. Naoman descended from the little bank where he sat, shrouded his face with his mantle of skins, and submitted to his fate. He fell dead at the feet of the white woman by a blow of the tomahawk."

Villa on the Hudson, Near Weehawken

FROM this admirably chosen spot, the Bay of New York appears with every accessory of beauty. The city itself comes into the left of the picture to an advantage seen from no other point of view, the flocks of river-craft scud past in all directions, men-of-war, merchantmen, steamers, and ferry-boats, fill up the moving elements of the panorama; and far away beyond stretches the broad harbour, with its glassy or disturbed waters, in all the varieties of ever-changing sea-view. It was on this side that Hudson, who had felt the hostility of the Manhattan Indians, found a friendlier tribe, and made his first amicable visit on shore. The Indian tradition, springing from that visit,* and describing the first intoxication they had ever experienced, is extremely amusing.

"A long time ago, before men with a white skin had ever been seen, some Indians, fishing at a place where the sea widens, espied something at a dis-

---

* It is disputed whether this scene of intoxication took place on the present site of New York, on the Jersey side, or at Albany.

VILLA ON THE HUDSON, NEAR WEEHAWKEN

tance moving upon the water. They hurried ashore, collected their neighbours, who together returned and viewed intensely this astonishing phenomenon. What it could be, baffled all conjecture. Some supposed it to be a large fish or animal, others that it was a very big house, floating on the sea. Perceiving it moving towards land, the spectators concluded that it would be proper to send runners in different directions to carry the news to their scattered chiefs, that they might send off for the immediate attendance of their warriors. These arriving in numbers to behold the sight, and perceiving that it was actually moving towards them (*i.e.* coming into the river or bay), they conjectured that it must be a remarkably large house, in which the Manitto (or Great Spirit), was coming to visit them. They were much afraid, and yet under no apprehension that the Great Spirit would injure them. They worshipped him. The chiefs now assembled at York Island, and consulted in what manner they should receive their Manitto: meat was prepared for a sacrifice; the women were directed to prepare the best of victuals; idols or images were examined and put in order; a grand dance they thought would be pleasing, and, in addition to the sacrifice, might appease him, if angry. The conjurers were also set to work, to determine what this phenomenon portended, and what the result would be. To these, men, women, and children, looked up for advice and protection. Utterly at a loss what to do, and distracted alternately by hope and fear, in this confusion a grand dance commenced. Meantime fresh runners arrived, declaring it to be a great house, of various colours, and full of living creatures. It now appeared certain that it was their Manitto, probably bringing some new kind of game. Others arriving, declared it positively to be full of people, of different colour and dress from theirs, and that one, in particular, appeared altogether *red*. This then must be the *Manitto*. They were lost in admiration; could not imagine what the vessel was, whence it came, or what all this portended. They are now hailed from the vessel in a language they could not understand; they answer by a shout or yell in their way. The house (or large canoe, as some render it) stops. A smaller canoe comes on shore, with the red man in it; some stay by his canoe, to guard it. The chiefs and wise men form a circle, into which the red man and two attendants approach. He salutes them with friendly countenance, and they return the salute after their manner. They are amazed at their colour and dress, particularly with him who, glittering in red, wore something (perhaps lace, or buttons) they could not comprehend. He *must* be the great Manitto, they thought; but why should he have a *white skin?* A large elegant *hockhack* (*gourd, i. e.* bottle, decanter, &c.) is brought by one of the supposed Manitto's servants, from which a substance is poured into a small cup or glass, and handed to the Manitto. He drinks, has the glass refilled, and handed to the chief near him; he takes it, smells it, and passes it to the next, who does the same. The glass in this manner is passed round the circle, and is about to be returned to the red-clothed man, when one of them, a great warrior, harangues them on the impropriety of returning the cup unemptied. It was handed to them, he said, by the Manitto, to drink out of as he had; to follow his example would please him—to reject it might provoke his wrath; and if no one else would, he would drink it himself, let what would follow; for it was better for one even to die, than a whole nation to be destroyed. He then took the glass, smelled at it, again addressed them, bidding adieu, and drank the contents. All eyes were now fixed (on the first Indian in New York who had tasted the poison which has since affected so signal a revolution in the condition of the native Americans). He soon began to stagger; the women cried, supposing him in fits; he rolled on the ground; they bemoan his fate; they thought him dying. He fell asleep. They at first thought he had expired, but soon perceived he still breathed. He awoke, jumped up, and declared he never felt more happy; he asked for more; and the whole assembly imitating him, became intoxicated."

In descending the river, after he had penetrated to Albany, Hudson ran his little craft ashore at Weehawken; but the ground was a soft ooze, and she was got off without damage, and proceeded to sea.

View of Meredith, New Hampshire

THIS beautiful town stands between the two lakes Winnipiseogee and Sullivan and is deeply surrounded on every side with the most luxuriant rural beauty. The neighbourhood of these exquisite lakes, studded throughout with small green islands, burdened with foliage,—the lofty mountains, near and distant,—the fertility of the soil, and the healthiness of the spot, form a nucleus of attraction which gives Meredith great preference over other towns in New Hampshire. The Winnipiseogee communicates, by the river of the

VIEW OF MEREDITH, NEW HAMPSHIRE

same name, with the Merrimack River, and is near five hundred feet above the level of the sea.

This is the only part of New England, as far as we are aware, in which Indians were regularly hunted by parties who went out for the purpose, and received a bounty for their scalps. We have alluded elsewhere to Captain Lovewell, who surprised and killed a large party of sleeping Indians, and was killed himself afterwards, in the famous "Lovewell fight." The following tragedy, which took place on the Merrimack, in what was, in those days, the neighbourhood of Meredith, shows the provocation to this apparent inhumanity.

In the year 1697, a party of Indians, arrayed in their war dresses, approached the house of Mr. Dustan. This man was abroad at his usual labour. Upon the first alarm, he flew to the house, with a hope of hurrying to a place of safety his family, consisting of his wife, who had been confined a week only in child-bed; her nurse, a Mrs. Mary Jeff, a widow from the neighbourhood; and eight children. Seven of his children he ordered to flee, with the utmost expedition, in the course opposite to that in which the danger was approaching; and went himself to assist his wife. Before she could leave her bed, the savages were upon them. Her husband, despairing of rendering her any service, flew to the door, mounted his horse, and determined to snatch up the child with which he was unable to part, when he should overtake the little flock. When he came up to them, about two hundred yards from his house, he was unable to make a choice, or to leave any one of the number. He therefore determined to take his lot with them, and to defend them from their murderers, or die by their side. A body of the Indians pursued, and came up with him; and from near distances fired at him and his little company. He returned the fire, and retreated, alternately. For more than a mile he kept so resolute a face to his enemy, retiring in the rear of his charge, returned the fire of the savages so often, and with so good success, and sheltered so effectually his terrified companions, that he finally lodged them all safe from the pursuing butchers, in a distant house. When it is remembered how numerous his assailants were, how bold when an overmatch for their enemies, how active, and what excellent marksmen, a devout mind will consider the hand of Providence as unusually visible in the preservation of this family. Another party of the Indians entered the house, immediately after Mr. Dustan had quitted it, and found Mrs. Dustan, and her nurse, who was attempting to fly with the infant in her arms. Mrs. Dustan they ordered to rise instantly; and before she could completely dress herself, obliged her and her companion to quit the house, after they had plundered it and set it on fire. In company with several other captives, they began their march into the wilderness; she feeble, sick, terrified beyond measure, partially clad, one of her feet bare, and the season utterly unfit for comfortable travelling. The air was chilly and keen, and the earth covered, alternately, with snow and deep mud. Her conductors were unfeeling, insolent, and revengeful: murder was their glory, and torture their sport. Her infant was in her nurse's arms; and infants were the customary victims of savage barbarity. The company had proceeded but a short distance, when an Indian, thinking it an incumbrance, took the child out of the nurse's arms, and dashed its head against a tree. Such of the other captives as began to be weary, and lag, the Indians tomahawked. The slaughter was not an act of revenge or of cruelty; it was a mere convenience; an effort so familiar as not even to excite an emotion. Feeble as Mrs. Dustan was, both she and her nurse sustained, without yielding, the fatigue of the journey. Their intense distress for the death of the child, and of their companions, anxiety for those whom they had left behind, and unceasing terror for themselves, raised these unhappy women to such a degree of vigour, that notwithstanding their fatigue, their exposure to cold, their sufferance from hunger, and their sleeping on damp ground, under an inclement sky, they finished an expedition of about one hundred and fifty miles, without losing their spirits, or injuring their health. The *weekwarm* to which they were conducted, and which belonged to the savage who had claimed them as his property, was inhabited by twelve persons. In the month of April this family set out, with their captives, for an Indian settlement still more remote; and informed them, that when they arrived at the settlement, they must be stripped, scourged, and run the gauntlet, naked, between two files of Indians, containing the whole number found in the settlement; for such, they declared, was the standing custom of their nation. This information made a deep impression on the minds of the captive women, and led them irresistibly to devise all the possible means of escape. On the 31st of the same month, very early in the morning, Mrs. Dustan, while the Indians were asleep, having awaked her nurse, and a fellow-prisoner (a youth taken some time before, from Worcester), despatched, with the assistance of her companions, ten of the twelve Indians; the other two escaped. With the scalps of these savages, they returned through the wilderness; and, having arrived safely at Haverhill, and afterwards at Boston, received a handsome reward for their intrepid conduct, from the legislature."

BALLSTON SPRINGS

Ballston Springs

THESE celebrated springs rise in a valley formed by a branch of the Kayade-rosseras Creek. In this valley, and on its acclivities, is built the village called Ballston Spa. The medicinal character of the waters was discovered (as was said of Saratoga) by the beaten track of the deer to the springs at certain seasons. Ballston is now a populous village during the summer, and, since the rail-road has connected it with Saratoga, these two resorts have become like one, and, together, assemble, during certain months, the greater proportion of the moving population of the country. A description of the kind of life led at these springs accompanies another drawing in this Series.

At the time of the breaking out of the revolutionary war this part of the country was very thinly settled. The inhabitants for the most part took the continental side; but at the battle of Hoosac, a few miles from Ballston, a man was taken prisoner by the Americans, whose history exhibits some fine traits of character. He was a plain farmer from this neighbourhood, named Richard Jackson, and had conscientiously taken the British side in the contest. Feeling himself bound of course to employ himself in the service of his sovereign, he no sooner heard that Colonel Baum was advancing, than he saddled his horse and rode to Hoosac, intending to attach himself to this corps. Here he was taken, in such circumstances as proved his intention beyond every reasonable doubt. He was, besides, too honest to deny it. Accordingly he was transmitted to Great Barrington, then the shire-town of Berkshire, and placed in the hands of General Fellows, high sheriff of the county, who immediately confined him in the county gaol. This building was at that time so infirm, that without a guard no prisoner could be kept in it who wished to make his escape. To escape, however, was in no degree consonant with Richard's idea of right; and he thought no more seriously of making an attempt of this nature, than he would have done had he been in his own house. After he had lain quietly in gaol a few days, he told the sheriff that he was losing his time, and earning nothing, and wished that he would permit him to go out and work in the day time, promising to return regularly at evening to his quarters in the prison. The sheriff had become acquainted with his character, and readily acceded to his proposal. Accordingly Richard went out regularly during the remaining part of the autumn, and the following winter and spring, until the beginning of May, and every night returned at the proper hour to the gaol. In this manner he performed a day's work every day, with scarcely any exception beside the Sabbath, through the whole period.

[187]

In the month of May he was to be tried for high treason. The sheriff accordingly made preparations to conduct him to Springfield, where his trial was to be held; but he told the sheriff that it was not worth his while to take this trouble, for he could just as well go alone, and it would save both the expense and inconvenience of the sheriff's journey. The sheriff, after a little reflection, assented to his proposal, and Richard commenced his journey; the only one, it is believed, which was ever undertaken in the same manner for the same object. In the woods of Tyringham he was overtaken by the Hon. T. Edwards, from whom I had this story.—"Whither are you going?" said Mr. Edwards. "To Springfield, Sir," answered Richard, "to be tried for my life." Accordingly he proceeded directly to Springfield, surrendered himself to the sheriff of Hampshire, was tried, found guilty, and condemned to die.

The council of Massachusets was at this time the supreme executive of the State. Application was made to this board for a pardon. The facts were stated, the evidence by which they were supported, and the sentence grounded on them. The question was then put by the president, "Shall a pardon be granted to Richard Jackson?" The gentleman who spoke first observed that the case was perfectly clear; the act alleged against Jackson was unquestionably high treason; and the proof was complete. If a pardon should be granted in this case, he saw no reason why it should not be granted in every other. In the same manner answered those who followed him. When it came to the turn of Mr. Edwards, he told this story with those little circumstances of particularity, which, though they are easily lost from the memory, and have escaped mine, give light and shade, a living reality, and a picturesque impressiveness, to every tale which is fitted to enforce conviction, or to touch the heart. At the same time he recited it without enhancement, without expatiating, without any attempt to be pathetic. As is always the case, this simplicity gave the narration its full force. The council began to hesitate. One of the members at length observed—"Certainly such a man as this ought not to be sent to the gallows." To his opinion the members unanimously assented. A pardon was immediately made out and transmitted to Springfield, and Richard returned to his family.

Never was a stronger proof exhibited, that honesty is wisdom.

The Narrows, from Fort Hamilton

NOT quite one hundred years after Verrazzano's discovery of the Bay of New York, during all which period we have no account of its having been visited by an European vessel, Hudson made the Capes of Virginia on his third cruise in search of the north-west passage. Standing still on a northward course, he arrived in sight of the Narrows, distinguishing from a great distance the Highlands of Neversink, which his mate, Robert Juet, describes in the journal he kept as a "very good land to fall with, and a pleasant land to see."

The most interesting peculiarity of our country to a European observer, is the freshness of its early history, and the strong contrast it presents of most of the features of a highly civilized land, with the youth and recent adventure of a newly discovered one. The details of these first discoveries are becoming every day more interesting: and to accompany a drawing of the Narrows, or entrance to the Bay of New York, the most fit illustration is that part of the journal of the great navigator which relates to his first view of them. The following extracts describe the Narrows as they were two hundred years ago: the drawing presents them as they are.

"At three of the clock in the afternoone we came to three great rivers. So we stood along to the northernmost, thinking to have gone into it, but we found it to have a very shoald barre before it, for we had but ten foot water. Then we cast about to the southward, and found two fathoms, three fathoms, and three and a quarter, till we came to the souther side of them, then we had five or six fathoms, and anchored. So we sent in our boat to sound, and they found no less water than foure, five, six, and seven fathoms, and returned in an hour and a halfe. So we weighed and went in, and rode in five fathoms, ose ground, and saw many salmons, and mullets, and rayes very great.

"The fourth, in the morning, as soone as the day was light, we saw that it was good riding farther up. So we sent our boate to sound, and found that it was a very good harbour; then we weighed and went in with our ship. Then our boat went on land with our net to fish, and caught ten great mullets, of a foot and a half long apeece, and a ray as great as foure men could hale into the ship. So we trimmed our boat, and rode still all day. At night the wind blew hard at the north-west, and our anchor came home, and we drove on shore, but took no hurt, thanked bee God, for the ground is soft sand and ose. This day the people of the country came aboard of us, seeming very glad of our comming, and brought greene tobacco, and gave us of it for knives and beads. They go in deere skins loose, well dressed. They have yellow copper. They

THE NARROWS, FROM FORT HAMILTON

desire cloathes, and are very civill. They have great store of maise, or Indian wheate, whereof they make good bread. The country is full of great and tall oaks.

"The fifth, in the morning, as soone as the day was light, the wind ceased; so we sent our boate in to sound the bay. Our men went on land there and saw great store of men, women, and children, who gave them tobacco at their coming on land. So they went up into the woods, and saw great store of very goodly oakes, and some currants.

"The sixth, in the morning, was faire weather, and our master sent John Colman with foure other men in our boate over to the north side, to sound the other river," (the Narrows.) "They found very good riding for ships, and a narrow river to the westward," (probably what is now called the Kells, or the passage between Bergen-Neck and Staten Island,) "between two islands. The lands, they told us, were as pleasant, with grasse and flowers, and goodly trees, as ever they had seen, and very sweet smells came from them. So they went in two leagues and saw an open sea, and returned; and as they came backe they were set upon by two canoes, the one having twelve, the other fourteen men. The night came on, and it began to raine, so that their match went out; and they had one man slain in the fight, which was an Englishman, named John Colman, with an arrow shot into his throat, and two more hurt. It grew so dark that they could not find the shippe that night, but laboured to and fro on their oares.

"The seventh was fair, and they returned aboard the ship, and brought our dead man with them, whom we carried on land and buried."

On the eighth, Hudson lay still, to be more sure of the disposition of the natives before venturing farther in. Several came on board, but no disturbance occurred, and on the ninth he got under weigh, passed the Narrows, and proceeded by slow degrees up the river destined to bear his name.

THE NOTCH-HOUSE, WHITE MOUNTAINS

(NEW HAMPSHIRE)

The Notch-House—White Mountains

A CONSIDERABLE tract of land in New Hampshire was granted to two individuals of the names of Nash and Sawyer, for the discovery of "the Notch." This pass, the only one by which the inhabitants of a large extent of country, north-westward of these mountains, can, without a great circuit, make their way to the eastern shore, was known to the savages, who used to conduct their prisoners, taken on the coast, through this gap to Canada. By the people of New Hampshire, it was either unknown, or had been forgotten. Nash discovered it; but Sawyer persuaded Nash to admit him to an equal share of the benefits resulting from the discovery. It was, however, little advantage to either. They were both hunters, and with the thoughtlessness of men devoted to that employment, squandered the property soon after it was granted.

The Notch-house is inhabited by a family of the name of Crawford, who have the reputation, given them by travellers to the Notch, of being giants in size and strength. Ethan, one of the brothers living a mile or two further up, is called the "Keeper of the Mountains." A manuscript journal of a pedestrian excursion to Mount Washington lies before us, in which the writer (a friend of ours, who is a small Titan himself, and whose estimate of thewe and sinew is to be taken with a grain of allowance) rather sneers at the proportions of the mountain-keeper. After walking from thirty to thirty-four miles a day, mostly up hill, our friend and his companion arrive at the Notch-house.

"About one o'clock," says the journal, "we reached the house of T. G. Crawford, where we must remain till we can ascend Mount Washington. These Crawfords are not such giants as I had been led to suppose. We have not, however, seen Ethan, the most celebrated of the race.

"Last night we had a thunder shower, with sharp lightning. The thunder sounds heavy, and rumbles or echoes among the mountains with a very impressive effect. Just at evening we visited a beautiful cataract called the *Flume*, about half a mile from the house, and took the finest shower-bath I ever enjoyed. To-day the weather is doubtful, and we shall not attempt the ascent till tomorrow. There is enough in this immediate neighbourhood to occupy a week. The variety and magnificence of the scenery in every direction would satisfy the most ardent lover of the picturesque. Crawford is a fine fellow: his house is excellent, his trout delicious, and his *neighbours perfectly quiet!* The album kept here is an amusing *omniana* of nonsense and astonishment, sentiment and piety.

"After dinner walked over to Ethan Crawford's, and saw the celebrated

'Keeper of the White Mountains.' Expected to find him a giant, but were disappointed: he is a large man, and strong in muscle, but I have seen fifty larger and stronger in my own town. There is nothing remarkable in his manners or conversation. His voice is stentorian, and his style is marked by a rude bluntness and an apparent consciousness that something original is expected of him. On our return had a fine view of Mount Washington and his fellow-peaks. The monarch's head was capp'd with clouds, while all the others stood bare, as if uncovered for respect."

Another traveller thus speaks of the scenery of this spot:—"We rode six miles farther, and came to a farm occupied by a man named Crawford. Here the mountains assumed the form of an immense amphitheatre, elliptical in its figure, from twelve to fifteen miles in length, from two to four in breadth, and crowned with summits of vast height and amazing grandeur. Compared with this scene all human works of this nature, that of Titus particularly, so splendidly described by Gibbon, are diminished into toys and gewgaws. Here more millions could sit than hundreds there; every one of whom could look down with a full view on the valley beneath.

"The south-eastern extremity of this form was, some years since, the scene of a melancholy circumstance. A young woman, who had been employed at Jefferson, in the service of Colonel Whipple, had fallen deeply in love with a young man in the service of the same gentleman. At the close of autumn they agreed to go together to Portsmouth. On some occasion or other she was induced, before the time fixed for their departure, to go over to Lancaster. When she returned, she found him unexpectedly gone, and determined to follow him. December was already advanced, the snow had fallen deep, and there was not a house for thirty miles on the road. She set out on foot, and walked twenty-three miles from the house she had left, and then, overcome probably with fatigue, wrapped herself in her cloak, and lay down under a bush, where she was found a month afterwards, stiffened with frost."

Wilkesbarre—Vale of Wyoming

THIS beautiful town is situated on the eastern bank of the Susquehanna, op-posite the village of Wyoming, celebrated in the "Gertrude" of Campbell. Like all the towns in this picturesque valley, it possesses fine points of pic-turesque beauty, and exhibits the thrift and agricultural prosperity which, all over the United States, contrast so strongly with the recent and unforgot-ten tales of the primitive wilderness.

There is a book, of which many copies do not now exist, entitled "Observa-tions made by John Bartram, in his Travels through Pennsylvania to the Lake Ontario," which presents a very wild picture of this part of the country in 1743. His companions were Mr. Weisar, a Mr. Evans, and a Delaware chief, called *Shickalamy*, and the object of their journey was to reconcile some dif-ferences between the English and the different Indian nations on that frontier. The dignity of their character as envoys from the English procured for them a kind reception, and the sight of many ceremonies not commonly seen by travellers. On their arrival on the banks of the Susquehanna, they were enter-tained by a hunting party of Indians, who served them up a roasted bear. *Apropos* to this, he describes the following superstition:—

"As soon as the bear is killed, the hunter places the small end of his pipe in its mouth, and, by blowing in the bowl, fills the mouth and throat full of smoke. He then conjures the departed spirit of the bear not to resent the in-jury done his body, nor to thwart his future sport in hunting. As he receives no answer to this, in order to know if his prayers have prevailed, he cuts the ligament under the bear's tongue. If these ligaments contract and shrivel up when cast into the fire, which is done with invocations and great solemnity, then it is esteemed a certain mark that the *manes* are appeased."

On the next day's journey, still following the winding bank of the east branch of the Susquehanna, they arrived at an Indian village, where the na-tives welcomed them by beating a rude drum. Assisting them to unsaddle their horses, they invited them into the principal wigwam, and cut long grass, and laid it on the floor for them to sit upon. The chiefs then came in with their pipes, (one of which, he says, was six feet long, with a stone head and a reed stem;) and immediately after they were regaled with roast venison, of which the morsel of honour was the neck, given to them for their share, to Mr. Bartram's great dissatisfaction. A superstitious ceremony took place here, the description of which is rather curious.

"They cut a parcel of poles, which they stick in the ground in a circle of

WILKESBARRE—VALE OF WYOMING

about five feet diameter, and then bring them together at the top, and tie them in the form of an oven. In this the conjuror placeth himself, and his assistants cover his cage over with blankets. To make it still more suffocating, hot stones are rolled in. The conjuror then cries aloud, and agitates his body in the most violent manner; and when nature has lost almost all her faculties, the stubborn spirit becomes visible to him, generally in the shape of some bird. There is usually a stake driven into the ground about four feet high, and painted, for the airy visitant to perch upon while he reveals what the invocant wisheth to know. Sometimes there is a bowl of water, into which they often look when nearly exhausted, to see whether the spirit is ready to answer their demands."

The next day he encounters another superstition:—"On our left, as we journeyed, we perceived a hill, where the Indians told us that corn, tobacco, and squashes were found on the following occasion. An Indian of a distant tribe, whose wife had eloped, came hither to hunt, intending, with his skins, to purchase another wife. Coming to this hill, he espied a young squaw, sitting alone. Going to her and inquiring whence she came, she answered that she came from heaven to provide sustenance for poor Indians, and if he came to that place twelve months after, he should find food there. He came accordingly and found corn, squashes, and tobacco, which were propagated from thence, and spread through the country; and this silly story is religiously held for truth among them."

He kept on up the valley of the Susquehanna, through woods, where, as he describes it, "the tops of the trees for miles together were so close to one another that there is no seeing which way the clouds drive, nor knowing which way the wind sets; and it seems as if the sun had never shone on the ground beneath since the creation." It is a description of a complete wilderness, till he reaches the borders of Lake Ontario—a tract of country that, in ninety years from the time he wrote, is seamed with rail-roads and canals, and teeming with towns, improvement and speculation.

SQUAWM LAKE

(NEW HAMPSHIRE)

Squawm Lake

The Indianesque, but not very pretty name, in which this lovely body of waters rejoices, has been once or twice changed, but the force of usage has uniformly triumphed. Dr. Dwight called it Sullivan's Lake, after Major-General Sullivan, formerly governor of the State; and the adjoining waters of Winnipiseogee, he named Lake Wentworth, after another governor; but both have fallen into disuse, and the original names have reverted.

The great defect in American Lakes, generally, is the vast, unrelieved expanse of water, without islands and promontories, producing a fatigue on the eye similar to that of the sea. Squawm and Winnipiseogee Lakes are exceptions to this observation. They are connected by so narrow an isthmus that five hundred dollars, it is said, would pay the expense of uniting them: and their islands together amount, it is said also, to exactly three hundred and sixty-five. As this singular coincidence has been remarked of several other lakes, however, the assertion seems rather apocryphal.

Some of the very loveliest scenery in the world lies about these two lakes, yet they are seldom visited. The country around is fertile, and sufficiently cultivated to soften the appearance of wilderness, which it might receive from the prevalency of forest, and the luxuriance of vegetation; but the mountains, which form its background from every point, shutting it in like an amphitheatre, seem to seclude it from the flow of population.

Nature is a capricious beauty, and, like most other beauties, has her best looks, and her favourable times, to be seen to advantage. Beautiful as she is at Squawm Lake in the first plenitude of spring, she is more beautiful in the first flush over her face of the bright colours of autumn. The autumnal tints of our forests are peculiar to America, but there are some parts of the country where, for various reasons, this phenomenon is much more beautiful than at others. The moisture of the land about these lakes, the extreme luxuriance of the sap in consequence, and the liability of the whole of this region to sudden changes of temperature, contribute to its brilliancy. The sharp frost of a single night effects a change very often that seems almost miraculous, and the multiplication of these gawdy colours in the mirror of the surrounding waters, the bright golden, crimson, and purple islands, and the gorgeous hillsides, all reflected and redoubled, make it a scene which the imagination never could pre-conceive. From a late publication we extract a description of this phenomenon, made from observation, and finished with some care.

"The first severe frost had come, and the miraculous change had passed

[199]

upon the leaves which is known only in America. The blood-red sugar maple, with a leaf brighter and more delicate than a Circassian lip, stood here and there in the forest like the sultan's standard in a host—the solitary and far-seen aristocrat of the wilderness; the birch, with its spirit-like and amber leaves, ghosts of the departed summer, turned out along the edges of the woods like a lining of the palest gold; the broad sycamore and the fan-like catalpa flaunted their saffron foliage in the sun, spotted with gold like the wings of a lady-bird; the kingly oak, with its summit shaken bare, still hid its majestic trunk in a drapery of sumptuous dyes, like a stricken monarch, gathering his robes of state about him, to die royally in his purple; the tall poplar, with its minaret of silver leaves, stood blanched like a coward in the dying forest, burthening every breeze with its complainings; the hickory paled through its enduring green; the bright berries of the mountain-ash, flushed with a more sanguine glory in the unobstructed sun; the gaudy tulip-tree, the sybarite of vegetation, stripped of its golden cups, still drank the intoxicating light of noon-day in leaves than which the lip of an Indian shell was never more delicately tinted; the still deeper-dyed vines of the lavish wilderness, perishing with the noble things whose summer they had shared, outshone them in their decline, as woman in her death is heavenlier than the being on whom in life she leaned; and alone and unsympathizing in this universal decay, outlaws from nature, stood the fir and the hemlock; their frowning and sombre heads darker and less lovely than ever, in contrast with the death-struck glory of their companions.

"The dull colours of English autumnal foliage give you no conception of this marvellous phenomenon. The change here is gradual; in America it is the work of a night—of a single frost!

"Oh, to have seen the sun set on hills bright in the still green and lingering summer, and to awake in the morning to a spectacle like this!

"It is as if a myriad of rainbows were laced through the tree-tops—as if the sun-sets of a summer—gold, purple, and crimson—had been fused in the alembic of the west, and poured back in a new deluge of light and colour over the wilderness. It is as if every leaf in these countless trees had been painted to outflush the tulip—as if, by some electric miracle, the dyes of the earth's heart had struck upward, and her crystals and ores, her sapphires, hyacinths, and rubies, had let forth their imprisoned colours to mount through the roots of the forests, and, like the angels that in olden time entered the bodies of the dying, re-animate the perishing leaves, and revel an hour in their bravery."

Sabbath-Day Point, Lake George

THE lovely waters of Lake George are known to the Catholics by the prettier and more appropriate name of Lake Sacrament. Its singular transparency, surpassing that of all other lakes in the world, probably suggested some tradition of its sacredness; and its water was carried to great distances to supply the consecrated fonts. The singular seclusion of its position, far aside from the general current of population, has assisted to preserve its character.

Loch Katrine, at the Trosachs, is a miniature-likeness of Lake George. It is the only lake in Europe that has at all the same style or degree of beauty. The small green islands, with their abrupt shores,—the emerald depths of the water, overshadowed and tinted by the tenderest moss and foliage,—the lofty mountains in the back-ground,—and the tranquil character of the lake, over which the wind is arrested and rendered powerless by the peaks of the hills and the lofty island-summits,—are all points of singular resemblance. Loch Katrine can scarce be called picturesque, except at the Trosachs, however; while Lake George, throughout all the mazes of its three hundred and sixty-five islands (there are said to be just this number), preserves the same wild and racy character of beauty. Varying in size, from a mile in length to the circumference of a tea-table, these little islets present the most multiplied changes of surface and aspect—upon some only moss and flowers, upon others a miniature forest, with its outer trees leaning over to the pellucid bosom of the lake, as if drawn downwards by the reflection of their own luxuriant beauty.

The forests on the shores of Lake George were formerly stocked plentifully with deer, who were hunted in rather a peculiar manner. The huntsmen were divided into two parties, one of which started them from their thickets on the edge of the lake. Upon hearing the approach of the dogs, they invariably took to the water and crossed to the opposite shore, from which a boat, directed by a boy stationed in a high tree, put out to meet them. A few blows with an oar conquered them easily, and they were towed ashore, or taken alive into the boat. Bears are hunted in the same manner, except that, being more inconvenient to close with, they are usually shot from the boat without ceremony.

The race of settlers who were to be found in these neighbourhoods not many years ago—half hunters, half farmers—has disappeared, or gone westward with the game. The celebrated theologian, Dr. Dwight, gives a graphic account of one of this class, whom he met in a first visit to Lake George, some-

SABBATH-DAY POINT, LAKE GEORGE

where about the year 1800. Landing on a point to dine, in his passage up the lake, he found a huntsman, with a buck lying beside him. "Before our departure," he says, "we heard the hounds advancing near to us. Our new companion instantly took fire at the sound. His eye kindled; his voice assumed a loftier tone; his stride became haughty; his style swelled into pomp, and his sentiments were changed rapidly from mildness to ardour, to vehemence, and to rage. I was forcibly struck with the sameness of the emotions produced by hunting and by war. The ardour of battle, the glitter of arms, and the shock of conflict, could scarcely have produced in a single moment more violent or fierce agitations than were roused in this man by the approach of the hounds, the confident expectation of a victim, and the brilliant prospect of a venatory triumph. To him who has been a witness of both objects, it will cease to be a wonder that the savage should make the chase a substitute for war, and a source of glory second only to that acquired in battle. Our hunter was not exempted, however, from the common lot of man. His partner came up with the hounds, but without a deer! The magnificence of our companion dwindled in a moment. The fire vanished from his eye; his voice fell to its natural key; and the hero shrank into a plain farmer."

No one, it has been well said, understands the character of the aboriginal tenants of America, who has seen them only as *vitiated* by contact with the settlers. I say vitiated; for, if they are not made better by proper protection and cultivation, they become much worse; as human nature, left to itself, is more susceptible of the contagion of vice, than of improvement in virtue. The Indian, thrown into temptation, easily takes the vices of the white man; and, in such exposure, his race melts away like the snow before a summer's sun.

The wild Indian, however, whose contact with the European race has not been enough to vitiate his habits, or subdue his self-importance—who still prowls the forest in the pride of his independence—who looks upon all nations and tribes, but his own, as unworthy of the contemptuous glance of his eye—whose dreams of importance become to him a constant reality, and actually have the same influence in the formation of his character as if they were all they *seem* to him—he regards himself as the *centre* of a world made purposely for him. Such a being (and the wild Indian is much more than this) who is not a creature of the imagination, but a living actor in the scenes of the earth, becomes at least an interesting object, if not, also, a *problem* yet to be solved in both moral philosophy and politics, and in the nature and character of man as a social being. His *bearing* may be imagined from the following description of the war-dance:—

[203]

"A hundred warriors now advance,
  All dressed and painted for the dance;
And sounding club and hollow skin,
A slow and measured *time* begin.
With rigid limb and sliding foot,
And murmurs low the time to suit,
For ever varying with the sound,
The circling band moves round and round.
Now slowly rise the swelling notes,
And every crest more lively floats.
Now tossed on high with gesture proud.
Then lowly 'mid the circle bowed;
While clanging arms grow louder still,
And every voice becomes more shrill,
Till fierce and strong the clamour grows,
And the wild *war-whoop* bids it close,
Then starts SKUNTONGA forth, whose band
Came far from Huron's storm-beat strand,
And loud recounts his *hunting* feats,
Whilst his dark club the measure beats."—ONTWA

Sabbath-day Point presents one of the most beautiful of the many views upon the lake. It received its name from Lord Amherst, who landed there with his suite to breakfast on a Sunday morning. It is about twenty-five miles from the head of the lake.

The Catterskill Falls

(From Below)

FROM the precipice whence our first view of this Fall is taken, the descent is steep and slippery to the very brink of the torrent, which it is necessary to cross on the wild blocks which lie scattered in its rocky bed. From thence, literally buried in forest foliage, the tourist will enjoy a very different, but, perhaps, more striking and picturesque view than the other. The stream, at a vast height above him, is seen leaping from ledge to ledge—sometimes lost, sometimes sparkling in sunshine, till it courses impetuously beneath the rock on which he is seated, and is lost in the deep unbroken obscurity of the forest. The rocky ledges above, worn by time, have the appearance of deep caverns, and beautifully relieve the fall of the light and silvery stream. In the winter, the vast icicles which are suspended from the ledges of rock, and shine like pillars against the deep obscurity of the caverns behind, afford a most romantic spectacle, one which has afforded a subject to Bryant for one of the most imaginative of his poems.

THE CATTERSKILL FALLS

"Midst greens and shades the Catterskill leaps
    From cliffs where the wood-flower clings;
All summer he moistens his verdant steeps
    With the sweet light spray of the mountain springs;
And he shakes the woods on the mountain side,
When they drip with the rains of autumn-tide.

"But when, in the forest bare and old,
    The blast of December calls,
He builds, in the starlight clear and cold,
    A palace of ice where his torrent falls,
With turret, and arch, and fretwork fair,
And pillars blue as the summer air.

"For whom are those glorious chambers wrought,
    In the cold and cloudless night?
Is there neither spirit nor motion of thought
    In forms so lovely and hues so bright?
Hear what the grey-haired woodmen tell
Of this wild stream, and its rocky dell.

THE CATTERSKILL FALLS
(FROM BELOW)

"'Twas hither a youth of dreamy mood,
    A hundred winters ago,
  Had wandered over the mighty wood,
    When the panther's track was fresh on the snow;
  And keen were the winds that came to stir
  The long dark boughs of the hemlock fir.

"Too gentle of mien he seemed, and fair,
    For a child of those rugged steeps;
  His home lay low in the valley, where
    The kingly Hudson rolls to the deeps;
  But he wore the hunter's frock that day,
  And a slender gun on his shoulder lay.

"And here he paused, and against the trunk
    Of a tall grey linden leant,
  When the broad clear orb of the sun had sunk
    From his path in the frosty firmament,
  And over the round dark edge of the hill
  A cold green light was quivering still.

"And the crescent moon, high over the green,
    From a sky of crimson shone,
  On that icy palace, whose towers were seen
    To sparkle as if with stars of their own;
  While the water fell, with a hollow sound,
  'Twixt the glistening pillars ranged around.

"Is that a being of life, that moves
    Where the crystal battlements rise?
  A maiden, watching the moon she loves,
    At the twilight hour, with pensive eyes?
  Was that a garment which seemed to gleam
  Betwixt the eye and the falling stream?

"'Tis only the torrent tumbling o'er,
    In the midst of those glassy walls,
  Gushing, and plunging, and beating the floor
    Of the rocky basin in which it falls:
  'Tis only the torrent—but why that start?
  Why gazes the youth with a throbbing heart?

"He thinks no more of his home afar,
    Where his sire and sister wait;
  He heeds no longer how star after star
    Looks forth on the night, as the hour grows late.
  He heeds not the snow-wreath, lifted and cast
  From a thousand boughs, by the rising blast.

"His thoughts are alone of those who dwell
    In the halls of frost and snow,
Who pass where the crystal domes upswell
    From the alabaster floors below,
Where the frost-trees bourgeon with leaf and spray,
And frost-gems scatter a silvery day.

"'And oh that those glorious haunts were mine!'
    He speaks, and throughout the glen
Their shadows swim in the faint moonshine,
    And take a ghastly likeness of men,
As if the slain by the wintry storms
Came forth to the air in their earthly forms.

"There pass the chasers of seal and whale,
    With their weapons quaint and grim,
And bands of warriors in glimmering mail,
    And herdsmen and hunters huge of limb—
There are naked arms, with bow and spear,
And furry gauntlets the carbine rear.

"There are mothers—and oh, how sadly their eyes
    On their children's white brows rest!
There are youthful lovers—the maiden lies
    In a seeming sleep on the chosen breast;
There are fair wan women with moon-struck air,
The snow-stars flecking their long loose hair.

"They eye him not as they pass along,
    But his hair stands up with dread,
When he feels that he moves with that phantom throng,
    Till those icy turrets are over his head,
And the torrent's roar, as they enter, seems
Like a drowsy murmur heard in dreams.

"The glittering threshold is scarcely passed,
    When there gathers and wraps him round
A thick white twilight, sullen and vast,
    In which there is neither form nor sound;
The phantoms, the glory, vanish all,
With the dying voice of the waterfall.

"Slow passes the darkness of that trance,
    And the youth now faintly sees
Huge shadows and gushes of light that dance
    On a rugged ceiling of unhewn trees,
And walls where the skins of beasts are hung,
And rifles glitter on antlers strung.

THE CATTERSKILL FALLS
(FROM ABOVE THE RAVINE)

"On a couch of shaggy skins he lies;
    As he strives to raise his head,
Hard-featured woodmen, with kindly eyes
    Come round him and smooth his furry bed,
And bid him rest, for the evening star
Is scarcely set, and the day is far.

"They had found at eve the dreaming one,
    By the base of that icy steep,
When over his stiffening limbs begun
    The deadly slumber of frost to creep;
And they cherished the pale and breathless form,
Till the stagnant blood ran free and warm."

Winter Scene on the Catterskills

THE great proportion of evergreen trees, shrubs, and creepers, in the American mountains, make the winter scenery less dreary than would be at first imagined; but even the nakedness of the deciduous trees is not long observable. The first snow clothes them in a dress so feathery and graceful, that, like a change in the costume of beauty, it seems lovelier than the one put off; and the constant renewal of its freshness and delicacy goes on with a variety and novelty which is scarce dreamed of by those who see snow only in cities, or in countries where it is rare.

The roads, in so mountainous a region as the Catterskills, are in winter not only difficult, but dangerous. The following extracts from a sleigh ride in a more level part of the country, will serve to give an idea of it. "As we got farther on, the new snow became deeper. The occasional farm-houses were almost wholly buried, the black chimney alone appearing above the ridgy drifts; while the tops of the doors and windows lay below the level of the trodden road, from which a descending passage was cut to the threshold, like the entrance to a cave in the earth. The fences were quite invisible. The fruit-trees looked diminished to shrubberies of snow-flowers, their trunks buried under the visible surface, and their branches loaded with the still falling flakes, till they bent beneath the burden. Nothing was abroad, for nothing could stir out of the road without danger of being lost; and we dreaded to meet even a single sleigh, lest, in turning out, the horses should 'slump' beyond their depth in the untrodden drifts. The poor animals began to labour severely, and sank at every step over their knees in the clogging and wool-like substance; and the long and cumbrous sleigh rose and fell in the deep pits like a boat in a heavy sea. It seemed impossible to get on. Twice we brought up with a terrible plunge, and stood suddenly still; for the runners had struck in too deep for the strength of the horses; and with the snow-shovels, which formed a part of the furniture of the vehicle, we dug them from their concrete beds. Our progress at last was reduced to scarce a mile in the hour, and we began to have apprehensions that our team would give out between the post-houses. Fortunately it was still warm, for the numbness of cold would have paralyzed our already flagging exertions.

"We had reached the summit of a long hill with the greatest difficulty. The poor beasts stood panting and reeking with sweat; the runners of the sleigh were clogged with hard cakes of snow, and the air was close and dispiriting. We came to a standstill, with the vehicle lying over almost on its side; and

WINTER SCENE ON THE CATTERSKILLS

I stepped out to speak to the driver and look forward. It was a discouraging prospect; a long deep valley lay before us, closed at the distance of a couple of miles by another steep hill, through a cleft in the top of which lay our way. We could not even distinguish the line of the road between. Our disheartened animals stood at this moment buried to their breasts; and to get forward, without rearing at every step, seemed impossible. The driver sat on his box, looking uneasily down into the valley. It was one undulating ocean of snow— not a sign of a human habitation to be seen—and even the trees indistinguishable from the general mass by their whitened and overladen branches. The storm had ceased, but the usual sharp cold that succeeds a warm fall of snow had not yet lightened the clamminess of the new-fallen flakes, and they clung around the foot like clay, rendering every step a toil."

"We heaved out of the pit into which the sleigh had settled, and for the first mile it was down hill, and we got on with comparative ease. The sky was by this time almost bare, a dark slaty mass of clouds alone settling on the horizon in the quarter of the wind; while the sun, as powerless as moonlight, poured with dazzling splendour on the snow; and the gusts came keen and bitter across the sparkling waste, rimming the nostrils as if with bands of steel, and penetrating to the innermost nerve with their pungent iciness. No protection seemed of any avail. The whole surface of the body ached as if it were laid against a slab of ice. The throat closed instinctively, and contracted its unpleasant respiration. The body and limbs drew irresistibly together, to economize, like a hedge-hog, the exposed surface. The hands and feet felt transmuted to lead; and across the forehead, below the pressure of the cap, there was a binding and oppressive ache, as if a bar of frosty iron had been let into the skull. The mind, meantime, seemed freezing up; unwillingness to stir, and inability to think of any thing but the cold, becoming every instant more decided.

"From the bend of the valley our difficulties became more serious. The drifts often lay across the road like a wall, some feet above the heads of the horses; and we had dug through one or two, and had been once upset, and often near it, before we came to the steepest part of the ascent. The horses had by this time begun to feel the excitement of the rum given them by the driver at the last halt, and bounded on through the snow with continuous leaps, jerking the sleigh after them with a violence that threatened momently to break the traces. The steam from their bodies froze instantly, and covered them with a coat like hoar-frost; and spite of their heat, and the unnatural and violent exertions they were making, it was evident, by the pricking of their ears, and the sudden crouch of the body when a stronger blast swept over, that the cold struck through even their hot and intoxicated blood.

"We toiled up, leap after leap; and it seemed miraculous to me that the now infuriated animals did not burst a blood-vessel, or crack a sinew, with every one of those terrible springs. The sleigh plunged on after them, stopping dead and short at every other moment, and reeling over the heavy drifts like a boat in a surging sea. A finer crystallization had meanwhile taken place upon the surface of the moist snow; and the powdered particles flew almost insensibly on the blasts of wind, filling the eyes and hair, and cutting the skin with a sensation like the touch of needle-points. The driver, and his maddened but almost exhausted team, were blinded by the glittering and whirling eddies; the cold grew intenser every moment, the forward motion gradually less and less; and when, with the very last effort apparently, we reached a spot on the summit of the hill, which from its exposed situation had been kept bare by the wind, the patient and persevering whip brought his horses to a stand, and despaired, for the first time, of his prospects of getting on."

The description, which is too long to extract entire, details still severer difficulties; after which the writer and driver mounted on the leaders, and arrived, nearly dead with cold, at the tavern. Such cold as is described here, however, is what is called "an old-fashioned spell," and occurs now but seldom.

Rogers' Slide, Lake George

THIS is an almost perpendicular precipice of great height, abutting directly upon the romantic waters of Lake George, and remarkable for the escape of an American officer, Major Rogers, who, pursued closely by a party of Indians when the lake was frozen over, descended this bluff, and escaped upon the ice. To look at it, the feat seems incredible; and so thought the pursuing Indians, who, arriving at the brow of the precipice, and not seeing his body at the bottom, attributed his disappearance to supernatural agency.

Much as we are in the habit of extolling the athletic make and superior physical qualities of the Indians of our country, the early annals prove the superiority in strength, and even in address, which was their strong point, to

[214]

ROGERS' SLIDE, LAKE GEORGE

have been oftenest on the side of the white settlers. There are two or three very stirring examples in the annals of a small town in New Hampshire: —

"Early in the morning of the 23d April, Ephraim Dorman left the fort to search for his cow. He went northwardly, along the borders of what was then a hideous and almost impervious swamp, lying east of the fort, until he arrived near to the place where the turnpike now is. Looking into the swamp, he perceived several Indians lurking in the bushes. He immediately gave the alarm, by crying, "Indians! Indians!" and ran towards the fort. Two, who were concealed in the bushes between him and the fort, sprang forward, aimed their pieces at him, and fired; but neither hit him. They then, throwing away their arms, advanced towards him: one he knocked down by a blow, which deprived him of his senses; the other he seized, and being a strong man, an able wrestler, tried his strength and skill in his favourite mode of 'trip and twitch.' He tore his antagonist's blanket from his shoulders, leaving him nearly naked. He then seized him by the arms and body, but, as he was painted and greased, he slipped from his grasp. After a short struggle, Dorman quitted him, ran towards the fort, and reached it in safety.

"Mrs. Clark was at a barn, near the Todd-house, about fifty rods distant. Leaving it, she espied an Indian near her, who threw away his gun, and advanced to make her prisoner. She gathered her clothes around her waist, and started for the fort. The Indian pursued: the woman, animated by cheers from her friends, outran her pursuer, who skulked back for his gun. Nathan Blake was at his barn, near where his son's house now stands. Hearing the cry of Indians, and presuming his barn would be burnt, he determined that his cattle should not be burnt with it. Throwing open his stable door, he let them loose, and presuming his retreat to the fort was cut off, went out at a back door, intending to place himself in ambush at the only place where the river could be crossed. He had gone but a few steps, when he was hailed by a party of Indians, concealed in a shop between him and the street. Looking back, he perceived several guns pointed at him, and at this instant several Indians started up from their places of concealment near him; upon which, feeling himself in their power, he gave himself up. He was then conducted to Lucbee, and thence to an Indian village, several miles north of that place, called Conissadawga. He was a strong, athletic man, and possessed many qualities which procured him the respect of the savages. He could run with great speed; and in all the trials to which he was put, (and they were many and severe,) he beat every antagonist.

"Not long after his arrival at the village, the tribe lost a chief by sickness.

[216]

As soon as his decease was made known, the women repaired to his wigwam, and with tears, sobs, and clamorous lamentations, mourned his death. The funeral ceremonies performed, the men sought Blake, dressed him in the Indian costume, and invested him with all the authority and privileges of the deceased, as one of the chiefs of the tribe, and as husband of the widow. In the family to which he now stood in the relation of father, there were, as he had often remarked, several daughters of uncommon beauty. Yet notwithstanding this good fortune, he still had difficulties to encounter. The tribe was divided into two parties, his friends and his enemies. The former consisted of the great mass of the tribe, who respected him for qualities to which they had not equal pretensions; the latter, of those who were envious of his success, and had been worsted in their contests with him. These, to humble his pride, sent far into the northern wilderness, and procured a celebrated Indian runner, to run against him. At the time assigned, the whole tribe assembled to witness the race; and a Frenchman, from Quebec, happened to be present. Perceiving the excitement among them, he advised Blake to permit himself to be beaten, intimating that fatal consequences might ensue if he did not. The race was run; and Blake, as advised by the Frenchman, permitted his antagonist to reach the goal a moment before he did. He persisted, however, after his return from captivity, in declaring that he might have beaten him, if he had tried. The event of the race restored harmony to the tribe, and Blake was permitted to live in peace."

The Gothic Church, New Haven

THE area occupied by the town of New Haven is estimated to be six times as great as that of a European town with the same number of inhabitants. It was originally laid out in parallelograms, and the houses are built upon the outer sides of the squares, with large gardens meeting in the centre. Almost every house stands separate, and surrounded by shrubbery and verdure; and it is the great peculiarity of the town, that all its streets are planted with rows of elms, grown at this day to remarkable size and luxuriance. It has the appearance of a town roofed in with leaves; and it is commonly said, that, but for the

THE GOTHIC CHURCH, NEW HAVEN

spires, a bird flying over would scarce be aware of its existence. Nothing could be more beautiful than the effect of this in the streets; for, standing where any of the principal avenues cross at right angles, four embowered aisles extend away as far as the eye can follow, formed of the straight stems and graceful branches of the drooping elm, the most elegant and noble of the trees of our country. The roads below are kept moist and cool with the roof overhead; the side-walks, between the trees and the rural dwellings, are broad and shady; the small gardens in front of most of the houses are bright with flowering shrubs; and the whole scene, though in the midst of a city, breathes of nature.

The style of domestic architecture in New Haven favours the rural character of the town. Built, as was remarked before, in the midst of a garden, each house looks like what would be termed in England a cottage, or, in streets where a more ambitious style prevails, like the sort of white villa common at watering places. The green Venetian blind is universal; the broad, open hall extends through the house, showing the gay alley of a garden in the rear; and, living in the midst of a primitive and friendly community, the inhabitants sit at their low windows along the street, or promenade, without fear of rude observation, on the shady pavement before their dwellings, preserving for the place altogether that look of out-of-doors life and gaiety which, with less elegance, distinguishes Naples and other cities of southern Europe. The prettiest of English rural towns have a general resemblance to it.

In the centre of New Haven were originally laid out two open squares, divided by a street kept sacred from private buildings. The upper green is a beautiful slope, edged with the long line of the college edifices. Between the two squares stand three churches, at equal distances; two of the common order of architecture for places of public worship in this country (immense brick buildings, with tall white spires); and a third, which is presented in the drawing, a Gothic episcopal church, of singular purity and beauty. Behind and before it, spread away the verdant carpets of the two enclosed "greens;" above its turret and windows hang the drooping fans of elms, half disclosing and half concealing its pointed architecture; and to its door, from every direction, tend aisles of lofty trees, overhanging the paths with shadow, as if the first thought of the primitive settlers had been to create visible avenues to the house of God. There is scarce a more beautiful place of worship, take it all in all, in the whole of Christendom.

The trees in the magnificent avenue in front of these churches were planted by a single individual, the Hon. James Hillhouse. His example decided the

[219]

character of the town, for it was followed in every street. To the enterprise of the same public-spirited gentleman, New Haven owes one of the most beautiful cemeteries in the world. The square in the rear of the churches was formerly, according to the English custom, used as a churchyard, and encumbered with graves, which soon threatened to overrun its limits. Mr. Hillhouse, some years since, purchased a field in the western skirt of the town, laid it out and planted it, and subsequently removed to it all the tombstones and remains from the Green; among them the headstone of the regicide Goffe. It is now one of the most beautiful of burial-places. The monuments are of white marble, or of a very rich *verd antique* found in the neighbourhood; and the natural elegance of the place has induced a taste and elegance into these monuments for the dead, found in no other spot of the same character.

The interior of the episcopal church is purely Gothic, and esteemed in the best taste. The material of the exterior is a brownish trap-rock from the neighbouring mountains, which, from its colour, resembles a very weather-beaten and time-worn stone, and gives a look of antiquity to the edifice. The cornices and abutments are of what a distinguished writer on the subject calls a sprightly freestone.

Niagara Falls

(From the Top of the Ladder on the American Side)

THIS is often the first near and general view of the Falls, and it is well calculated to produce the most astonishing impression on any one suddenly introduced to it. Supposing him to have arrived from Lockport, by a tedious progress through the forests, the visitor is conducted through a beautiful wood, presenting scenery of the softest character. But, with the roar of the cataract in his ear, he hurries rapidly through, till he stands on the very verge of the Fall, at the point where its mighty waters descend in one solemn unbroken mass into a gulf of spray, rising in clouds from the tortured waves beneath, and driven about by the gusts, till sometimes the whole river beneath, and the opposite shores, are momentarily concealed. As this misty curtain is with-

NIAGARA FALLS

(FROM THE TOP OF THE LADDER ON THE AMERICAN SIDE)

drawn, the whole scene is disclosed. Beyond the American fall, which is immediately before him, and the wooded steeps of Goat Island, he sees the sublime curve of the Horse-shoe Fall; from below the centre of which, where the greatest mass of water descends, arises a tall and beautiful column of silvery vapour far into the sky.

At this spot is the entrance of the long covered ladder by which the descent to the ferry is accomplished. At an opening in it, half way down the precipice, people usually stop (in spite of their hurry, and that absorbing matter, the care of their baggage) to enjoy the only view, perhaps, which brings them near to the falling column in the midst of its descent. It is, indeed, "horribly beautiful." No one has better described the effect sometimes produced on the mind at Niagara, than Basil Hall.

"On Sunday night, the 8th of July, we returned to the Falls, and walked down to the Table Rock, to view them by moonlight. Our expectations, as may be supposed, were high, but the sight was more impressive than we had expected. It possessed, it is true, what may be called a more sober kind of interest than that belonging to the wild scene behind the sheet of water above described. I may mention one curious effect:—it seemed to the imagination not impossible that the Fall might swell up, and grasp us in its vortex. The actual presence of any very powerful moving object is often more or less remotely connected with a feeling that its direction may be changed; and when the slightest variation would evidently prove fatal, a feeling of awe is easily excited. At all events, as I gazed upon the cataract, it more than once appeared to increase in its volume, and to be accelerated in its velocity, till my heated fancy became strained, alarmed, and so much overcrowded with new and old images,—all exaggerated; and in spite of the conviction that the whole was nonsense, I felt obliged to draw back from the edge of the rock; and it required a little reflection, and some resolution, to advance again to the brink.

"During the delightful period that the Falls formed our head-quarters, we made various excursions to several interesting objects in the neighbourhood. Of these, the most amusing were, a trip to Buffalo, a flourishing American town at the eastern end of Lake Erie, where the great New York canal commences; and a visit to the Welland canal, which joins Lake Erie with Lake Ontario."

Sawmill at Centre Harbour, Lake Winnipiseogee

In the early records of the first settlement of Keene, in this state, on the river Asduelot, (in the Indian language, *a collection of many waters,*) is an account of some of their difficulties; among which was the establishment of a saw-mill. "A vote was passed," says the record, "offering one hundred acres of middling good land, and twenty-five pounds, to any person or persons who would engage to build a saw-mill, and saw boards for the proprietors at twenty shillings per thousand." The next year "another meeting was appointed at the *house lot* of Joseph Fisher, but was adjourned to the *house* of Nathan Blake, the first erected in the township." A committee was here appointed, "to agree with a man to build a great mill, and they were authorized to offer not exceeding forty pounds encouragement therefor." These early annals are highly interesting, and we cannot better associate drawings of scenes of cultivated life at the present day, than by portraying some of the steps by which the comfort and civilization of the state have been attained.

"No person," says the record, "had hitherto attempted to remain through the winter on the township. Those who came in the summer to clear their lands, brought their provisions with them, and erected temporary huts to shelter them from the weather. In the summer of 1736, at least one house was erected; and three persons, Nathan Blake, Seth Heaton, and William Smeed, (the two first from Wrentham, and the last from Deerfield,) made preparations to pass the winter in the wilderness. Their house was at the lower end of the street. Blake had a pair of oxen and a horse, and Heaton a horse. For the support of these, they collected grass in the open spots; and in the first part of the winter they employed them in drawing logs to the saw-mill, which had just been completed. Blake's horse fell through the ice of Beaver-Brook, and was drowned. In the beginning of February their own provisions were exhausted, and, to obtain a supply of meal, Heaton was despatched to Northfield. There were a few families at Winchester, but none able to furnish what was wanted. Heaton procured a quantity of meal; but before he left Northfield, the snow began to fall; and when, on his return, he arrived at Winchester, it was uncommonly deep, and covered by a sharp crust. He was told 'that he might as well expect to die in Northfield and rise again in Upper Asduelot, as ride thither on horseback.' Recollecting the friends he had left there, he nevertheless determined to make the attempt; but had proceeded only a short distance when he found that it would be impossible to succeed. He then returned, and directed his course towards Wrentham. Blake and Smeed,

SAWMILL AT CENTRE HARBOUR, LAKE WINNIPISSEOGEE

hearing nothing from Heaton, gave the oxen free access to the hay, left Asduelot, and, on snow-shoes, proceeded either to Deerfield or Wrentham. Anxious for their oxen, they returned early in the spring. They found them near the Branch, south-east of Carpenter's, much emaciated, but feeding upon twigs and such grass as was bare. The oxen recognised their owner, and exhibited such pleasure at the meeting as drew tears from his eyes.

"About this time, John Andrews came from Boxford to settle in Upper Asduelot. He sent back Ephraim Donnan and Joseph Ellis with a team of eight oxen and a horse, to bring up his furniture. The route they came, which was probably then the best, if not the only one, led through Concord, Worcester, Brookfield, Belchertown, Hadley, Hatfield, Deerfield, Northfield, Winchester, Swanzey, and on the banks of the Asduelot, to the house lots. When they passed through Swanzey, it rained hard, and they did not reach the station until night. As it continued to rain, was very dark, and as the water, which already covered the meadows, rose rapidly, they, apprehensive of being drowned, unyoked their oxen, chained their cart to a tree, and hastened to the settlement, then a mile distant. As soon as day-light appeared, the next morning, a boat was despatched in search of the cattle and furniture; when, passing over Bullard's Island, a man cried to them for help. It was Mark Ferry, the hermit. Wearied with the noise and bustle of the settlement, he had retired to a cave, which he had dug into the bank of the river, where he constantly resided. The water had now driven him from his dwelling, and compelled him to seek refuge on a stump, where he then sat, with a calf in his arms, over which he had drawn a shirt. The boatman answered, "we must take care of the *neat cattle* first," and passed on. They soon came to the cart, which was afloat. Proceeding further, and guided by the sound of the bells, which the cattle as usual wore, they found them on several little hillocks— some with only their heads out of water. They forced them into the water, and guided them, swimming, to high land, where they left them until the flood subsided. Hearing cries for help below them, they proceeded to Crissen's House, in the borders of Swanzey, to the chamber and to the top of which the family had been driven. These they took off, and, on their return home, took Ferry and his calf into the canoe. This, which was known by the name of Andrew's flood, was the highest ever known in the township. The water came within a few feet of the street north of Captain Blake's old house."

THE LITTLE FALLS ON THE MOHAWK

The Little Falls on the Mohawk

THE cavities worn in the rocks about these Falls, afford great matter of speculation to the geologist. The rock is *gneiss*, and these circular pots are worn evidently by the attrition stones kept in agitation by the current of a river. The astonishing part of it is, that these cavities are, some of them, more than a hundred feet above the present level of the Mohawk, proving that river to have been thus much higher in former times, and of course a lake, whose waters must have extended far and wide over the broad interval above. The narrow passage which it makes through the hills just below, shut in by perpendicular precipices on each side, would be sufficient to have made the theory probable without the assistance of these appearances.

These cavities are very numerous, and the largest are about eight feet deep, and fifteen in diameter. The rocks exhibit evidences of having been washed by water still higher. There are analogous traces of lakes on the Connecticut and Hudson rivers, which break through the mountains in a similar manner, the first between Mount Tom and Mount Holyoke, and the latter at the Highlands; but the depth and number of these rock-worn cavities are peculiar to Little Falls.

In approaching this part of the Mohawk from the east, the stranger is first delighted with the bold abutments on the river of two dark precipices, whose summits are laden with foliage, and which rise so abruptly from the undulating banks of the Mohawk, that they seem designed as barriers to the pass. The river glides between, darkened by their shadow; and close under the face of one precipice shoots the rail-car, while as close under the opposing one glides the silent passage-boat of the canal. Emerging to the sunshine beyond, the river spreads out in its thousand windings, as if rejoicing in the space of which it is so soon to be deprived, and in a moment or two (if you are travelling by steam) your course is arrested amid the foaming and busy scenery of the Falls, the picturesque and the hideous, the wildly beautiful and the merely useful, so huddled together that the artist who would draw either the architecture or the scenery by itself, would scarce find a bit large enough for a vignette.

Alluring as the picturesque and fertile valley of the Mohawk must have been, it was not till after the revolution that it was sought by white men with a view to settle. For some years after the war, it was still the beaver country of the aborigines, or the place of their wigwams; and the country round about, now stocked with villages, and without a red-face to be seen, was a hunting-ground, in which ranged bears, foxes, wolves, deer, and other game, the Indians themselves calling it *couxsachraga*, or the dismal wilderness. The town of Mohawk, where the tribe dwelt up to the year 1780, is but thirty-six miles west of Albany.

General Sir William Johnson lived not many miles below Little Falls, and from this spot to Canada Creek a tract of fourteen miles was given to him on his marriage with a Mohawk girl, by King Hendricks, the faithful Indian ally of the whites. It is a curious fact, that, during the war of the revolution, a son of Sir William Johnson, in the English service in Canada, made an incursion at the head of a party of hostile Indians on the very lands once owned by his father.

The Mohawks contended very fiercely for the honour of original descent. The Iroquois, who were more powerful, they considered as interlopers; and, in the following tradition, give the basis of their pedigree: —

"Before man existed, there were three great and good spirits; of whom one was superior to the other two, and is emphatically called the Great and Good Spirit. At a certain time, this exalted being said to one of the others, '*Make a man!*' He obeyed; and taking *chalk*, formed a paste of it, and moulding it into the human shape, infused into it the animating principle and brought it to the Great Spirit. He, after surveying it, said, '*It is too white!*'

"He then directed the other to make a trial of his skill. Accordingly, taking *charcoal*, he pursued the same process, and brought the result to the Great Spirit; who, after surveying it, said, 'It is too black!'

"Then said the Great Spirit, 'I will now try myself.' And, taking *red earth*, he formed a human being in the same manner, surveyed it and said, 'This is a proper man!'"

It is possible that this is traditionary, but it is more probable that it was invented after the arrival of whites, and the introduction of blacks into the country, neither of which races the Indians had before seen.

Bridge at Norwich, Connecticut

Two Indian rivers, the Shetucket and Yautick, unite at this place to form the Thames, and in the fork of the junction lies the picturesque and prosperous town of Norwich. From the hilly nature of the ground, the buildings have a remarkably fine appearance, the streets rising one above the other, and the style of the houses denoting taste and opulence. In the rear of the hill on which the town stands is a level plain, on which are laid out several handsome streets, planted with avenues of trees. The prospects are extensive and various; and, altogether, there are few towns in the world which have so many advantages and attractions.

The Thames is navigable for large vessels as high as Norwich, and its trade with the West Indies was once considerable. That has declined, and the capital of the inhabitants is now invested principally in manufactories, for which the fine water-power of the neighbourhood furnishes peculiar facilities. As a birth-place of distinguished individuals, Norwich has produced Mrs. Sigourney, the sweetest of American poetesses; and it stands upon the natal ground and possessions of the celebrated Uncas, chief of the Mohegans. The burial-place of the kings of this warlike tribe is still to be seen here.

No spot could have been selected with more felicity than that on which Uncas formerly lived. It is a high point of land, commanding a noble and extensive view of the Thames, here a large river, and of the country on both sides. It was, therefore, well fitted for the discovery of an enemy's approach, and furnished every convenience to hostile excursions. At the same time, it bordered on a never-failing supply of provisions, furnished by the scale and shellfish, with which both the river and the neighbouring ocean have ever been richly stored.

Uncas was originally a petty sachem; a Pequod by birth; a subject and a tributary to Sassacus. When the English made war upon the Pequods, Uncas was unfriendly to this chieftain, and would have quarrelled with him, had he not been kept in awe by the talents and prowess of this formidable warrior. Of the English he appears to have entertained, from the first, a very respectful opinion; and, when he saw them determined upon a war with his master, concluded to unite his forces and his fortune with theirs. His dread of Sassacus was, however, so great, that when Captain Mason marched against the Pequods, he did not believe him to be serious in his professed design of attacking that terrible nation, nor did he even engage in the conflict, until after Mason and his little band of heroes had stormed the Pequod fortress.

[229]

BRIDGE AT NORWICH, CONNECTICUT

Upon the death of Sassacus, Uncas became the sachem of the remaining Pequods, as well as of the Mohegans. In this character he claimed, perhaps rightfully enough, as there was no other acknowledged heir, all the territory which had been possessed by that tribe. This tract included almost the whole of the eastern division of Connecticut, from the middle of the Syno range. He understood his own interest too well to quarrel with the English, and had a sufficient share of cunning to support his claims with very plausible reasons. They were, therefore, very generally allowed.

From this time he became the most formidable, and altogether the most prosperous Indian chieftain in Southern New England. Over his subjects he exercised a more efficacious and unresisted government than perhaps was ever exercised by any other sachem. Nor was his control confined to them; but extended, in a considerable degree, to several of the tribes on the western side of the Connecticut. To his enemies he became scarcely less formidable than Sassacus had been before him. At the head of four or five hundred men, he met Miantonomoh, a brave and sagacious chief of the Narrhagansetts, coming to attack him with twice the number; and, after having in vain challenged him to single combat, defeated his army, took him prisoner, and put him to death. On this occasion he cut a piece of flesh from his shoulder, roasted and eat it, and, with the true spirit of a savage, declared that it was the sweetest meat which he had ever tasted in his life.

The avarice, ambition, and restlessness of this man, frequently embroiled him with his neighbours, and were sometimes troublesome to his English allies. The natives considered them as the friends of Uncas, and implicated them more or less in his mischievous conduct. When he found the English resentful, and himself severely censured, he made such submissions, promises, and presents as he thought necessary to restore their good-will, and secure his future peace. But he was not indebted for these advantages to his address alone. On several occasions he rendered them real and important assistance; and to their interests he adhered faithfully and uniformly. No Indian among the New England tribes, except Massasait, exhibited an equally steady attachment to the Colonists, or so regular an adherence to his engagements. Hence he enjoyed their public friendship, and the good-will of individuals among them, until the day of his death.

Uncas died at an advanced age, in his own house, and left his power and his property to his children. Onecho, his eldest son, commanded a party of Mohegans in a war which the English carried on against the Narrhagansetts in 1676. The family, however, soon declined in their importance by the general declension of their tribe, and the sale of their property to the English. Some years since, a man, descended from Uncas, came from North Carolina, or Tennessee, where he was settled, and obtained permission of the Connecticut legislature to sell his patrimonial share in this tract. This man had received a military commission from the British government; and it is said, was well dressed, well informed, sensible, and gentlemanly in his deportment. He was probably the only respectable descendant of Uncas then living.

Undercliff
(The Seat of General Morris)

THE pen of the poet and the pencil of the artist have so frequently united to record the grandeur and sublimity of the Hudson, and with such graphic fidelity, that little of interest remains unsaid or unsketched. But when every point of its bold and beautiful scenery might be made the subject of a picture, and every incident of its past history the theme of a poem, it requires no great research to discover new and prominent objects of attraction. Perhaps there is no portion of this beautiful river which partakes more of the picturesque, or combines more of the wild and wonderful, than the vicinity of the present View; and when time shall touch the history of the present with the wand of tradition, and past events shall live in the memory of the future as legends, romance will never revel in a more bewitching region. Fiction shall then fling its imaginative veil over the things we have seen—covering, but not concealing them—and, in the plenitude of poetic genius, people the drama of futurity with a thousand exquisite creations, clothed in the venerated garb of antiquity.

Undercliff, the mansion of General George P. Morris, which forms the principal object in the engraving, is situated upon an elevated plateau, rising from the eastern shore of the river; and the selection of such a commanding and beautiful position at once decides the taste of its intellectual proprietor. In the rear of the villa, cultivation has placed her fruit and forest trees with a profuse hand, and fertilized the fields with a variety of vegetable products. The extent of the grounds is abruptly terminated by the base of a rocky moun-

tain, that rises nearly perpendicular to its summit, and affords in winter a secure shelter from the bleak blasts of the north. In front, a circle of greensward
is refreshed by a fountain in the centre, gushing from a Grecian vase, and encircled by ornamental shrubbery; from thence a gravelled walk winds down a
gentle declivity to a second plateau, and again descends to the entrance of the
carriage road, which leads upwards along the left slope of the hill, through
a noble forest, the growth of many years, until suddenly emerging from its
sombre shades, the visitor beholds the mansion before him in the bright blaze
of day. A few openings in the wood afford an opportunity to catch a glimpse of
the water, sparkling with reflected light; and the immediate transition from
shadow to sunshine is perculiarly pleasing.

Although the sunny prospects from the villa, of the giant mountains in
their eternal verdure—the noble stream, when frequent gusts ruffle its surface
into a thousand waves—the cluster of white cottages collected into the distant
village, are glorious; it is only by the lovely light of the moon, when nature
is in repose, that their magic influence is fully felt. We were fortunate in having an opportunity to contemplate the scene at such an hour: the moon had
risen from a mass of clouds which formed a line across the sky so level that
fancy saw her ascending from the dark sea, and her silvery light lay softened
on the landscape; silence was over all, save where the dipping of a distant oar
was echoed from the deep shadows of the rocks. Sometimes the white sail of
a sloop would steal into sight from the deep gloom, like some shrouded spirit
gliding from the confines of a giant's cavern, and recalled the expressive lines
by Moore:—

> "The stream is like a silvery lake,
>   And o'er its face each vessel glides
> Gently, as if it feared to wake
>   The slumber of the silent tides."

In the view of Undercliff, the artist has been peculiarily happy in producing an effect at once brilliant and chaste. The broken foreground is agreeably
relieved by the sparkling transparency of the water: the receding figures on
the shore are judiciously introduced to mark the perspective. The projecting
bluff in the middle distance is thrown into shadow, and stands out in fine contrast from the light horizon, while the lights upon the solitary rock, the entrance gate, the mansion, and the vessels, produce the effect of a setting sun;
and the whole subject is treated with masterly skill. We only regret that art
has not power to convey the kindly hospitalities hourly exercised in the interior of the mansion.

UNDERCLIFF NEAR COLD-SPRING

(THE SEAT OF GENERAL GEORGE P. MORRIS)

To enumerate the matchless and minute beauties of Undercliff, would occupy more space than the limits of our descriptive pages will permit. Its superiority, however, may be summed up in one expressive sentence, to which it is justly entitled, and which has been conceded to it by common consent—"*The Gem of the Hudson River.*" To the belles-lettres reader the "Gem" will acquire additional value by reflecting the light of literature: it is the home of a fine poet, and graceful prose writer. General Morris has been for many years the editor of the "New York Mirror," a weekly journal, which circulates more extensively among the *élite* than any other periodical in the country. The typographic neatness of its execution, the talent of its original contributions, and the elegance of its embellishments, have placed upon it a permanent seal of popularity, and seem to have given a tone to taste, and a refinement to fashion.

General Morris has recently published a volume of lyrical effusions, called "The Deserted Bride, and other Poems." Many of them have been written among the fairy beauties of Undercliff, and under the inspiration of that true poetic feeling which such enchanting scenes are so likely to elicit. Where so many gems of genius enrich a work, it becomes difficult to decide upon that most worthy of selection. It is not our province or intention to review the volume, but we cannot resist the inclination to make a few extracts, because they seem as beautiful accessories to the subject, and create an added interest in the engraving. Where scenes are so replete with the poetry of nature, they are best illustrated by the poetry of numbers; but we were particularly delighted with the following lines, addressed to his young daughter. The natural simplicity of the subject is well expressed by the purity of its poetic images, and breathes the refinement of paternal affection.

IDA

"Where Hudson's wave, o'er silvery sands,
  Winds through the hills afar,
Old Cro'nest like a monarch stands,
  Crowned with a single star:
And there, amid the billowy swells
  Of rock-ribbed, cloud-capt earth,
My fair and gentle IDA dwells,
  A nymph of mountain birth.

"The snow-curl that the cliff receives,
  The diamonds of the showers,
Spring's tender blossoms, buds and leaves,
  The sisterhood of flowers:
Morn's early beam, eve's balmy breeze,
  Her purity define;

[235]

But IDA's dearer far than these,
 To this fond breast of mine.

"My heart is on the hills. The shades
 Of night are on my brow:
Ye pleasant haunts and silent glades,
 My soul is with you now!
I bless the star-crowned islands where
 My IDA's footsteps roam:
Oh for a falcon's wing to bear
 Me onward to my home!"

General Morris is not less successful in the lighter and livelier freaks of poetic fancy, as we hope to prove by a quotation from "The New York Mirror," in which the moral of the lines is not their least merit. The melodies of the various birds which roost among the wild recesses of the rocks, or haunt the mountain forest, or sweep along the waters, are set forth hourly in sounds of "unwritten music." But the cry "most musical, most melancholy," comes at the twilight hour from the clear throat of the whip-poor-will, at intervals, through the summer's night: nor is it ever heard or seen by day; it may be called the sad unknown. The words, "whip-poor-will," are divided into three shrill, distinct notes, and express the sounds as perfectly as if uttered by the human voice. The poetry annexed, is equally expressive of the melancholy mystery which seems to mark the mourning burden of its lonely song.

TO THE WHIP-POOR-WILL

"Why dost thou come at set of sun,
 Those pensive words to say?
Why whip poor Will?—What has he done?
 And who is Will, I pray?

"If poverty's his crime, let mirth
 From out his heart be driven:
That is the deadliest sin on earth,
 And never is forgiven!

"Art Will himself?—It must be so—
 I learn it from thy moan,
For none can feel another's woe
 As deeply as his own.

"Yet wherefore strain thy tiny throat,
 While other birds repose?
What means thy melancholy note?
 The mystery disclose.

"Still 'whip-poor-will!'—Art thou a sprite,
 From unknown regions sent
To wander in the gloom of night
 And ask for punishment?

"Is thine a conscience sore beset
 With guilt—or, what is worse,
Hast thou to meet writs, duns, and debt—
 No money in thy purse?

"If this be thy hard fate indeed,
 Ah well may'st thou repine:
The sympathy I give, I need—
 The poet's doom is thine.

"Art thou a lover, Will?—Hast proved
 The fairest can deceive?
Thine is the lot of all who've loved
 Since Adam wedded Eve.

"Why come from yon leaf-shaded hill,
    A suppliant at my door?—
Why ask of me to whip poor Will?
    And is Will really poor?

"Hast trusted in a friend, and seen
    No friend was he in need?
A common error—men still lean
    Upon as frail a reed.

"Hast thou, in seeking wealth or fame,
    A crown of brambles won?
O'er all the earth 'tis just the same
    With every mother's son!

"Hast found the world a Babel wide,
    Where man to mammon stoops?
Where flourish arrogance and pride,
    While modest merit droops?

"What, none of these?—Then, whence thy pain
    To guess it who's the skill?
Pray have the kindness to explain
    Why I should whip poor Will?

"Dost merely ask thy just desert?
    What, not another word?—
Back to the woods again, unhurt—
    I will not harm thee, bird!

"But treat thee kindly—for my nerves,
    Like thine, have penance done;
Treat every man as he deserves—
    Who shall 'scape whipping?—None.

"Farewell, poor Will—not valueless
    This lesson by thee given:
'Keep thine own counsel, and confess
    Thyself alone to heaven!'"

We cannot close our description without one more extract from the delightful volume before us.

THE OAK

"Woodman, spare that tree!
    Touch not a single bough!
In youth it sheltered me,
    And I'll protect it now.
'Twas my forefather's hand
    That placed it near his cot;
There, woodman, let it stand,
    Thy axe shall harm it not!

"That old familiar tree,
    Whose glory and renown
Are spread o'er land and sea,
    And wouldst thou hack it down?
Woodman, forbear thy stroke!
    Cut not its earth-bound ties;
Oh spare that aged oak,
    Now towering to the skies!

"When but an idle boy
    I sought its grateful shade;
In all their gushing joy
    Here, too, my sisters played.
My mother kissed me here;
    My father pressed my hand—
Forgive this foolish tear,
    But let that old oak stand!

"My heart-strings round thee cling,
    Close as thy bark, old friend!
Here shall the wild-bird sing,
    And still thy branches bend.
Old tree! the storm still brave!
    And, woodman, leave the spot;
While I've a hand to save,
    Thy axe shall harm it not."

BOSTON, AND BUNKER HILL

(FROM THE EAST)

Boston, and Bunker Hill

(From the East)

THIS view is taken from a long cape, sometimes cut off by water overflowing the marshes, and called William's Island. Five or six years ago, it was a thinly cultivated and neglected spot, scarce known, except to adventurous boys, who pulled across from the city wharfs, and to the one or two farmers who inhabited it. Now, with the suddenness which attends speculation in our country, it is grown suddenly into a consequential suburb, with a showy hotel and steam ferry, and citizens and strangers resort to it to eat French dinners, and pass the hot weeks of the summer.

Boston, from this point of view, is very picturesque. The town rises gradually from the water's edge to the height surmounted by the State House, whose lofty cupola brings to a point all the ascending lines of the picture; Dorchester Heights rise gracefully on the left limit of the bay, and Bunker Hill, famous in American story, breaks the horizon on the right. In the centre lie the forest of shipping, and the fine ranges of commercial buildings on the water side; and, turning from this view, the harbour, with its many small islands, stretches away behind to the sea, tracked by steamers, and sprinkled by craft of every size and nation. Like every other bay in the world, that of Boston has been compared to Naples; but it has neither its violet sky, nor its volcano, yet it may be mentioned in the same day.

Close under the eye of the spectator here, lies that part of the town formerly the fashionable quarter, but now very much what Red Lion Square, and its precincts, are to London. There is still existing (or there was, some six or eight years since,) the house of Governor Hutchinson, of which the mouldings were brought from London, and in which the drawing-room panels were portraits of his family, in their youth. This is still a very roomy and well-built, and must once have been a rather luxurious house. We are apt to fancy that our strait-laced ancestors from England lived parsimoniously, and denied themselves the elegances of modern luxury; but antiquarian researches exhibit a different state of things. "In the principal houses," says the discourse of a learned gentleman on this subject, "there was a great hall, ornamented with pictures and a great lantern, and a velvet cushion in the window-seat which looked into the garden. On either side was a great parlour, a little parlour, or study. These were furnished with great looking-glasses, Turkey carpets, window curtains and valance, pictures, and a map, a brass clock, red leather-back chairs, and a great pair of brass andirons. The chambers were well supplied with feather beds, warming-pans, and every other article that would now be thought necessary for comfort or display. The pantry was well filled with substantial fare and dainties—prunes, marmalade, and Madeira wine. Silver tankards, wine-cups, and other articles of plate, were not uncommon; and the kitchen was completely stocked with pewter, iron, and copper utensils. Very many families employed servants, and in one we see a Scotch boy valued among the property, and invoiced at 14*l*."

In the matter of dress, our grandames seem to have pushed the ruling passion of the sex even through the rigid crust of Puritanism. In a tract, called the "Simple Cobler of Agawam," some righteous round-head thus expresses his indignation at their fashions:—

"Methinks it should break the hearts of Englishmen to see so many goodly Englishwomen imprisoned in French cages, peering out of their hood-holes for some men of mercy to help them with a little wit, and nobody relieves them. We have about five or six of them in our colony; if I see any of them accidentally, I cannot cleanse my phansie of them for a month after.

"It is a more common than convenient saying, that 'nine taylors make a man:' it were well if nineteen could make a woman to her mind. If taylors were men, indeed, well furnished but with mere moral principles, they would disdain to be led about like asses by such mymick marmosets. It is a most unworthy thing for men that have bones in them, to spend their lives in making fiddle-cases for women's phansies.

"It is known more than enough that I am neither niggard nor cynic to the true bravery of the true gentry. I am not much offended if I see a trimme far trimmer than she that wears it; but when I hear a nugiperous gentle dame inquire what dress the queen is in, with egge to be in it in all haste, whatever it be, I look to her as the very gizzard of a trifle, the product of a quarter of a cypher, the epitome of nothing, fitter to be kickt, if she were of a kickable substance, than either honoured, or humoured."

Mount Jefferson
(From Mount Washington)

IN looking in this direction from the elevated summit of Mount Washington, the eye drops upon a region of climate entirely different from that on its southeastern side. The towns of Lancaster and Jefferson, though something north of the White Mountains, enjoy a benign, tranquil atmosphere, such as is not known for two or three hundred miles farther south, and with the beauty of the scenery and the number of water-courses, it is a little Arcadia in the bosom of the north. The peculiar climate felt here, is owing to the proximity of the White Mountains, which form a wall of thirty miles from north to south, either checking entirely the easterly winds, or elevating them into a region far above the surface. The westerly winds, again, impinging against the mountains, (but in an elevated part,) are arrested, leaving the towns below in the same tranquillity as is felt by a person coming near a large building in a high wind.

The snow rarely lies permanently here until after the tenth or fifteenth of December, and generally leaves it about the middle of March: at this time the earth is usually free from frost. A stick forced through the snow in the month of February enters the earth without difficulty, the snow falling so early as to prevent the frost from penetrating to any depth, and dissolving the little which had previously existed. Hence the pastures become suddenly green, and cattle are safely turned into them in the middle of April; the time of pasturage is, therefore, as long here as in Connecticut. In this manner that tedious period, known as the breaking up of the frost, is here chiefly prevented; and the warm season is annually lengthened, so far as the purposes of gardening and agriculture are concerned, about a month every year.

There is a broad tract running across the State at this point, embracing both sides of the mountains, which is generally called *Upper Coos*. What the meaning of this term is, would be difficult to say; but Dwight supposes, from its application to places where there are remarkable alluvial intervals, and where there are no distinguishing objects, except a peculiar winding of rivers, that one or the other of these must be denoted by the term.

In the year 1776, a farmer planted himself on the richest and most beautiful of these lands, a large share of which he left to his descendants. Valuable as his acquisition has since become, however, his first step required uncommon enterprise, industry, and perseverance. His separation from society may

MOUNT JEFFERSON
(FROM MOUNT WASHINGTON)

be understood from the fact, that, for several years after he came here to live, he carried all his corn one hundred and twenty-four miles to be ground. There was not a single road in the neighbourhood. All his communication with the world was either through the wilderness, or down the channel of the Connecticut; and this he was obliged to enter at the distance of twenty miles from his house. When any member of his family was ill, he had neither physician nor nurse, nor other medicine than his own limited stock.

Rains and snows, in this part of the country almost universally come from the western side of the heavens, and chiefly from the north-west. Snow falls here in a singular manner. A light fleecy shower descends frequently for a few minutes in the morning, when the sky becomes perfectly clear, and the day perfectly fine. In this manner it has been known to fall thirty successive days, and yet to cover the ground scarcely to the depth of six inches. By this gradual accumulation, it has sometimes arisen in the forests to the height of thirty inches; commonly it has not exceeded eighteen. Travelling in the winter, therefore, is easy and pleasant in this neighbourhood, and the weather generally delightful.

The imperfect state of settlements in a country still comparatively new, prevents many persons from forming just views of the splendour of the scenery. In a landscape of any great extent, the proportion of wild forest throws a gloom over the whole, and the eye, accustomed to the haunts of man, demands instinctively a more smiling scene of cultivation and habitation. In a more limited view, the appearance of girdled trees, of drowned woods, burnt or fallen stumps, rough enclosures, and stony land, are blemishes which an unaccustomed eye can with difficulty overcome. It requires the prospective glance of an American to see the form of nature, which is now in dishabille, restored to her neat drapery, glowing with vegetation, and decked with flowers. The outline of her fair proportions is enough for him; and so that is beautiful, as in this country it almost every where is, he can finish the portrait to his fancy, and make a flowery Tempe of a prostrate wilderness.

MOUNT TOM, AND CONNECTICUT RIVER

Mount Tom, and Connecticut River

THIS fine mountain rises nobly from the fertile Interval of the Connecticut, giving a character of boldness and majesty to scenery that were else merely soft and lovely. The river at this point broke down the barrier that evidently at one time held it back from the sea; and the broad lands that were then left bare by the liberated waters, were destined to form a strip of verdure and fertility, extending the whole length of New England.

The expansions of the Valley of the Connecticut on either side of Mount Tom, are landscapes of great beauty. The word *interval*, which describes the wide-spreading meadows extending from the banks of the river in these expansions, has a peculiar use in America, and seems to define a formation of alluvial land not seen to the same extent in other countries. In the Southern States the same description of land is called a *flat*, or a *bottom*. They are formed by the deposit of particles of soil brought down into the main river by its tributaries, or by occasional streams created by the melting of the snow, or heavy rains. A shoal is first formed, which, as it accumulates, rises gradually above the ordinary surface, while the stream itself, if it flows like the Connecticut through a soft soil, is continually deepening its bed, and leaving these newly-formed banks out of the reach of accidental floods.

The existence of some cause to check the current, is absolutely necessary to the formation of intervals. Wherever such cause is found, intervals are found proportioned to the room furnished on the side of the stream for their formation, and the lightness of the soil about the tributary streams. These causes exist on the Connecticut in falls and points of land, and in the narrowness of the channel at particular parts shut in by mountains.

These lands are subject to many changes. Every new obliquity of the current wears away some part of the Interval, against which its force is directed. In the progress of such changes, the inhabitants of the Connecticut have already seen large tracts gradually removed from one side to the other. The former channel in the mean time has been filled up, so as, in many instances, to leave no trace of its existence, and a new one has been made through the solid ground.

The soil of the intervals is, of course, of the richest quality: there is, however, a material difference in their fertility. The parts which are lowest are commonly the best, as being the most frequently overflowed, and therefore most enriched by the successive deposits of slime. Of these parts, that division which is farthest down the river is the most productive, as consisting of finer

[245]

particles, and being more plentifully covered with this manure. In the spring, these grounds are regularly overflowed. In the months of March and April, the snows, which in the northern parts of New England are usually deep, and the rains, which at this time of the year are generally copious, raise the river from fifteen to twenty feet, and extend the breadth of its waters in some places a mile and a half, or two miles. Almost all the slime conveyed down the current at this season is deposited on these lands; for here, principally, the water becomes quiescent, and permits the earthy particles to subside. This deposit is a rich manure. The lands dressed with it are preserved in their full strength, and being regularly enriched by the hand of nature, cannot but be highly valuable.

The form of these lands is naturally beautiful. A river passing through them becomes almost, of course, winding. The border is necessarily curved, from the evenness of the impression of the river on a soft soil; and the edge is fringed with shrubs. A great part of them are formed into meadows, which are more profitable, and, at the same time, more agreeable to the eye than any other mode of culture. The magnificent elms, for which this country is remarkable, stand singly in the fields; while orchards and groves serve to break the uniformity. As they are seldom enclosed for miles together, there is a look also of extent and wildness about them, as if they produced their vegetation, "ploughed only by the sunbeams," like a paradise spontaneously verdant and fertile.

Valuable as these intervals on the Connecticut have become, they were bought cheaply enough by the first proprietors. One of the first settlers of the neighbourhood of Mount Tom, was a tailor, who, for a trifling consideration, purchased a tract on the river, forming a square of three miles on a side. A carpenter came to settle in the valley, and having constructed a rude wheel-barrow, the tailor offered him for it, *either a suit of clothes, or the whole of his land!* He accepted the latter, and became the possessor of one of the finest farms on the bank of the Connecticut.

SILVER CASCADE, IN THE NOTCH OF THE WHITE MOUNTAINS

Silver Cascade, in the Notch of the White Mountains

FOR a mountainous region, usually fertile in such accidents of nature, the neighbourhood of the "White Hills" has few waterfalls; of those that are met with in the "Notch," the Silver Cascade is by far the most beautiful; but to be seen to advantage it should be visited after heavy rains. The stream is scanty, but its course from among the deep forest, whence its springs issue into the light, is one of singular beauty. Buried beneath the lofty precipices of the gorge, after ascending towards the Pulpit Rock, by the side of the turbulent torrent of the Saco, the ear is suddenly saluted by soft dashings of this sweetest of cascades; and a glance upwards reveals its silver streams issuing from the loftiest crests of the mountain, and leaping from crag to crag, or spread in a broad thin sheet of liquid light over the edge of some projecting ledge, till it reaches the road, across which it passes, forming a still and transparent pool immediately beneath, before it joins the Saco in the depths of the gorge. It is a beautiful vision in the midst of the wildest and most dreary scenery; and its sudden appearance—for nothing of it is seen till the tourist is immediately under it—is a moment of deep delight to him from the suddenness of the contrast. The lover of nature loves to linger among the wild beauties of this region; and some of the finest ideas of the American painters have been gleaned amongst its solitudes. We believe that the engraving, from a painting by Doughty, will be very interesting to our subscribers.

View of New York, from Weehawken

WEEHAWKEN is slighted by the traveller ascending to the bolder and brighter glories of the Highlands above; and few visit it except—

"The prisoner to the city's pent-up air,"

who, making a blest holiday of a summer's afternoon, crosses thither to set his foot on the green grass, and mount the rocks for a view of our new-sprung

[248]

VIEW OF NEW YORK, FROM WEEHAWKEN

Babylon and its waters. There is no part of "the country" which "God made" so blest in its offices of freshening the spirit, and giving health to the blood, as the rural suburb of a metropolis. The free breath drawn there, the green herb looked on before it is trodden down, the tree beautiful simply for the freedom of its leaves from the dust of the street, the humblest bird or the meanest butterfly, are dispensers of happiness in another measure than falls elsewhere to their lot. Most such humble ministers of large blessings have their virtue for "its own reward;" but it has fallen to the lot of Weehawken to find a minstrel, and no mean one, among those for whose happiness and consolation it seems made to bloom. A merchant-poet, whose "works" stand on shelves in Wall Street, but whose rhymes for pastime live in literature, and in the hearts of his countrymen, thus glorifies his suburban Tempe:—

"Weehawken! in thy mountain scenery yet,
    All we adore of Nature in her wild
And frolic hour of infancy, is met,
    And never has a summer morning smiled
Upon a lovelier scene than the full eye
Of the enthusiast revels on—when high

"Amid thy forest-solitudes he climbs
    O'er crags that proudly tower above the deep,
And knows that sense of danger, which sublimes
    The breathless moment—when his daring step
Is on the verge of the cliff, and he can hear
The low dash of the wave with startled ear,

"Like the death music of his coming doom,
    And clings to the green turf with desperate force,
As the heart clings to life; and when resume
    The currents in his veins their wonted course
There lingers a deep feeling, like the moan
Of wearied ocean when the storm is gone.

"In such an hour he turns, and on his view
    Ocean, and earth, and heaven, burst before him;
Clouds slumbering at his feet, and the clear blue
    Of summer's sky in beauty bending o'er him;
The city bright below; and far away
Sparkling in light, his own romantic bay.

"Tall spire, and glittering roof, and battlement,
    And banners floating in the sunny air,
And white sails o'er the calm blue waters bent,
    Green isle, and circling shore, are blended there
In wild reality. When life is old,
And many a scene forgot, the heart will hold

[250]

"Its memory of this; nor lives there one
  Whose infant breath was drawn, or boyhood's days
Of happiness were passed beneath that sun,
  That in his manhood's prime can calmly gaze
Upon that bay, or on that mountain stand,
Nor feel the prouder of his native land."*

Weehawken is the "Chalk Farm" of New York, and a small spot enclosed by rocks, and open to observation only from the river, is celebrated as having been the ground on which Hamilton fought his fatal duel with Aaron Burr. A small obelisk was erected on the spot, by the St. Andrew's Society, to the memory of Hamilton, but it has been removed. His body was interred in the churchyard of Trinity, in Broadway, where his monument now stands.

It is to be regretted that the fashion of visiting Hoboken and Weehawken has yielded to an impression among the "fashionable" that it is a vulgar resort. This willingness to relinquish an agreeable promenade because it is enjoyed as well by the poorer classes of society, is one of those superfine ideas which we imitate from our English ancestors, and in which the more philosophic continentals are so superior to us. What enlivens the Tuileries and St. Cloud at Paris, the Monte-Pincio at Rome, the Volksgarten at Vienna, and the Corso and Villa Reale at Naples, but the presence of innumerable "vulgarians?" They are considered there like the chorus in a pantomime, as producing all the back-ground effect as necessary to the *ensemble*. The place would be nothing—would be desolate, without them; yet in England and America it is enough to vulgarize any—the most agreeable resort, to find it frequented by the "people!"

*"Fanny," a poem, by Fitz-Greene Halleck.

[251]

PRESIDENT'S HOUSE, FROM THE RIVER

President's House

(From the River)

THE residence of the Chief Magistrate of the United States resembles the country-seat of an English nobleman, in its architecture and size; but it is to be regretted that the parallel ceases when we come to the grounds. By itself it is a commodious and creditable building, serving its purpose without too much state for a republican country, yet likely, as long as the country exists without primogeniture and rank, to be sufficiently superior to all other dwelling-houses to mark it as the residence of the nation's ruler.

The President's House stands near the centre of an area of some twenty acres, occupying a very advantageous elevation, open to the view of the Potomac, and about forty-four feet above high water, and possessing from its balcony one of the loveliest prospects in our country—the junction of the two branches of the Potomac which border the district, and the swelling and varied shores beyond of the States of Maryland and Virginia. The building is one hundred and seventy feet front, and eighty-six deep, and is built of white free-stone, with Ionic pilasters, comprehending two lofty stories, with a stone balustrade. The north front is ornamented with a portico, sustained by four Ionic columns, with three columns of projection—the outer intercolumniation affording a shelter for carriages to drive under. The garden-front on the river (presented in the drawing) is varied by what is called a rusticated basement-story, in the Ionic style, and by a semi-circular projecting colonnade of six columns, with two spacious and airy flights of steps leading to a balustrade on the level of the principal story.

The interior of the President's House is well disposed, and possesses one superb reception-room, and two oval drawing-rooms, (one in each story,) of very beautiful proportions. The other rooms are not remarkable; and there is an inequality in the furniture of the whole house, (owing to the unwillingness and piecemeal manner with which Congress votes any monies for its decoration,) which destroys its effect as a comfortable dwelling. The oval rooms are carpeted with Gobelin tapestry, worked with the national emblems; and are altogether in a more consistent style than the other parts of the house. It is to be hoped that Congress will not always consider the furniture of the President's House as the scape-goat of all sumptuary and aristocratic sins, and that we shall soon be able to introduce strangers, not only to a comfortable and well-appointed, but to a properly-served and neatly-kept, presidential mansion.

[253]

At the present moment (the last month of General Jackson's administration) the venerable President is confined to his room, and occupies a small chamber in the second story, near the centre of the house, on the front presented in the drawing. In a visit made to him by the writer a few days since, he was sitting at a table by the side of his bed, with a loose dressing-gown drawn over his black coat, and a sheet of half-written paper before him. He rose, with the pen in his hand, to receive a lady from another country, whose introduction to him was the principal object of the visit, and entered into conversation with that grace and dignified ease which mark his manners so peculiarly. He spoke of his approaching retirement, and the route he should pursue to reach the Hermitage, (his seat in Tennessee,) and expressed a strong wish to avoid all publicity in his movements, and to be suffered to pass tranquilly to his retreat. General Jackson is much changed since a reception given to the writer six years ago. He was then thin and spare, but stood erect and firm, and had a look of iron vigour—the effect, perhaps, of his military attitude, and the martial expression of face which belongs to him. He had since lost several of his front teeth, and though the bold and full under lip still looks as if it could hold up the world on its firm arch, it is the mouth of an old man, and in any other face would convey an idea of decrepitude. The fire still burns in the old warrior's eye, however, and his straight and abundant white hair, which has been suffered to grow untrimmed during his illness, adds to the stern energy which is never wanting even to his most quiet expression. Peace and veneration go with him to his retirement!

View on the Susquehanna, at Liverpool

THE musical Indian name of this lovely river, spite of the canals, rail-roads, and county towns, that have supplanted the wild forest, and the rude wigwam in its valley, recalls irresistibly to the fancy the associations of aboriginal life, and the swift but bloody transit from an Indian hunting-ground to European civilization. In the county-town of Liverpool may be found, at this day, all the transcendental marks of national refinement—such as milliners who get the fashions from Paris, farmers who drink champagne, lawyers who dream of the presidency, and young ladies who read Shelley and Chateaubriand; but it is only forty-five or fifty years ago that the Susquehanna and the head waters of the Ohio were ranged by the warlike Shawanee; and there was scarce a white man's house west of Wyoming which had not been the scene, to a greater or less extent, of the barbarities we now find it so difficult to realize.

Among the authentic records of this region of country is a story of the captivity and escape of two children, which seems to me one of the most curious, and shows at the same time of what stuff the early settlers of these borders were made.

The names of these boys were John and Henry Johnson, the former thirteen years of age, the latter eleven. They had been rambling in the woods at a short distance from home, and getting tired, sat down to rest upon a log. After sitting a few minutes, two Indians approached, whom they took for whites, till they were too close upon them to admit of escape, and they were made prisoners. The sun set after they had followed their captors for an hour, and the Indians kindled a fire, and sharing with them their roasted meat and parched corn, lay down to sleep, each with one of the boys folded in his arms.

Henry, the youngest, had abandoned himself to his grief as they travelled on over the hills, but the elder kept a stout heart, and encouraged him with the hope of yet eluding the vigilance of the savages. The practice of terrifying children by threats of the red man with his tomahawk and scalping-knife had filled the mind of the younger, however, and he was only pacified when fatigue made the coarse food welcome, and the heat of the fire and the accustomed hour for repose overcame him with sleep. He lay down with the red arms of the savage around him, and was soon lost in the deep slumbers of childhood.

John, too, lay down, and pretended to sleep; and in a few minutes, the Indian, who had locked him in his arms, relaxed his hold. He disengaged him-

VIEW ON THE SUSQUEHANNA, AT LIVERPOOL

self softly and walked to the fire; and to try the soundness of their sleep, he stirred the half-burnt faggots, and rekindled the blaze. Not a limb stirred, and not a breathing was interrupted. He gently pulled his brother and awoke him, and they both stood by the fire, with their captors sleeping soundly at their feet. "I think," said John, smiling, "we may go home now." "They will catch us again," said the younger, despairingly. "Then, before we go, we'll kill them," said the other.

The Indians had one gun, which rested against a tree, with their tomahawks on the ground beside it. John reflected a moment, and then, getting a rest for the gun upon a decayed log near the head of one of the savages, he cocked it, took aim at the ear of the sleeping man, and then calling to Henry, placed his hand on the trigger. Ordering him to pull without moving the gun when he gave him a sign, he took the tomahawk, and stood astride the Indian in whose arms he had been encircled. At the given signal he struck, and the gun was discharged. The blow of the tomahawk descended on the back of his victim's neck, and he attempted to rise, but the bold boy repeated his blows, while the younger one cried out, "Lay on!—I've done for this one!" and both the savages were, in the next moment, lying motionless before them. The discharge of the gun had carried away the jaw of the other, and stunned him.

They started on their way back, taking with them the gun and tomahawk as trophies, and arrived at home just before day-break. The neighbours had all been in search for them, and when they told their tale, it was at first disbelieved. John, however, had hung up his hat as a mark to find the place, and led them back the way he had come, where they found the tomahawked Indian lying in his blood. The other had disappeared, but was tracked to a short distance, where, as the chronicle quietly expresses it, "they agreed to leave him, *as he must die at any rate*."

DESERT ROCK LIGHT-HOUSE, AND MOUNTAIN

Desert Rock Light-House, and Mountain

VERY much the same sort of incredulity with which one reads a traveller's account of the deliciousness of the Russian summer comes over him, *(malgré* all the information to the contrary,) when it is proposed to him to admire any thing so near the cradle of the east wind as Penobscot River. We know, indeed, that spring visits that region of the world—as far, at least, as the British boundary line. We could be made, upon reflection, to presume that the grass grows, and the sun shines there—the farmers are warm in haying-time, and the flowers come to maturity in season for the bees to provide against winter; but, in point of fact, when Penobscot River is mentioned, we shudder at our remembrance of the acrid blasts that have swept over us from that quarter, and image the scenery forth-drest in the drapery so well described by the captain of the Penobscot whaler—a fog so thick, that having driven his jack-knife into it on the eve of sailing for the Pacific, he found it sticking in the same spot on his return from a three years' cruise.

There *is* beautiful scenery in Maine, however; and Mr. Doughty, from one of whose pictures the accompanying drawing was taken, made a tour in search of it, and filled a portfolio with sketches which (the most of them) might belong to any Tempe for their summer look. They were taken from the neighbourhood of Desert Rock, and within view of Mount Desert, (shown in the drawing,) though the names of their neighbours sound unpromising.

Such spots as this are expected, like the knife-grinder, to have a story to tell, and this, unlike the knife-grinder, answers to expectation. The Light-house in the fore-ground stands upon a rock, about twelve miles from land; and near it lies a low reef, hidden at high tides, with a channel between it and the loftier rock. Some years before the erection of the Light-house, a homeward-bound vessel ran upon the breakers in a storm, and went to pieces. The storm having just commenced, and the sea not running as yet very high, several of the crew succeeded in getting upon the rock, where they found a partial shelter under a projecting shelf to leeward. The storm increased in violence, and after three days of unintermitted fury, during which they had seen no friendly sail even in the distance, the miserable survivors, perishing with hunger, abandoned themselves to despair. On the fourth night, they were crowded together in their narrow place of shelter, their eyes fixed on the black darkness covering the sea, when a vivid flash of lightning revealed to them a large ship careening straight for the rock, and apparently in complete ignorance of the danger. In the same instant all was black again, and they waited in the most breathless agony for the shock. A minute elapsed, and simultaneously, with a gleam that made the whole sea as bright as day, the ship appeared on the crest of a mountain-wave bounding over the reef, and with one cry from the man at the helm, as he discovered the rock before him, she launched into the channel on the breaking wave, and they heard her no more. They spoke of her to each other as lost, and betook themselves to their silent despair. The tempest stilled toward morning, and the sun rose clear, and till noon again they bore the gnawings of despairing hunger, and watched the desolate sea in vain for a passing sail. Soon after noon a boat suddenly pulled into the channel between the rocks, friendly voices hailed the exhausted mariners, and with daring humanity they were successfully taken off. The ship they had seen in the night was lying-to not far from the opposite side of the rock, and they were soon on board of her, where, with proper treatment, they recovered from their exhaustion, and arrived safe in port. The pilot had seen them by the same gleam which revealed to him his danger, and after being saved by the recoil of the wave, which threw the ship into the current of the channel between the reefs, he lay-to till morning, when finding the vessel had drifted far south of the rock, he returned upon her course, and with the first abatement of the waves, manned his boat for the dangerous service he succeeded in.

Successful as Mr. Doughty is in sketches of this description, his forte lies in scenery of a softer and inland character—in the lonely forest-brook, the misty wood-lake, the still river, the heart of the quiet wilderness. In painting these features of Nature, he has (in his peculiar style) no rivals among American painters—perhaps none in England. His landscapes can scarcely be appreciated by those who have not seen the untouched and graceful wilderness of America; but of travellers who have, they touch the heart and fill the memory afresh. He is a most sweet and accomplished artist; and when the time comes for America to be proud of her painters, Doughty will be remembered among the first.

Washington's House, at Mount Vernon

THE house erected on this consecrated spot is of wood, cut in imitation of free-stone. The centre part was built by Lawrence Washington, brother to the General. The wings were added by General Washington. It is named after Admiral Vernon, in whose expedition the former served. The house is two stories high, and ninety-six feet in length, with a portico fronting the river, extending the whole length of the house, surmounted with a cupola. The grounds are in the same state as left by General Washington.

The house contains on the ground floor, six rooms, and a spacious passage: four of these are of the ordinary size. At the north-east is a large room, with a handsomely sculptured ceiling, which contains a marble mantel-piece, sent to General Washington from Italy, and a very fine organ, on which instrument Mrs. Washington was an accomplished performer. The room at the south-east end of the house is used as a family dining-room, and contains busts of Necker, Paul Jones, and General Washington; also a handsome library, fitted in the wall, with glass cases. The books were chiefly collected by General Washington.

The house fronts north-west, the rear looking to the river. In front of the house is a lawn, containing five or six acres of ground, with a serpentine walk around it, fringed with shrubbery, and planted with poplars. On each side of the lawn stands a garden; the one on the right is a flower-garden, and contains two green-houses, (one built by General Washington, the other by Judge Washington,) a hot-house, and a pinery. It is laid out in handsome walks, with box wood borders, remarkable for their beauty. It contains also a quantity of fig-trees, producing excellent fruit. The other is a kitchen-garden, containing only fruit and vegetables.

About two hundred yards from the house, in a southerly direction, stands a summer-house, on the edge of the river-bank, which is here lofty and sloping, and clothed with wood to the water's edge. The summer-house commands a fine prospect of the river and the Maryland shore; also of the White House, at a distance of five or six miles down the river, where an engagement took place with the British vessels which ascended the river during the last war.

The estate, as owned by Judge Washington, consisted of between three and four thousand acres, since divided between his nephews. The timber of the woods, in which the fallow deer once abounded, is composed of white and black oak, with dogwood, hickory, ash, cedar, &c. The soil is thin and

WASHINGTON'S HOUSE, AT MOUNT VERNON

rather poor, cultivated chiefly in Indian corn, rye, barley, &c. There are two fisheries on the place, where shad and herring are caught in large quantities. Mount Vernon is healthy during all the year except the autumn, when bilious fevers and agues prevail.

A distinguished writer visited Mount Vernon some years since, and gave a more particular account of the grounds than is to be found elsewhere. "We were conducted," he says, "over long gravel walks, bordered with box, which is arranged and trimmed into the most fanciful figures, and which, at the age of twenty years and upwards, still possesses the vigour and freshness of youth. At the extremity of these extensive alleys and pleasure-grounds, ornamented with fruit-trees and shrubbery, and clothed in perennial verdure, stands two hot-houses, and as many green-houses, situated in the sunniest part of the garden, and shielded from the northern winds by a long range of wooden buildings for the accommodation of servants. From the air of a frosty December morning, we were suddenly introduced into the tropical climate of these spacious houses, where we long sauntered among groves of the coffee-tree, lemons and oranges, all in full bearing, regaling our senses with the flowers and odours of spring.

"One of the hot-houses is appropriated entirely to rearing the pine-apple, long rows of which we saw in a flourishing and luxuriant condition. Many bushels of lemons and oranges, of every variety, are annually grown, which, besides furnishing the family with a supply of these fruits at all seasons, are distributed as delicacies to their friends, or used to administer to the comfort of their neighbours in cases of sickness. The coffee-plant thrives well, yields abundantly, and, in quality, is said to be equal to the best Mocha. The branches under which we walked were laden with the fruit, fast advancing to maturity. Among the more rare plants we saw the night-blooming cereus, the guava, aloes of a gigantic growth, the West India plantain, the sweet cassia in bloom, the prickly pear, and many others.

"At every step in these pleasure-grounds, the thought occurred that the illustrious projector is no more. In passing the house, the chamber in which he died was pointed out to us; and imagination, aided by these memorials, soon presented the scene in such distinct and vivid colours, that we seemed almost to follow his remains to the grave."

VILLAGE OF LITTLE FALLS, MOHAWK RIVER

Village of Little Falls, Mohawk River

THIS thriving town sits above the north bank of the Mohawk, amid some of the most exquisite scenery of the world. The falls afford great facilities for manufactures of all kinds, and the Erie canal and rail-road both pass through it, up the Valley of the Mohawk, making it altogether the busiest spot, as it is the loveliest on the great route westward. It is impossible to conquer the wildness of the scenery here, however; and spite of mills and aqueducts, and smoking steam-engines, the soul of the banished Mohawk might return and haunt with comfort the bold precipices and impassive rocks that frown down upon his ancient abode, and still find the water untamed, and the mountains beautiful.

Of the small relics of Indian history that exist, there is a scrap which proves the supremacy of the Mohawk over even the far-off tribes of Connecticut. In the year 1656, a Podunk Indian, named Weaseapano, murdered a Sachem, who lived near Mattabeseck, (now Middletown.) Seaquassin, the existing Sachem of his tribe, complained of the outrage to the magistracy of Connecticut, and said that the Podunk Indians entertained the murderer, and protected him from the merited punishment. Seaquassin, at the same time, engaged Uncas in his cause, who also complained that Tontonimo enticed away many of his men, and protected an Indian who had murdered a Mohegan. Upon these complaints, the magistrates summoned the parties before them. Seaquassin and Uncas, after observing that the murderer was a mean fellow, and that the man murdered was a great Sachem, insisted that *ten men*, friends of Weaseapano, should be delivered up to be put to death, as a satisfaction for the crime. Tontonimo insisted that the satisfaction demanded was excessive; particularly as the murdered Sachem had killed Weaseapano's uncle. The governor endeavoured to convince the complainants that the demand was excessive, observing that the English, in cases of murder, punished only the principal, and such as were accessary to the crime.

Tontonimo then proposed to make satisfaction by the payment of wampum, but it was refused. They fell, however, in their demands from ten men to six. The proposition was rejected by Tontonimo. The magistrates then urged him to deliver up the murderer: this he promised to do. But while the subject was in agitation, he privately withdrew from the court with the rest of the Podunk Sachems, and retired to the fortress belonging to his nation. Both the magistrates and the complainants were offended at this behaviour of Tontonimo. However, the magistrates appointed a committee to persuade the Indians to

[265]

continue at peace with each other. At their solicitation, Uncas at length consented to accept the murderer, and promised to be satisfied if he should be delivered up; but the Podunk Indians told the English that they could not comply with this condition, because the friends of Weaseapano were numerous and powerful, and would not agree to the proposal.

The governor then addressed them in form, urging them to continue in peace, and endeavouring to persuade the complainants to accept of wampum. This they again refused, and withdrew; after it had been agreed on all hands that the English should not take any part in the controversy, and after the Indians had promised that they would not injure the persons or possessions of the English on either side the river.

Soon after, Uncas assembled an army for the purpose of avenging his wrongs; but being met near Hoccanum river by an equal number of the Podunks, and considering the issue of a battle as doubtful, he prudently retired, after having sent a message to Tontonimo, in which he declared, that if the Podunk Sachem persisted in withholding the murderer from justice, he would send to the Mohawks to come and destroy both him and his people.

Not long after, the crafty Mohegan accomplished his purpose in the following manner. He sent a trusty warrior, furnished with some Mohawk weapons, to Podunk, directing him to set fire in the night to a house near the fort, and then to leave the weapons on the ground in the vicinity, and immediately return. The warrior executed his commission. When the Podunks came in the morning to examine the ruins they found the weapons, and knowing them to belong to the Mohawks, were so alarmed with the apprehension that Uncas was about to execute his threat, that they delivered up the murderer, and sued for peace.

Harper's Ferry

(From the Blue Ridge)

THE scenery at Harper's Ferry is, perhaps, the most singularly picturesque in America. The Views already given display its beauties, as seen from below. To attain that given in the present number, it was necessary to climb the Blue

HARPER'S FERRY

(FROM THE BLUE RIDGE)

Ridge, by a narrow winding path, immediately above the bank of the Potomac. The view from this lofty summit amply repays the fatigue incurred by its ascent. The junction of the two rivers is immediately beneath the spectator's feet; and his delighted eye resting first upon the beautiful and thriving village of Harper's Ferry, wanders over the wide and woody plains, extending to the Alleghany mountains. President Jefferson, who has given the name to a beautiful rock immediately above the village, has left a powerful description of the scenery of Harper's Ferry, which we shall give to our readers.

"The passage of the Potomac through the Blue Ridge, is, perhaps, one of the most stupendous scenes in nature. You stand on a very high point of land; on your right comes up the Shenandoah, having ranged along the foot of the mountain a hundred miles to seek a vent. On your left approaches the Potomac, in quest of a passage also; in the moment of their junction, they rush together against the mountain, rend it asunder, and pass off to the sea. The first glance of this scene hurries our senses into the opinion that this earth has been created in time; that the mountains were formed first, that the rivers began to flow afterwards, that in this place particularly they have been dammed up by the Blue Ridge of mountains, and have formed an ocean which filled the whole valley; that, continuing to rise, they have at length broken over at this spot, and have torn the mountain down from its summit to its base. The piles of rock on each hand, but particularly on the Shenandoah—the evident marks of their disrupture and avulsion from their beds by the most powerful agents of nature, corroborate the impression. But the distant finishing which nature has given to the picture, is of a very different character; it is a true contrast to the fore-ground; it is as placid and delightful as that is wild and tremendous; for the mountain being cloven asunder, she presents to your eye, through the cleft, a small catch of smooth blue horizon, at an infinite distance in the plain country, inviting you, as it were, from the riot and tumult roaring around, to pass through the breach and participate of the calm below. Here the eye ultimately composes itself; and that way, too, the road happens actually to lead. You cross the Potomac above the junction, pass along its side through the base of the mountain for three miles, its terrible precipices hanging in fragments over you, and, within about twenty miles, reach Fredericktown, and the fine country round that. This scene is worth a voyage across the Atlantic; yet here, as in the neighbourhood of the Natural Bridge, are people who have passed their lives within half a dozen miles, and have never been to survey these monuments of a war between rivers and mountains, which must have shaken the earth itself to its centre."

[268]

Barhydt's Lake, Near Saratoga

I DROVE to Barhydt's Lake, with the accomplished artist whose name is at the bottom of the drawing, on one of the finest days of early September. With a pair of crop ponies, whose *going*, simply, we acknowledged we had never seen beaten on the smooth roads of England, and a day over our heads of the most inspiriting freshness, we dashed through the pine woods of Saratoga in a light waggon, and pulled up at Barhydt's door in twenty minutes from leaving the Springs.

The old man sat under his Dutch *stoup*, smoking his pipe, and suffered us to tie our ponies to his fence without stirring; and in answer to our inquiries if there was a boat on the lake, simply nodded an assent, and pointed to the water's edge. Whether this indifference to strangers is indolence merely, or whether Herr Barhydt does not choose to be considered an inn-keeper, no one is enough in his secrets to divine. He will give you a dram, or cook you a dinner of trout, and seems not only indifferent whether you like his fish or his liquor, but quite as indifferent whether and what you pay him. In his way, Herr Barhydt is kind and courteous.

We descended to the lake, and after pulling up to the upper extremity where the view is taken, we returned to partake of the old Dutchman's hospitality, and have a little conversation with him. Among other things, we asked him if he was aware that he had been put in a book.

"I've hearn tell on't," said he; "a Mr. Wilkins, or Watkins, has writ something about me, but I don't know why. *I never did him no harm as I know on.*"

We had not the book to show the injured old gentleman his picture, but as it happens to lie by us now, and really contains a very literal description of the spot, we will copy out the extract: —

"Herr Barhydt is an old Dutch settler, who, till the mineral springs of Saratoga were discovered some four miles from his door, was buried in the depth of a forest unknown to all but the prowling Indian. The sky is supported above him, (or looks to be,) by a wilderness of straight columnar pine-shafts, gigantic in girth, and with no foliage except at the top, where they branch out like round tables spread for a banquet in the clouds. A small ear-shaped lake, sunk as deep into the earth as the firs shoot above it, and clear and unbroken as a mirror, save the pearl-spots of the thousand lotuses holding up their cups to the blue eye of heaven, sleeps beneath his window; and around him in the forest, lies, still unbroken, the elastic and brown carpet of the faded pine-tassels, deposited in yearly layers since the continent first rose from the flood,

BARHYDT'S LAKE, NEAR SARATOGA

and rotted a foot beneath the surface to a rich mould that would fatten the Symplegades to a flower-garden. With his black tarn well stocked with trout, his bit of a farm in the *clearing* near by, and an old Dutch Bible, Herr Barhydt lived a life of Dutch musing, talked Dutch to his geese and chickens, sung Dutch psalms to the echoes of the mighty forest, and, except on his far-between visits to Albany, which grew rarer and rarer as the old Dutch inhabitants dropped faster away, saw never a white human face from one maple-blossoming to another.

"A roving mineralogist tasted the waters of Saratoga, and, like the work of a lath-and-plaster Alladin, up sprung a thriving village around the fountain's lip; and hotels, tin-tumblers, and apothecaries, multiplied in the usual proportion to each other, but out of all precedent with every thing else for rapidity. Libraries, newspapers, churches, livery-stables, and lawyers, followed in their train; and it was soon established, from the plains of Abraham to the Savannahs of Alabama, that no person of fashionable taste or broken constitution could exist through the months of July and August without a visit to the chalybeate springs and populous village of Saratoga. It contained seven thousand inhabitants before Herr Barhydt, living in his forest seclusion only four miles off, became aware of its existence. A pair of loons, philandering about the forest on horseback, popped in upon him one June morning, and thenceforth there was no rest for the soul of the Dutchman. Everybody rode down to eat his trout, and make love in the dark shades of his mirrored lagoon; and, at last, in self-defence, he added a room or two to his shanty, enclosed his cabbage-garden, and set a price on his trout dinners. The traveller, now-a-days, who has not dined at Barhydt's, with his own champagne cold from the tarn, and the white-headed old settler 'gargling' Dutch about the house in his maniform vocation of cook, ostler, and waiter, may as well not have seen Niagara."

Fair Mount Gardens, Philadelphia

THE walks here, though not extensive, are delightful, from the views they command over the Schuylkill. In the early days of William Penn, this side of

[271]

FAIRMOUNT GARDENS, PHILADELPHIA

the river was covered by a thick wood; and so late as Franklin's time, (who "frequented it," says the analist, "with his companions, Osborne, Watson, and Ralph,") the banks afforded a secluded and rural retreat, much resorted to by swimmers. The name of Schuylkill, given it by the Dutch, is said to express "Hidden River," as its mouth is not visible in ascending the Delaware. The Indians called it by a name, meaning "The Mother;" and a small branch of the Schuylkill, higher up, called "Maiden Creek," was named by them, *Ontelaunee*, meaning "the little daughter of a great mother."

The Schuylkill and Delaware, in former days, were the scenes of feats in swimming and skating, which are not emulated in these graver times. The colonial annals record the achievements of George Tyson, a fat broker, weighing one hundred and ninety pounds; and "Governor Mifflin, and Joe Claypoole," descend on the page of history as the best skaters of Pennsylvania. The annalist enters on this theme with great unction. "During the old-fashioned winters, when about New-year's day every one expected to see or hear of an *ox-roast* on the river, upon the thick-ribbed ice, which, without causing much alarm among the thousands moving in all directions upon its surface, would crack and rend itself by its own weight without separating, in sounds like thunder, among the then multitudinous throngs of promenaders, sliders, and skaters, visible all about the river, as far as the eye could reach. Of the many varieties of skaters of all colours and sizes mingled together, and darting about here and there, upward and downward, mingled and convolved, a few were at all times discernible as being decidedly superior to the rest for dexterity, power, and grace; namely, Governor Mifflin, Joe Claypoole, and others, not forgetting, by the way, a black Othello, who, from his apparent muscle and powerful movement, might have sprung, as did the noble Moor, from "men of royal size." In swiftness he had no competitor; he outstripped the wind; the play of his elbows in alternate movements with his low-gutter skates, while darting forward and uttering occasionally a wild scream peculiar to the African race while in active exertion of body, was very imposing in appearance and effect. Of the gentlemen skaters before enumerated, George Heyl took the lead in graceful skating, and in superior dexterity in cutting figures and *High Dutch* within a limited space of ice. On a large field of glass he might be seen moving about elegantly, and at perfect ease, in curve lines, with folded arms, being dressed in a red coat, as was the fashion, and buckskin tights, his bright broad skates in an occasional turn flashing upon the eye. Then, again, to be pursued by others, he might be seen suddenly changing to the back and heel-forward movement, offering them his hand,

and, at the same time, eluding their grasp by his dexterous and instantaneous deviations to the right and left, leaving them to their hard work of striking out after him with all their might and main."

Among the recorded amusements of Philadelphia, however, the "Meschianza" is the most remarkable. This was a tilt and tournament, with other entertainments, given to Sir William Howe, by the officers of his army, on quitting his command to return to England. The company were enbarked on the Delaware, in a grand regatta of three divisions; and with a band of music to each, and an outer line of barges to keep off the crowd of the uninvited, they proceeded to the neighbouring country-seat of Mr. Wharton. The tilting-ground was a lawn of one hundred and fifty yards on each side, lined with troops, and faced with several pavilions; and in front of each sat seven young ladies, dressed in Turkish costume, and wearing on their turbans the prizes for the victors. At the sound of a trumpet, "*seven white knights*, habited in white and red silk, and mounted on grey chargers, richly caparisoned," made their appearance, followed by seven esquires, and a herald in his robe. After saluting the ladies, the herald proclaimed their challenge in the name of the "*Knights of the blended Rose*." At the third repetition of the challenge, a black herald made his appearance, and accepted the challenge in the name of the "*Knights of the Burning Mountain*." Immediately after entered the black knights, with tunics representing a mountain in flames, and the motto, "I burn for ever;" and the tournament began. They fought with spears, pistols, and swords, and the contest was long and desperate; but whether the white or black knights had the victory is not recorded.

After the tilt, the company ascended a flight of steps to a banqueting-room, and after the banquet, a ball-room was flung open, "decked with eighty-five mirrors, festoons of flowers, and a light and elegant style of painting." Four drawing-rooms on the same floor contained sideboards with refreshments. The knights and their ladies opened the ball, and at twelve o'clock followed fire-works, and a supper, which was spread in a saloon of two hundred and ten by forty feet, ornamented with fifty-six large pier glasses, and containing alcoves with side-tables. There were one hundred branch lights, eighteen lustres, three hundred wax tapers on the supper tables, four hundred and thirty covers, and twelve hundred dishes. They were waited on by a great number of black slaves in oriental dresses, with silver collars and bracelets.

The queen of the "Meschianza," concludes the annalist, with a remark which contains a moral, "was a once beautiful Mrs. L——, *now blind and fast waning from the things that be*."

Sing-Sing Prison, and Tappan Sea

An American prison is not often a picturesque object, and, till late years, it suggested to the mind of the philanthropist only painful reflections upon the abuses and thwarted ends of penitentiary discipline. To the persevering humanity of Louis Dwight, and to the liberal association that sustained him, we owe the change in these institutions which enables us to look on them without pain and disgust as places of repentance and reformation, rather than as schools for vice, and abodes of neglect and idleness. It is a creditable thing to our country to have led the way in these salutary changes; and there are many who have felt their patriotism more flattered by the visits of persons from Europe sent out by their governments to study our systems of prison discipline, than by many an event sounded through the trumpet of national glory.

The Tappan Sea spreads its broad waters at this part of the Hudson, looking, like all scenes of pure natural beauty, as if it was made for a world in which there could neither exist crime nor pain. Yet there stands a vast and crowded prison on its shores to remind us of the first—and for the latter, who ever entered upon these waters without a recollection of poor André? It may be doubted whether in the history of our country the fate of an individual has ever excited more sympathy than his. The rare accomplishments which he possessed, the natural elegance of his mind, the unfitness of his open character for the degrading circumstances under which he was taken, and his mild constancy at the approach of his melancholy fate, endear him, without respect to party, to the memories of all who read his story. André was taken on the eastern shore of the river at Tarrytown, and executed on the opposite side, at Tappan.

The story of Captain Hale has been regarded as parallel to that of Major André. This young officer had received a university education, and had but recently taken his degree when the war of the revolution commenced. He possessed genius, taste, ardour, was a distinguished scholar, and to all this was added, in an eminent degree, the winning address and native grace of a gentleman. No young man of his years put forth a finer promise of usefulness and celebrity.

Upon the first news of the battle of Lexington, he obtained a commission in the army, and marched with his company to Cambridge, where his promptness, activity, and assiduous attention to discipline, were early observed. After considerable service, the theatre of action was changed, and the army was removed to the southward. The battle of Long Island was fought, and the

[275]

SING-SING PRISON, AND TAPPAN SEA

American forces were drawn together in the city of New York. At this moment it became extremely important for Washington to know the situation of the British army on the heights of Brooklyn, its numbers, and the indications as to its future movements. Having expressed a wish to this effect, Colonel Knowlton called together the younger officers, stated to them the wish of the General, and left it to their reflections, without naming any individual for the service. The undertaking was particularly hazardous; but it was immediately determined upon by Hale, who resisted all opposition on the part of his friends, and crossed over the river to the enemy's ground. His disguise was well contrived, and he had obtained all necessary information, when he was arrested in the boat by which he was attempting to return. He was taken before the British commander, was condemned as a spy, and hanged the following morning. The circumstances of his death, however, were widely different from those of André. The Provost-marshal was a refugee, and behaved towards him in the most unfeeling manner, refusing him the attendance of a clergyman, and the use of a Bible in his last moments, and destroying the letters he had written to his mother and friends. In the midst of these barbarities Hale was collected and calm. To the last he displayed his native elevation of soul, and his dignity of deportment.

"But," says a distinguished writer of biography, "whatever may have been the parallel between these two individuals while living, it ceased with their death. A monument was raised and consecrated to the memory of André by the bounty of a grateful sovereign. His ashes have been removed from their obscure resting-place, transported across the ocean, and deposited with the remains of the illustrious dead in Westminster Abbey. Where is the memento of the virtues, the patriotic sacrifice, the early fate of Hale?"

WASHINGTON, FROM THE PRESIDENT'S HOUSE

Washington

(From the President's House)

DISTANCE lends more enchantment to a view of Washington than to most other views. Covering a good deal of ground, possessing two or three very fine points in itself, and lying in the centre of a superb outer circle of scenery, it has all the qualities which a draftsman could desire for his sketch. Thus much was seen or anticipated by the sagacious eye of the great patriot whose name it bears. Every one knows, however, that the location of the President's House was the result of after speculation, or rather the result of a dispute between the owners of estates, two miles distant from each other, each desirous of locating all the public buildings on his own land, but who, like children quarrelling for a sugar-toy, pulled the subject of dispute in two. The Capitol was already placed on one elevation, and the President's House carried off two miles to another. The consequence is, that the town itself, which, being a merely legislative metropolis, could never be very large, stretches and straddles between these two distant points, trying in vain to grow into compactness, and form the continuous and close-built street of a city.

The common sagacity acquired by travel is of little use to the stranger arriving for the first time in Washington. Visiting it during the session of Congress, he thinks himself very safe in requesting to be set down at the hotel nearest the Capitol, presuming, naturally, that this must be the great centre of convenience, as well as of interest. He accordingly takes a pigeon-hole at Gadsby's Hotel, a vast white wooden caravanserai, accommodating many hundreds of people; and on the first day, walks half a mile to the Capitol, and wonders why the deuce the hotel was not built on some of the waste lots immediately at the foot of the hill. In a day or two, however, the secretaries and diplomatists begin to call on him, and the party-giving inhabitants shower upon him the "small rain" of pink billets. He sets apart a day for returning his visits; and, inquiring the addresses of his friends, is told that it is impossible to direct him, but *the hackney coachmen all know*. He calls a carriage, and the first thing is a drive of two miles directly away from the Capitol. He passes the President's House, and getting off the Macadamized road, begins to pitch and plunge through miry lanes and waste lots, passing occasionally a house which lacks nothing of being in the country but trees, garden, and fences. It looks as if it had rained naked brick houses upon an open plain, and every man had made a street with reference to his own front door. The much shaken and

[279]

more bewildered victim consumes his morning and his temper, and has made by dinner-time but six out of forty calls, all imperatively due, and all to be traced through the same irregular and ill-defined geography. He pays a price for his hackney coach which would keep a chariot and two posters for twice the time in London, and the next day moves into the disjointed settlement on the other side of President's Square, abandons the Capitol, except on great occasions, and makes all visits by proxy that are not for a dance, or a dinner.

Malgré all these inconveniences, however, Washington is by much the most agreeable place in the United States for winter society. The great deficiency in all our cities, the company of highly cultivated and superior men, is here supplied. Female society, in any city or village, is seldom wanting in interest or cultivation; for women refine and elevate themselves with or without the advantages of metropolitan intercourse. But the men of our cities, devoted usually to one engrossing and repressing pursuit, have little time and less inclination to form themselves for intellectual intercourse. The ordeal through which a legislator must have come who finds himself at Washington, however, implies force of character at least, and oftenest, high talent, while the leaders and principal opposers of the ruling party, are, more necessarily than in any other country, men of exalted abilities and great experience of men and the world. The smaller lines which define polished society in May Fair, and the Faubourg St. Germain, may be wanting, but the stamen and spirit of high and cultivated intercourse, such as may well please the most fastidious, is seen in all the society in which the stranger would mingle during the session.

View of Baltimore

THE hospitable and wealthy metropolis of Maryland owes its location to the principle, that "second thoughts are best." The two brothers of Lord Baltimore, one of whom, Leonard Calvert, had been appointed governor of the province, landed with his two hundred colonists on the north side of the Potomac, and there founded the town of St. Mary's, the intended capital of Maryland. Little remains of St. Mary's now, though it enjoyed its prospective

VIEW OF BALTIMORE

honours for several years; and, as the historian says, "the worthy burghers cleared the adjacent lands, lived at peace with their Indian neighbours, and dozed away life, amid their tobacco-fields, with a comfortable and satisfactory sense of their own mark and importance." The principal event in its history, is an attack upon it by a certain Captain Ingle, who, in the course of a rebellion, seized upon the public records, and drove the governor over the Potomac into Virginia.

The first settler within the limits of the present capital, was a Mr. Gorsuch, who, twenty-eight years after the founding of St. Mary's, *patented* some land on Whetstone Point, the present review-ground for the Baltimore militia. Among the earliest who followed, was Charles Carroll, of Carrollton, whose descendant and namesake signed the Declaration of Independence. It is recorded that Charles and Daniel Carroll sold the sixty most eligible acres in the town for forty shillings an acre, which the commissioners paid for in tobacco, at a penny a pound. It was then surrounded with a board-fence, with two gates for carriages, and one for foot passengers; and "provision was made to keep this notable rampart in repair." Thus Baltimore grew and prospered, till at this day it is one of the most enlightened and agreeable capitals of the United States, the third in size, and with a population rising eighty thousand. A humorous antiquarian gives the following sketchy account of it in one of its phases.

"It was a treat to see this little Baltimore town just at the termination of the war of Independence—so conceited, bustling, and *débonair*—growing up like a saucy chubby boy, with his dumpling cheeks and short grinning face, fat and mischievous, and bursting, incontinently, out of his clothes in spite of all the allowance of tucks and broad selvages. Market Street had shot, like a Nuremberg snake out of its toy-box, as far as Congress Hall, with its line of low-browed, hipped-roofed, wooden houses, in disorderly array, standing forward and back, after the manner of a regiment of militia, with many an interval between the files;—some of these structures were painted blue and white, and some yellow; and here and there sprang up a more magnificent mansion of brick, with windows like a multiplication table, and great wastes of wall between the stories, with occasional court-yards before them, and reverential locust-trees, under whose shade bevies of truant school-boys, ragged little negroes, and grotesque chimney-sweeps, *shyed coppers*, and disported themselves at marbles.

"This avenue was enlivened with apparitions of grave matrons and stirring damsels, moving erect in stately transit, like the wooden and pasteboard figures of a puppet-show; our present grandmothers, arrayed in gorgeous brocade and taffeta, luxuriantly displayed over hoops, with comely bodices, laced around that ancient piece of armour, the stay, disclosing most perilous waists; and with sleeves that clung to the arm as far as the elbow, where they took a graceful leave, in ruffles that stood off like the feathers of a bantam. And such faces as they bore along with them!—so rosy, so spirited, and sharp!—with the hair all drawn back over a cushion, until it lifted the eyebrows, giving an amazingly fierce and supercilious tone to the countenance, and falling in cataracts upon the shoulders. Then they stepped away with such a mincing gait, in shoes of many colours, with formidable points to the toes, and high and tottering heels, fancifully cut in wood; their tower-built hats garnished with tall feathers that waved aristocratically backward at each step, as if they took a pride in the slow paces of the wearer.

"In the train of these goodly groups came the beaux and gallants, who upheld the chivalry of the age; cavaliers of the old school, full of starch and powder, most of them the iron gentlemen of the revolution, with leather faces—old campaigners, renowned for long stories, fresh from the camp, with their military erectness and dare-devil swagger; proper roystering blades, who had just got out of the harness, and began to affect the manners of civil life. Who but they!—jolly fellows, fiery, and loud!—with stern glances of the eye, and a brisk turn of the head, and a swash-buckler strut of defiance, like game cocks; all in three-cornered hats and wigs, and light-coloured coats, with narrow capes and marvellous long backs, with the pockets on each hip, and small-clothes that hardly reached the knee; and striped stockings, with great buckles in their shoes, and their long steel chains that hung conceitedly, half way to the knee, with seals in the shape of a sounding board to a pulpit. And they walked with such a stir, striking their canes so hard upon the pavement, as to make the little town ring again. I defy all modern coxcombry to produce any thing like it. There was such a relish about it—and particularly when one of these weather-beaten gallants accosted a lady in the street, with a bow that required a whole side pavement to make it in, with the scrape of his foot, and his cane thrust with a flourish under his left arm till it projected behind, along with his cue, like the pallisades of a *chevaux-de-frize;* and nothing could be more piquant than the lady, as she reciprocated the salutation with a curtsey that seemed to carry her into the earth, with her chin bridled to her breast—and such a volume of dignity!"

VIEW OF THE EXCHANGE AND GIRARD'S BANK, PHILADELPHIA

View of the Exchange and Girard's Bank, Philadelphia

THE most accomplished architect of the United States, William Strickland, Esq., is a citizen of Philadelphia; and to his excellent taste is the city in a great measure indebted for its superiority over the other capitals of our country in the architecture of public buildings. The view seen in the drawing is taken from Third Street, in the business-part of the city, and presents the rear of the Exchange, a new structure by Mr. Strickland, and the façade of a much older building, a chaste and beautiful specimen of the Corinthian order, occupied many years by the United States Bank. It has since been appropriated to the uses of a bank, of which the entire capital was furnished by Stephen Girard, the wealthiest citizen of Philadelphia, lately deceased. The Exchange (of which a minute description is given in another part of the work) is a copy of the choragic monument at Athens, commonly called the Lantern of Demosthenes.

Philadelphia is, and ever has been, fortunate in her citizens; and it may be said with truth that there is not a metropolis in the world where the effects of a liberal and enterprising public spirit are so clearly manifest. This is particularly true of all that ministers to the comfort of the inhabitant—such as excellence of markets, abundance of water, cleanliness of streets, baths, public conveyances, &c. The wooden, or block pavement, common in Russia, is now under experiment in the principal street, and promises to add another to the luxuries of the city; and among the later instances of liberal and refined taste, is the purchase by the city of a beautiful estate on the banks of the Schuylkill, and its appropriation to the purposes of a cemetery. It occupies very high ground, of an uneven surface, plentifully shaded with venerable trees, and is already, perhaps, the most lovely burial-place in the world, after the Necropolis of Scutari.

Philadelphia is the favourite residence of foreigners among us; and though, in all its features, unlike foreign capitals, it possesses more than all other cities of the United States, the advantage of highly educated and refined society. I speak here of that which is constant and resident; as Washington, during the Session of Congress, and Boston, during one or two of the hot months, become in turn the focus of the foreign and floating society of the country. Perhaps the climate of Philadelphia may have had its effect in making it the home of those accustomed to the equable temperatures of the continent; for

Boston, nine months of the year, is uninhabitable from its acrid winds and clammy cold; and Washington, on the other hand, is unhealthy during a considerable part of the summer. New York, though the metropolis of the country, is more a place of transit than residence, to those not engaged in its business or commerce—a result partly of the unhealthfulness of its water and the effluvia of its streets, but partly, too, of the unsettled and shifting character of its society.

The commercial prospects of Philadelphia have brightened lately with the success of Atlantic steam navigation. Hitherto the delay in getting up the Delaware to a city so far from the sea, has made competition with New York in the sailing-packet lines impossible; but with vessels independent of winds and tides, the difficulty is obviated, and the enterprise of her merchants is already at work—companies formed and capital advanced for building steamships—and Philadelphia promises fair to vie with New York as a grand commercial emporium. The vast internal improvements of Pennsylvania, which have gone on nobly for the last few years, will now have double value, and aptly meet the wants of the new accession of trade.

It has always been a subject of regret that the noble design of William Penn to extend a broad pier along the Delaware, the length of the city, was never carried into effect: it is the one objection to the admirable arrangement of Philadelphia. It is to be hoped that, in the new need for wharf-room, the liberal spirit of the merchants will remember the wish of the great founder, and remove the unsightly edifices which now crowd into the river. With a man like Mr. Biddle in the municipality, no good or great change need be despaired of.

View of the Principal Front of the Capitol at Washington

THE Capitol presents a very noble appearance, as the spectator advances to it in the point of view taken by the artist; and from what is shown of the proportions and size of the building, a very imposing effect is produced. Its height, the ascending terraces, the monument and its fountain, the grand balustrade of freestone which protects the offices below, and the distinct object which it forms, standing alone on its lofty site, combine to make up the impression of grandeur, in which its architectural defects are lost or forgotten.

The waste lands which lie at the foot of Capitol Hill might be marshes in the centre of a wilderness for any trace of cultivation about them; but they are appropriated for a botanical garden, when Congress shall find time to order its arrangement and cultivation. This, however, and other features of desolation which belong to so thinly settled a metropolis, are said, by the defenders of Washington's foresight, to answer one of his chief ends, in the location of the Capitol far from any commercial centre—that to prevent intimidation or interference from the people, the legislative capital should be thinly peopled, and in the power exclusively of the legislators themselves. The district of Columbia, accordingly, which was presented and set apart to the General Congress, by the different states, has a sort of civic government, of which the President of the United States held, in the first instance, the office of Mayor, and by its distance from the sea, and the natural independence of its position, it is impossible it should ever become a commercial or a thickly populated mart.

In a little volume written by a descendant of Washington, an account is given of the first survey of the Potomac, by the great patriot, with reference to the navigation above tide-water.

"The canoe, or pirogue," says the author, "in which General Washington and a party of friends first made the survey of the Potomac, was hollowed out of a large poplar tree, on the estate of Colonel Johnson, of Frederick county, Maryland. This humble bark was placed upon a waggon, hauled to the margin of the Monocacy river, launched into the stream, and there received its honoured freight. The General was accompanied by Governor Johnson, one of the first commissioners for the location of the city of Washington, and several other gentlemen. At nightfall, it was usual for the party to land and seek quarters of some of the planters, or farmers, who lived near the banks of the

VIEW OF THE PRINCIPAL FRONT OF THE CAPITOL AT WASHINGTON

river, in all the pride and comfort of old-fashioned kindliness and hospitality. Putting up for a night at a respectable farmer's, the General and the two Johnsons were shown into a room, having but two beds. 'Come, gentlemen!' said Washington, 'who will be my bedfellow?' Both declined. Colonel Johnson often afterwards declared, that greatly as he should have felt honoured by such intimacy, the awe and reverence with which the chief had inspired him, even in their daily and unreserved intercourse, would have made the liberty seem little short of profanation.

"While the party were exploring in the vicinity of Harper's Ferry, news arrived of the burning at the stake of Colonel Crawford, by the Indians at Sandusky. Washington became excited to tears at hearing the recital, for Crawford had been one of the companions of his early life, and had often been his rival in athletic exercises. The unfortunate man was brave as a lion, and had served with great distinction in the war of the revolution. Tears soon gave way to indignation, and Washington, pointing to a lofty rock which juts over the stream, at its remarkable passage through the mountain, exclaimed, with a voice tremulous from feeling, 'By Heaven, were I the sole judge of these Indians, it would be slight retaliation to hurl every spectator of his death from that height into the abyss.'"

To the reader who venerates the name of the great Patriot, no anecdote, however trifling, told in connexion with the monuments of his greatness, can be unappropriate or uninteresting.

THE NARROWS, LAKE GEORGE

The Narrows, Lake George

BETWEEN some of its beautiful islands, and between the islands and the main, Lake George assumes the character of calm river scenery. From the undisturbed state of the vegetation on the shore, however, and the absence of the deposit left by the freshets, to which running streams are liable, the scenery is lovelier than that of most rivers, and differs from them, as the shores of the tideless Mediterranean differ from those of the disturbed Atlantic. There is scarce one of these beautiful islands that has not some association or legend of interest, and this story is recorded of Diamond Island, the one most visited and admired:—A party of pleasure had been visiting the island on a little sailing excursion, and having lingered longer upon that beautiful spot than they were conscious of, as night drew on, concluded to encamp for the night,—it being already too late to return to the fort. "From the shore where we lay hid," said Cane, "it was easy to watch their motions; and perceiving their defenceless situation, as soon as it was dark we set off for the island, where we found them asleep by their fire, and discharged our guns among them. Several were killed, among whom was a woman, who had a sucking child, which was not hurt. This we put to the breast of its dead mother, and so we left it. But Major Hopkins was only wounded, his thigh-bone being broken; he started from his sleep to a rising posture, when I struck him," said Barney Cane, "with the butt of my gun, on the side of his head; he fell over, but caught on one hand; I then knocked him the other way, when he caught with the other hand; a third blow, and I laid him dead. These were all scalped except the infant. In the morning, a party from the fort went and brought away the dead, together with one they found alive, although he was scalped, and the babe, which was hanging and sobbing at the bosom of its lifeless mother."

Even this tale of barbarity to a mother, yields in horror to the sufferings of Massy Harbisson, from whose journal of captivity, take for example the following passages;—"The Indians, when they had flogged me away along with them, took my oldest boy, a lad of about five years of age, along with them, for he was still at the door by my side. My middle little boy, who was about three years of age, had by this time obtained a situation by the fire in the house, and was crying bitterly to me not to go, and making bitter complaints of the depredations of the savages.

"But these monsters were not willing to let the child remain behind them; they took him by the hand to drag him along with them, but he was so very unwilling to go, and made such a noise by crying, that they took him up by the feet, and dashed his brains out against the threshold of the door. They then scalped and stabbed him, and left him for dead. When I witnessed this inhuman butchery of my own child, I gave a most indescribable and terrific scream, and felt a dimness come over my eyes next to blindness, and my senses were nearly gone. The savage then gave me a blow across my head and face, and brought me to my sight and recollection again. During the whole of this agonizing scene, I kept my infant in my arms.

"As soon as their murder was effected, they marched me along to the top of the bank, about forty or sixty rods, and there they stopped and divided the plunder they had taken from our house; and here I counted their number, and found them to be thirty-two, two of whom were white men, painted as Indians.

"Here I beheld another hard scene, for as soon as we had landed, my little boy, who was still mourning and lamenting about his little brother, and who complained that he was injured by the fall in descending the bank, *was murdered*.

"One of the Indians ordered me along, probably that I should not see the horrid deed about to be perpetrated. The other then took his tomahawk from his side, and with this instrument of death *killed and scalped him*. When I beheld this second scene of inhuman butchery, I fell to the ground senseless, with my infant in my arms, it being under, and its little hands in the hair of my head. How long I remained in this state of insensibility, I know not.

"The first thing I remember was my raising my head from the ground, and my feeling myself exceedingly overcome with sleep. I cast my eyes around, and saw the scalp of my dear little boy, fresh bleeding from his head, in the hand of one of the savages, and sunk down to the earth again, upon my infant child. The first thing I remember after witnessing this spectacle of woe, was the severe blows I was receiving from the hands of the savages, though at this time I was unconscious of the injury I was sustaining. After a severe castigation, they assisted me in getting up, and supported me when up.

"In the morning one of them left us, to watch the trail or path we had come, to see if any white people were pursuing us. During the absence of the Indian, who was the one that claimed me, the other, who remained with me, and who was the murderer of my last boy, took from his bosom his scalp, and prepared a hoop, and stretched the scalp upon it. Those mothers who have not seen the like done by one of the scalps of their own children, (and few, if any, ever had so much misery to endure,) will be able to form but faint ideas of the feelings which then harrowed up my soul!"

The Natural Bridge, Virginia

THE description of Jefferson first attracted the attention of travellers to this remarkable spot, unequalled probably in the world. Of recent descriptions the best is that by Miss Martineau, which is so characteristic and interesting, that we can add nothing to it.

"At a mile from the bridge, the road turns off through a wood. While the stage rolled and jolted along the extremely bad road, Mr. L—— and I went prying about the whole area of the wood, poking our horses' noses into every thicket, and between any two pieces of rock, that we might be sure not to miss our object; the driver smiling after us, whenever he could spare attention from his own not very easy task, of getting his charge along. With all my attention, I could see no precipice, and was concluding to follow the road without any more vagaries, when Mr. L——, who was a little in advance, waived his whip, as he stood beside his horse, and said, 'Here is the bridge!' I then perceived that we were nearly over it, the piled rocks on either hand forming a barrier, which prevents a careless eye from perceiving the ravine which it spans. I turned to the side of the road, and rose in my stirrup to look over; but I found it would not do. I went on to the inn, deposited my horse, and returned on foot to the bridge.

"With all my efforts, I could not look down steadily into what seemed the bottomless abyss of foliage and shadow. From every point of the bridge I tried, and all in vain. I was heated and extremely hungry, and much vexed at my own weakness. The only way was to go down and look up; though where the bottom could be, was past my imagining, the view from the top seeming to be of foliage below foliage for ever.

"The way to the glen is through a field opposite the inn, and down a steep, rough, rocky path, which leads under the bridge, and a few yards beyond it. I think the finest view of all is from this path, just before reaching the bridge. The irregular arch of rock, spanning a chasm of one hundred and sixty feet in height, and from sixty to ninety in width, is exquisitely tinted with every shade of grey and brown; while trees encroach from the sides, and overhang from the top; between which and the arch there is an additional depth of fifty-six feet. It was now early in July; the trees were in their brightest and thickest foliage; and the tall beeches under the arch contrasted their verdure with the grey rock, and received the gilding of the sunshine, as it slanted into the ravine, glittering in the drip from the arch, and in the splashing and tumbling waters of Cedar Creek, which ran by our feet. Swallows were flying

THE NATURAL BRIDGE, VIRGINIA

about under the arch. What others of their tribe can boast of such a home?

"We crossed and re-crossed the creek on stepping-stones, searching out every spot to which any tradition belonged. Under the arch, thirty feet from the water, the lower part of the letters G. W. may be seen, carved in the rock. When Washington was a young man, he climbed up hither, to leave this record of his visit. There are other inscriptions, of the same kind; and above them a board, on which are painted the names of two persons, who have thought it worth while thus to immortalize their feat of climbing highest. But their glory was but transient, after all. They have been outstripped by a traveller, whose achievement will probably never be rivalled; for he would not have accomplished it, if he could by any means have declined the task. Never was a wonderful deed more involuntarily performed. There is no disparagement to the gentleman in saying this: it is only absolving him from the charge of foolhardiness.

"This young man, named Blacklock, accompanied by two friends, visited the Natural Bridge; and, being seized with the ambition appropriate to the place, of writing his name highest, climbed the rock opposite to the part selected by Washington, and carved his initials. Others have perhaps seen what Mr. Blacklock had overlooked—that it was a place easy to ascend, but from which it is impossible to come down. He was forty feet or more from the path; his footing was precarious; he was weary with holding on, while carving his name, and his head began to swim when he saw the impossibility of getting down again. He called to his companions that his only chance was to climb up upon the bridge, without hesitation or delay. They saw this, and with anguish agreed between themselves that the chance was a very bare one. They cheered him, and advised him to look neither up nor down. On he went, slanting upwards from under the arch, creeping round a projection, on which no foothold is visible from below, and then disappearing in a recess filled up with foliage. Long and long they waited, watching for motion, and listening for crashing among the trees. He must have been now one hundred and fifty feet above them. At length their eyes were so strained that they could see no more; and they had almost lost all hope. There was little doubt that he had fallen while behind the trees, where his body would never be found. They went up to try the chance of looking for him from above. They found him lying insensible on the bridge. He could just remember reaching the top, when he immediately fainted. One would like to know whether the accident left him a coward, in respect of climbing, or whether it strengthened his confidence in his nerves."

VIEW OF THE PASSAIC FALLS

View of the Passaic Falls

A DESCRIPTION of these beautiful Falls having been given in another page of the work, it may be worth while to step a little aside from the immediate subject of the drawing, in search of historic incident. The annals of New Jersey present nothing more interesting than the military operations of Washington, within its border; and among these stands conspicuous the battle at Monmouth Court House. On the news of the alliance between America and France, the British Government ordered its forces to be concentrated at New York. The royal army, in consequence, evacuated Philadelphia, and took up their march through New Jersey, where Washington resolved to hazard a battle. "The British army," says the historian, "marched in two divisions,— the van commanded by General Knyphausen, and the rear by Lord Cornwallis; but the British commander-in-chief, judging that the design of the American General was to make an attempt on his baggage, put it under the care of General Knyphausen, that the rear division, consisting of the flower of the British army, might be ready to act with vigour. This arrangement being made, General Knyphausen's division marched, in pursuance of orders, at break of day, on the 28th of June; but the other division, under Lord Cornwallis, attended by the Commander-in-chief, did not move until eight, that it might not press too closely on the baggage. General Lee appeared on the heights of Freehold, soon after the British had left them; and, following them into the plain, made dispositions for intercepting their covering party in the rear. While he was advancing to the front of a wood, adjoining the plain, to reconnoitre the enemy in person, Sir Henry Clinton was marching back his whole rear division, to attack the Americans. Lee now perceived that he had mistaken the force which formed the rear of the British; but he still proposed to engage on that ground. While both armies were preparing for action, General Scott, mistaking an oblique march of an American column for a retreat, left his position, and repassed a morass in his rear. Lee, dissatisfied with the ground on which the army was drawn up, did not correct the error of Scott, but directed the whole detachment to repass the morass, and regain the heights. During this retrograde movement, the rear of the army, which at the first firing had thrown off their packs, and advanced rapidly to the support of the front, approached the scene of action; and General Washington, riding forward, met the advanced corps, to his extreme mortification and astonishment, retiring before the enemy. On coming up to Lee, he spoke to him in terms of disapprobation; but, though warm, he lost not for a moment that self-

[297]

command, than which, at so critical a moment, nothing could be more essential to the command of others. He instantly ordered Colonel Stewart's and Lieutenant-Colonel Ramsay's battalions to form on a piece of ground, which he judged suitable for giving a check to the enemy; and, having directed General Lee to take proper measures with the residue of his force to stop the British columns on that ground, he rode back himself to arrange the rear division of the army. His orders were executed with firmness. A sharp conflict ensued; and though Lee was forced from the ground on which he had been placed, he brought off his troops in good order, and was then directed to form in the rear of Englishtown. The check which he had given to the enemy procured time to make a disposition of the left wing, and second line of the American army, in the wood, and on the eminence to which Lee was retreating. Lord Stirling, who commanded the left wing, placed some cannon on the eminence, which, with the cooperation of some parties of infantry, effectually stopped the advance of the British in that quarter. The enemy attempted to turn the left flank of the Americans, but were repulsed. They also made a movement to the right, but were there repelled by General Greene, who had taken a very advantageous position. Wayne, advancing with a body of troops, kept up so severe and well-directed a fire, that the British soon gave way, and took the position which Lee had before occupied, where the action commenced immediately after the arrival of General Washington. Here the British line was formed on very strong ground. Both flanks were secured by the woods and morasses, and their front could only be reached through a narrow pass. The day had been intensely hot, and the troops were greatly fatigued; yet General Washington resolved to renew the engagement. He ordered Brigadier-General Poor, with his own and the Carolina brigade, to gain the enemy's right flank, while Woodford, with his brigade, should turn their left. The artillery was ordered at the same time to advance and play on them in front. These orders were promptly obeyed: but there were so many impediments to be overcome, that before the attack could be commenced, it was nearly dark. It was therefore thought most advisable to postpone further operations until morning; and the troops lay on their arms in the field of battle. General Washington, who had been exceedingly active through the day, and entirely regardless of personal danger, reposed himself at night in his cloak, under a tree, in the midst of his soldiers. His intention of renewing the battle was frustrated. The British troops marched about midnight, in such profound silence, that the most advanced posts, and those very near, knew nothing of their departure until morning."

[298]

Northumberland, on the Susquehanna

(At the Junction of the East and West Branches)

THE comfort and prosperity of the towns on this and other central rivers, in the middle states, have been dearly bought by the sacrifices of the pioneers, who went in advance of civilization, and over whose graves the grass is hardly yet matted with time. It is necessary to look back constantly to the recent date of the chronicles of those border contests, to realize that centuries have not elapsed since these flourishing fields were contended for, hand to hand, by the white and the red man.

It was only in 1778, that the increasing inroads on the settlements in this part of the country compelled many of the inhabitants to abandon their farms, and congregate at the rude forts scattered along the frontier, where they could resist, to more advantage, the dangers which threatened them. An exciting tale is recorded of a contest between an old man and two Indians, under the following circumstances.

David Morgan, the hero of the story, was upwards of sixty years of age. He owned a small farm about a mile from one of the forts; and on the day of the adventure, not feeling very well, he had sent his son and daughter to feed the cattle, at the deserted barn, and had gone to bed, in the fort. As he slept, he dreamed that he saw his children making towards him, scalped. The fancy was so vivid, that he started from his sleep, and, finding they had not returned, took his gun, and walked out rapidly to find them. He reached the farm in great agitation, but the children were there, and he sat down on a log to recover his composure. He had not sat long, before two Indians came out of the house, and made towards his son and daughter, who were at a little distance, preparing the ground for melons. Fearing to alarm them too much, and thus deprive them of the power of escaping, he kept his seat; and, in his usual tone of voice, apprised them of their danger, and told them to run towards the fort. The savages raised a terrific cry, and started in pursuit: but the old man showing himself at the same instant, they took to the shelter of the trees. Morgan then attempted to follow his children; but in a minute or two, finding that the savages gained upon him, he turned to fire. They instantly sprang behind trees, and the old man did the same, taking aim at one of the Indians, whose refuge, a small sapling, did not entirely cover his body. As he was on the point of firing, the savage felt his exposure, and dropped behind a prostrate log, close at his feet. The next instant the reserved shot took effect, be-

NORTHUMBERLAND, ON THE SUSQUEHANNA

neath the log, and the Indian rolled over, stabbing himself twice in the breast.

Having disposed of one of his foes, Morgan abandoned the shelter of his tree, and took to flight. The Indian pursued, and the race was continued about sixty yards, when, looking over his shoulder, the old man saw the gun raised, within a few paces of him. He sprang aside, and the ball whizzed harmlessly by. It was now a more equal contest; and Morgan struck at the Indian with his gun, receiving at the same instant a blow from a tomahawk, which severed one of the fingers from his left hand. They closed immediately, and the Indian was thrown; but overturned the old man, with a powerful effort; and, sitting on his breast, uttered his yell of victory, and felt for his knife. A woman's apron, which he had stolen from the farm-house, and tied around his waist, embarrassed him; and Morgan seized one of his hands between his teeth, and, getting hold, himself, of the handle of the knife, drew it so sharply through the Indian's fingers, as to wound him severely. In the struggle, they regained their feet, and still retaining his hold on the fingers in his mouth, Morgan gave him a stab, which decided the contest. The savage fell, and, afraid that others of the tribe might be lurking near, the exhausted old man made the best of his way to the fort.

A party immediately went out to the spot where the struggle had taken place, but the fallen Indian was not to be seen. They tracked him by his blood to a fallen tree, where he was endeavouring to stanch his wounds with the stolen apron. On their approaching him, he affected to smile, and endeavoured to conciliate them, crying out, in his broken English, "How do, broder? how do, broder?" There was little mercy in store for him, however. To the shame of our white race, it is recorded that "they tomahawked and scalped him: and afterwards flaying both him and his companion, they converted their skins into saddle-seats and pouches!"

Pulpit Rock, White Mountains

THE name given to this fine fragment of the White Mountains, indicates very fairly the favourite vein of association in the minds of the first Puritan settlers of New Hampshire; but it looks as much like a pulpit as many other rocks in the bold scenery of New England, of which we know at least a dozen by the same name. Settled by the same class of stern religionists as Massachusetts, New Hampshire has not upon its history the same blot of fanaticism. The tragical era of persecution for witchcraft in Massachusetts had no corresponding abomination in New Hampshire. The two or three cases on record are rather amusing—particularly that inserted in the historical collections, under the title of "The Complaint of Susan Trimmings, of Little Harbour, Piscatagua." The complaint and evidence were as follows:—

"On Lord's-day, 30th of March, at night, going home with Goodwife Barton, she separated from her at the freshet next her house. On her return, between Goodman Evens's and Robert Davis's, she heard a rustling in the woods, which she at first thought was occasioned by swine; and presently after, there did appear to her a woman, whom she apprehended to be old Goodwife Walford. She asked me where my consort was; I answered, I had none. She said, thy consort is at home by this time: lend me a pound of cotton. I told her I had but two pounds in the house, and I would not spare any to my mother. She said I had better have done it; that my sorrow was great already, and it should be greater; for I was going a great journey, but should never come there. She then left me; and I was struck *as with a clap of fire* on the back, and she vanished towards the waterside, in my apprehension, in the *shape of a cat*. She had on her head a white linen hood tied under her chin, and her waistcoat and petticoat were red, with an old green apron, and a black hat upon her head."—Taken upon oath, 18th April, 1656.

"Her husband (Oliver) says, she came home in a sad condition. She passed by me with her child in her arms, laid the child on the bed, sat down on the chest, and leaned upon her elbow. Three times I asked her how she did. She could not speak. I took her in my arms and held her up, and repeated the question. She forced breath, and something stopped in her throat as if it would have stopped her breath. I unlaced her clothes, and soon she spake and said, 'Lord, have mercy upon me, this wicked woman will kill me.' I asked her what woman? she said, Goodwife Walford. I tried to persuade her it was only her weakness. She told me no; and related as above, that her back was as a flame of fire, and her lower parts were as it were numb, and without feeling. I pinched her, and she felt not. She continued that night, and the day and night following, very ill, and is still bad of her limbs, and complains still daily of it.

"A witness deposed, June 1656, that he was at Goodman Walford's, 30th March, 1656, at the time mentioned by Mrs. Trimmings, and that Good-

PULPIT ROCK, WHITE MOUNTAINS

wife Walford was at home till quite dark, as well as she ever was in her life.

"*Nicholas Rowe* testified that Jane Walford, shortly after she was accused, came to the deponent in bed in the evening, and put her hand upon his breast, so that he could not speak, and was in great pain till the next day. By the light of the fire in the next room it appeared to be Goody Walford, but she did not speak. She repeated her visit about a week after, and did as before, but said nothing.

"*Eliza Barton* deposed that she saw Susannah Trimmings at the time she was ill, and her face was coloured and spotted with several colours. She told the deponent the story, who replied, that it was nothing but her *fantasy;* her eyes looked as if they had been scalded.

"*John Puddington* deposed that three years since, Goodwife Walford came to his mother's. She said that her own husband called her an old witch; and when she came to her cattle, her husband would bid her begone, for she did overlook the cattle; which is as much as to say, in our country, *bewitching*.

"*Agnes Puddington* deposes, that, on the 11th of April, 1656, the wife of W. Evens came to her house, and lay there all night; and a little after sun-set, the deponent saw a yellowish cat; and Mrs. E. said she was followed by a cat wherever she went. John came and saw a cat in the garden—took down his gun to shoot her; the cat got up on a tree, and the gun would not take fire, and afterwards would not stand cocked. She afterwards saw three cats; the yellow one vanished away on a plain ground; she could not tell which way they went.

"*John Puddington* testifies to the same effect.

"Three other deponents say they heard Eliza, the wife of Nicholas Rowe, say, that *there were three men witches at Strawberry Bank;* one was Thomas Lurpin, who was drowned; another, old Hans; and the third should be 'nameless,' because he should be blameless. Goodwife Walford was bound over to the next Court.

"*Court of Associates*, *June*, 1656.

"Jane Walford being brought to this court upon suspicion of being a witch, is to continue bound until the next court, to be responsive.

"This complaint was probably *dropped* at the *next term*. Goodwife Walford brought an action of slander in the County Court, 22d of March, 1669, against one Robert Coutch, and laid her damages at one thousand pounds.

"Declaration in an action of slander for saying that the said Jane was a witch, and he could prove her one, which is greatly to her damage.

"Verdict for plaintiff, Walford, five pounds, and costs of court."

[304]

View of Hudson, and the Catskill Mountains

A WEDGE-SHAPED promontory, or bluff, pushes forward to the river at this spot; and on its summit, which widens into a noble plain, stands the city of Hudson. The business of the place is chiefly done in a simple street, which runs at right angles from the river. Its growth at first was remarkably rapid; but the resources of the surrounding country were found inadequate to second its prosperity, and its trade has accordingly been nearly stationary for a number of years. The enterprise of the citizens, however, has found a new source of wealth in the whale fishery.

It is supposed that the Halve-Mane, the vessel in which the great discoverer made his first passage up the Hudson, reached no farther than two leagues above the city which bears his name, and that the remainder of the exploring voyage was made in the shallop. His reception here was in the highest degree hospitable. "He went on shore in one of their canoes, with an old Indian, who was the chief of forty men, and seventeen women: these he saw in a house made of the bark of trees, exceedingly smooth and well-finished within and without. He found a great quantity of Indian corn and beans, enough of which were drying near the house to have loaded three ships, besides what was growing on the fields. On coming to the house, two mats were spread to sit on, eatables were brought in, in red bowls, well made; and two men were sent off with bows and arrows, who soon returned with two pigeons. They also killed a fat dog, and skinned it with shells. They expected their visitors would remain during the night, but the latter determined to return on board. The natives were exceedingly kind and good-tempered; for when they discovered Hudson's determination to proceed on board, they, imagining it proceeded from fear of their bows and arrows, broke them to pieces, and threw them into the fire."

On his return down the river, Hudson stopped again for four days opposite the site of the future city. The historical collections give a very particular account of every day's movements in this interesting voyage. "On the report of those whom he had sent to explore the river," says the historian, "Hudson found that it would be useless to proceed with his ship any farther, or to delay his return. He had passed several days in a profitable traffic, and a friendly intercourse with the natives; among whom were probably those from each side of the river—the *Mahicanni*, as well as the Mohawks. At noon of the 23d of September, he therefore went down six miles to a shoal: having but little

VIEW OF HUDSON, AND THE CATSKILL MOUNTAINS

wind, the tide laid his ship on the bar until the flood came, when she crossed it, and was anchored for the night.

"The next day, after proceeding seven or eight leagues, she grounded on a bank of ooze in the middle of the river, where she was detained till the ensuing morning, when the flood, at ten o'clock, enabled Hudson to anchor her in deep water. Thus the ship once more was interrupted in her passage opposite the spot where a city now commemorates the name of Hudson.

"Here he remained, by reason of adverse winds, four days. On the day of his arrival, 'they went on land and gathered good store of chestnuts;' but whether on the east or west side of the river, is not mentioned. But the day following they went on land, 'to walk on the west side of the river, and found good ground for corn, and other garden herbs, with good store of goodly oaks and walnut-trees, and chestnut-trees, yew-trees, and trees of sweet wood, in great abundance, and great store of *slate for houses, and other good stones*.' Nothing is said of any inhabitants while they were thus visiting the site, which is now that of the village of Athens, opposite Hudson. But, next morning (26th), after the carpenter, mate, and four of the company, had gone on shore to cut wood, while the vessel lay at anchor, two canoes came up the river from the place where they first found 'loving people,' (Catskill landing,) and in one of them was the old chief whom Hudson had caused to be made intoxicated at Albany. He had followed our strange visitors thirty miles, to the base of the Catskill mountains, with the double view of again testifying to Hudson the sincerity of his friendship, and of gratifying the love of the marvellous, by relating his own adventures to the mountaineers, and drawing them from their retreat to witness the floating phenomenon. The old chief now introduced with him 'an old man, who brought more stropes of beads, and gave them to our master, and showed him all the country thereabout, as though it were at his command!' They tarried, greatly pleased with the unaccountable curiosities they discovered on board. Hudson 'made the two old men dine with him, and the old man's wife; for they brought two old women, and two young maidens of the age of sixteen or seventeen years with them, who behaved themselves very modestly.'

"After dinner, and upon exchange of presents, the guests retired, inviting Hudson by signs to come down to them; for the ship was within two leagues of the place where they dwelt."

The concluding circumstances of this interesting return down the Hudson, will accompany another view in the series.

Scene Among the Highlands on Lake George

HAVING dwelt upon the scenery of this celebrated Lake in other pages of this work, let us glance here at the events which took place upon its borders during the war between the French and the British colonies, in 1755.

The Baron de Dieskau had arrived from France, in company with De Vaudreuil, Governor General of Canada, bringing with him three thousand regular troops, destined to make war on the English colonies. Landing at Quebec, his first instructions were to reduce Osnego, but intelligence reaching the Governor that a considerable force was collecting at Lake Sacrament (now Lake George) with the probable intention of invading Canada, Baron Dieskau changed his route, and proceeded up Lake Champlain.

The provincial army was commanded by Colonel, afterwards Sir William, Johnson; and it was in alliance with a considerable body of Indians, under the command of the celebrated chief Hendrick, the great Mohawk Sachem. In Johnson's official report he is called "a valiant warrior, and a faithful friend."

After a fruitless attempt to surprise and take Fort Edwards, Dieskau advanced toward the head of Lake George. On the first intimation of his approach, a council of war was called by Colonel Johnson, and it was determined that a party should go out to meet him. The number of men fixed upon was mentioned by Johnson to Hendrick. The Sachem replied, "If they are to fight, they are too few; if they are to be killed, they are too many." The number was accordingly increased. General Johnson, also, proposed to divide them into three parties. Hendrick took three sticks, and putting them together, said to him, "Put these together, and you cannot break them; take them one by one, and you will break them easily." The hint succeeded, and Hendrick's sticks probably saved the whole army from destruction.

The detached party consisted of twelve hundred, commanded by Colonel Williams. He met the enemy about four miles from Lake George. Dieskau had been informed of his approach by scouts, and arranged his men on both sides of the road in a half-moon, to receive them. The whole country was a forest, and Williams impetuously marched directly into the hollow. At the same instant, a tremendous fire was opened on him in front, and on both his flanks; and Johnson and Hendrick fell among the heaps of the slain, the latter displaying the highest courage and valour. His death was embittered by the disgrace of receiving the mortal wound in his back, and his last breath was spent in lamenting it.

SCENE AMONG THE HIGHLANDS, ON LAKE GEORGE

The overpowered detachment fell back in good order upon the entrenchments, and the enemy advanced to the position of General Johnson, which was upon the shore of Lake George. They began the engagement by firing in platoons upon the centre, but did little injury. After an hour or two of manœuvering and skirmishing, the English leaped over their breast-works, and charged upon the enemy. They broke, and fled in every direction; and Dieskau was found by a soldier, resting on a stump, with scarcely an attendant. As he was feeling for his watch to give it to the soldier, the man, thinking he was feeling for a pistol, discharged his musket through his hips. He was carried into camp in a blanket by eight men, with the greatest care and tenderness, but in extreme agony. For some reason or other, the flying enemy was not pursued, and few were taken prisoners. They had fought with great bravery, and had kept the field till one-third of their number was cut down— a thousand being left dead on the field.

On their retreat, the French army was met by a party of provincial militia, amounting in all to a hundred and fifty men. With the loss of only six men, (among whom was the second in command, Captain M'Ginnes,) this small body of men succeeded in driving the French from their ground, and possessing themselves of all the ammunition and baggage of the flying army. His Majesty was so well pleased with the result of this battle, that he created General Johnson a baronet, and Parliament voted him a present of 5000*l*.

The Sachem Hendrick had lived a life of unsullied bravery, and died fighting gallantly. He was at this time from sixty to seventy years of age. His head was covered with white locks, and, what is uncommon among Indians, he was corpulent. Immediately before the march, he mounted a rock and addressed his people. He had a voice of great depth and power, and could be heard distinctly half a mile. His eloquence is represented as fiery and impressive to a degree, unusual even among this nation of orators. It is said, that when his death was announced to his son, the young chief gave a single groan; but immediately recovered himself, and striking his hand on his breast, rose with great dignity and said, his father was still alive in his son's bosom.

Dieskau was conveyed from Albany to New York, and thence to England, where he soon after died.

Schuylkill Water-Works, at Philadelphia

THE Water-works of Philadelphia rank among the most noble public under-takings of the world. The paucity of water in the city first set to work the sagacious mind of Dr. Franklin, who, by will, bequeathed a portion of a long accumulated legacy to bring a greater supply of this necessary element from Wissahiccon Creek. This was found, after a while, to be insufficient; and a plan was proposed, and carried into operation, to form a reservoir on the east bank of the Schuylkill, from which water was to be thrown by a steam-engine into a tunnel, conveyed to a central position, and raised by a second engine to a higher reservoir, which supplied all the pipes in the city. An experience of ten years satisfied the corporation that a sufficient supply could not be ob-tained by this method. The steam-engines were liable to frequent accidents, and the derangement of one stopped the supply of the whole city. After several other futile experiments, the present extensive yet simple water-works were proposed, and three hundred and fifty thousand dollars voted at once by the city corporation for the commencement of the undertaking.

The Schuylkill opposite Philadelphia, is about nine hundred feet in breadth. It is subject to sudden *freshets*, (an American word, unknown in this use in England, and meaning an overflow of a river current,) but its average depth is thirty feet at high water. It was necessary to back the river up about six miles; and a dam was then created by cribs and masonry, running diagonally across, with several ingenious contrivances to prevent damage by ice and spring freshets. An overfall of one thousand two hundred and four feet, form-ing a beautiful feature of the scenery, is thus created, and a water-power upon the wheels sufficient to raise eleven millions of gallons in twenty-four hours. The reservoirs, elevated above the top of the highest house in the city, crown the ornamental hill which overhangs the river at this place; and water can thus be conveyed to every quarter of Philadelphia, and made to spring, as if by a magic touch, in the highest chamber of the inhabitant. It is of a deli-ciously soft and pleasant quality; and those who are habituated to wash in the "city of brotherly love," are spoiled for the less agreeable lavations afforded by other towns in America.

Fair Mount is a beautiful spot; and standing, as it does, just on the skirt of the town, it serves the additional use of a place of pleasant and healthful pub-lic resort. The buildings containing the pump-rooms have considerable pre-tensions to architecture; and the *façades* and galleries extend along the river, forming a showy object from every point of view, but from the absence of any

[311]

SCHUYLKILL WATER-WORKS, AT PHILADELPHIA

grand design in the whole, failing of a general fine effect, and presenting what a Londoner would call rather a teagardenish appearance. Steps and terraces conduct to the reservoirs, and thence the view over the ornamented grounds of the country seats opposite, and of a very picturesque and uneven country beyond, is exceedingly attractive. Below, the court of the principal building is laid out with gravel walks, and ornamented with fountains and flowering trees; and within the edifice there is a public drawing-room, of neat design and furniture; while in another wing are elegant refreshment-rooms—and, in short, all the appliances and means of a place of public amusement.

It may as well be remarked here, that this last advantage is less improved in America than it would be in any other country. The Water-works of Fair Mount, though within fifteen minutes' walk of every citizen's dwelling in Philadelphia, are (comparatively to its capacities) unfrequented. In several visits made to them in fine weather, we scarce saw more than three or four persons in the grounds; and those seemed looking for other company, more than enjoying the refreshing fountains and lovely prospects around them. As a people, we have no habit of amusement in America. Business and repose are the only two states of existence we know. How far Europeans have the better of us in this respect—how much our morals improve, or our health suffers, from the distaste for places of public relaxation and resort, are questions the political economists have not yet condescended to settle.

VIEW OF THE UNITED STATES BANK, PHILADELPHIA

View of the United States Bank, Philadelphia

THIS is one of those chaste and beautiful buildings which have given the public architecture of Philadelphia a superiority over that of every other city of our country. It needs but that its fair marble should be weather-fretted and stained, to express perfectly to the eye the model of one of the most graceful temples of antiquity. The severe simplicity of taste which breathes through this Greek model, however, is not adapted to private buildings; and in a certain kind of simplicity, or rather of want of ornament, lies the fault found by every eye in the domestic architecture of this city. The chess-board regularity of the streets, so embarrassing to a stranger, as well as tiresome to the gaze, require a more varied, if not a more ornate style. The hundreds of houses that resemble each other in every distinguishable particular, occasion a bewilderment and fatigue to the unaccustomed eye, which a citizen of Philadelphia can scarcely comprehend.

The uniformity and plainness which William Penn has bequeathed in such an abiding legacy to Philadelphia, however, is seen but by a faint *penumbra* in the dress of the inhabitants, or in their equipages, style of living, and costliness of furniture and entertainment. A faint shadow of original simplicity there still certainly exists, visible through all the departures from the spirit of Quakerism; and it is a leaven of taste and elegance in the ferment of luxury which has given Philadelphia emphatically a character for refinement. A more delightful temper and tone of society, a more enjoyable state of the exercise and mode of hospitality, or a more comfortable metropolis to live in, certainly does not exist this side the water. A European would prefer Philadelphia to every other residence in the United States.

Is it possible to realize, that, on the site of this refined capital, only a hundred and fifty years ago, lived a people in such strong contrast to the above, (save only in hospitality,) as are described by William Penn in the following terms!—

"The natives I shall consider in their persons, language, manners, religion, and government, with my sense of their original. For their persons, they are generally tall, straight, well-built, and of singular proportion; they tread strong and clever, and mostly walk with a lofty chin. Of complexion, black, but by design, as the gypsies in England: they grease themselves with bear's fat, clarified; and using no defence against sun or weather, their skins must needs be swarthy. Their eye is little and black, not unlike a straight-looked Jew. The thick lip and flat nose, so frequent with the East Indians and Blacks, are not common to them; many of them have fine Roman noses.

"Their language is lofty, yet narrow; but like the Hebrew, in significa-tion full. Like short-hand in writing, one word serveth in the place of three, and the rest are supplied by the understanding of the hearer; imperfect in their tenses, wanting in their moods, participles, adverbs, conjunctions, and interjections.

"Of their customs and manners there is much to be said: I will begin with children. So soon as they are born, they wash them in water; and while very young, and in cold weather, they plunge them in the rivers, to harden and embolden them. The children will go very young—at nine months, commonly: if boys, they go a fishing till ripe for the woods, which is about fifteen; then they hunt, and after having given some proofs of their manhood by a good return of skins, they may marry; else it is a shame to think of a wife. The girls stay with their mothers, and help to hoe the ground, plant corn, and carry burdens: and they do well to use them to that young, which they must do when they are old; for the wives are the true servants of the husbands, other-wise the men are very affectionate to them.

"When the young women are fit for marriage, they wear something upon their heads for an advertisement, but so as their faces are hardly to be seen but when they please. The age they marry at, if women, is about thirteen and fourteen; if men, seventeen and eighteen; they are rarely elder.

"Their houses are mats, or barks of trees, set on poles, in the fashion of an English barn, but out of the power of the winds, for they are hardly higher than a man: they lie on reeds, or grass. In travel, they lodge in the woods, about a great fire, with the mantle of duffils they wear by day wrapt about them, and a few boughs stuck round them.

"Their diet is maize, or Indian corn, divers ways prepared; sometimes roasted in the ashes; sometimes beaten and boiled with water, which they call *homine;* they also make cakes not unpleasant to eat. They have likewise sev-eral sorts of beans and peas that are good nourishment; and the woods and rivers are their larder."

Brock's Monument from the American Side

LEWISTON is seldom seen to advantage by the traveller, who, in his eagerness to reach Niagara, if going thither, or in the fulness of his recollections, if
returning, pays it very little attention. The village itself is as dull and indif-
ferent-looking a place as one would chance to see; but it stands at the outlet of
Niagara river into Lake Ontario, and its neighbourhood on all sides is picturesque and beautiful.

Across the river, on the heights of Queenstown, stands the Monument of
General Brock, who died fighting very gallantly on this spot. A slight *resumer*
of the hard-fought battle of Queenstown, which was creditable to the courage
and spirit of both countries, will be in place accompanying this view.

The American forces on the Niagara river consisted of about five thousand eight hundred men, under the command of Colonel Van Rensellaer.
Eighteen hundred of these were at Black Rock, twenty-eight miles distant,
and the remainder at Fort Niagara, under the General's personal command.
Several skirmishes on the St. Lawrence had resulted in favour of the Americans, and the forces at Lewiston were very anxious to have an opportunity for
action.

Directly opposite to the camp, on the other side of the river, lay Queenstown, strongly fortified, and garrisoned by a large force, waiting the orders
of General Brock, then in Michigan. It was supposed that preparations were
making for a general attack on the frontier. The possession of this place was
considered very important to the Americans, as it was the port for all the
merchandise of the country above, and a depôt of public stores for the line of
English posts on Niagara and Detroit rivers. It has besides, an excellent harbour, and good anchorage.

An attack on Queenstown was projected for the night of the 11th of October. It failed, however, in consequence of a tremendous storm, and of the loss
of a boat containing all the oars for the ferriage. Better arrangements were
completed by the night of the 12th, and on the morning of the 13th, three
hundred regular troops, and three hundred militia, were ready at dawn of
day to cross to the attack.

The river here is one sheet of violent eddies, and the boating very difficult
and laborious. A battery, mounting two eighteen-pounders and two sixes,
protected the embarkation, and the boats put off. The enemy had been apprised of these preparations, and a brisk fire of musquetry immediately
opened along the shore, on the Canada side, which, from the slow progress of

BROCK'S MONUMENT FROM THE AMERICAN SIDE

the boats, did great execution. One of the boats was hit by a grape shot, which threw the pilot and oarsmen into such confusion, that they were carried down by the stream and obliged to return, and two others dropped below the landing, and fell into the hands of the enemy. Colonel Van Rensellaer, however, succeeded in landing with about a hundred men, under a tremendous fire, and immediately ascended the precipitous bank of the river. Before reaching the summit, he received four balls, and two of his officers were killed, and three wounded. Retiring under the shelter of the bank, Colonel Van Rensellaer had still sufficient strength to give the order for storming the fort; and about sixty men, commanded by Captain Ogilvie, seconded by Captain Wool, who was previously wounded, mounted the rocks on the right of the fort, gave three cheers, and with three desperate charges obtained entire possession; they then carried the heights, and spiked the cannon.

Reinforcements had by this time crossed the river, and the Americans formed on the heights, under the command of Colonel Christie. General Brock, who was on his way to Queenstown, having been met by an express, arrived with a reinforcement of regulars from Fort George, and immediately led his men into the rear of the captured battery. Captain Wool detached one hundred and sixty men to meet him, but the detachment was driven back. It was reinforced once more, and driven again to the brow of the precipice overhanging the river. An American officer at this time, despairing of the attempt, was about raising a white handkerchief on a bayonet, when Captain Wool tore it off, and ordered the men once more to charge. At this moment, Colonel Christie came up with a reinforcement, and repeating Captain Wool's orders, the American force, amounting then to about three hundred, pushed forward and entirely routed the British 49th, who were aided by the 41st, and who had hitherto been called the Egyptian Invincibles. General Brock was attempting to rally these two regiments, when he received three balls, and died almost immediately.

The British formed again in an hour or two, and were reinforced by several hundred Indians from Chippeway, and other regiments of their own from other posts. Attempting to re-embark and retreat before a force so much superior, the boats were found insufficient, and the American regiments, after fighting nearly twelve hours, surrendered prisoners of war, to the number of seven hundred.

On the burial of General Brock the succeeding day, the batteries on the American side fired during the ceremony, as a tribute of respect to a gallant soldier.

VILLAGE OF CATSKILL, HUDSON RIVER

Village of Catskill, Hudson River

CATSKILL is more known as the landing-place for travellers bound to the mountains above, than for any remarkable events in its own history, or any singular beauties in itself. It is a thrifty little village, in which the most prosperous vocations are those of inn-keeper and stage-proprietor, and, during the summer months, these two crafts at Catskill entertain and transport to the hotel on the mountain half the population of the United States—more or less. The crowded steamers stop at the landing on their way up and down; and a busier scene than is presented on the wharf twice in the day, for a minute and a half, could not easily be found.

I have often thought in passing, of the contrast between these numerous advents and the landing of Hendrick Hudson on this very spot, in his voyage of discovery up the river. He found here, he says, "a very loving people, and a very old man," by whom he and his crew were very kindly entertained. From the first step of a white man's foot on the soil to the crowded rush of passengers from a steam-boat—from a savage wilderness to the height of civilization and science, it is but a little more than two hundred years of rapid history. Compare the old Indian canoe in which Hudson went from his vessel to the land, with a steamer carrying on its deck near a thousand souls; compare the untutored population which then swarmed upon the shore to the cultivated and refined crowds who come and go in thousands on the same spot, and the contrast is as astonishing as the extinction of the aboriginal race is melancholy.

It is surprising how few details connected with the races that inhabited the older settlements of our country are reached even by the researches of Historical Societies. The materials for the future poets and historians of America, are, in this department, singularly meagre, though it might almost be supposed that the very tracks of the retreating tribes might at this early day be still visible on the soil. Wherever any particulars of the intercourse between the first settlers and the Indians are preserved, they are highly curious, and often very diverting. In a book on the settlements of this country, written by Capt. Nathaniel Uring, who visited it in 1709, there is an amusing story connected with the history of one of the forts, built, by permission of the Indians, to secure the settlers against sudden incursion.

"It happened one day," says the Captain, relating the story as it was told him by the Governor, "as the carpenter was cutting down a large timber-tree for the use of the fort, that great numbers of Indians stood round it, gazing, and admiring the wonderful dexterity of the carpenter, and greatly surprised at the manner of cutting it; having, before the arrival of the Europeans, never seen an axe, or any such like tools. The carpenter, perceiving the tree ready to fall, gave notice to the Indians by language or signs to keep out of its reach when it fell; but either for want of understanding the carpenter, or by carelessness of the Indians, a branch of the tree, in its fall, struck one of them, and killed him; upon which they raised a great cry. The carpenter, seeing them much out of humour at the accident, made his escape into the fort; and soon after, the Indians gathered together in great numbers about it, and demanded justice of the Europeans for the death of their brother, and desired to have the man who was the occasion of his being killed, that they might execute him, and revenge their brother's death. The governor endeavoured to excuse the carpenter, by representing to them that he was not to blame, and told them that if their brother had observed the notice given him by the carpenter, he had not been hurt; but that answer would not satisfy the Indians; they increased their numbers about the fort, and nothing less than the execution of the carpenter would content them.

"The Europeans endeavoured to spin out the time by treaty, and thought to appease them by presents, hoping those, and time together, might make them easy; but finding that would not do, and not being able longer to defend themselves against such numbers as besieged them, they consulted how to give the Indians satisfaction.

"The carpenter being a useful man, they considered that they could not spare him without the greatest inconvenience; but seeing there was an absolute necessity of doing something, they found out an expedient, which was this:—there was in the fort an old weaver who had been bed-rid a long time; *they concluded to hang up the weaver, and make the Indians believe it was the carpenter.*

"Having come to this resolution, the governor let the Indians know, that, since nothing else would satisfy them, though their demand was unjust, yet, to show them how ready they were to live in amity and friendship with them, that in the morning they should see the carpenter hanging upon a certain tree in their view.

"In the night they carried the poor old weaver and hanged him in the room of the carpenter, which gave full satisfaction to the Indians, and they were again good friends."

View from Gowan's Heights, Brooklyn

THE Bay of New York and Staten Island, are, from this elevated point of view, laid out beautifully beneath the eye, but the picturesque interest of the spot yields to the historic. Directly below these heights was fought the battle so disastrous to the revolutionary forces, between the detachments commanded by Sullivan and Putnam, and the English army, under Generals Howe and Clinton. As the defence of Long Island was intimately connected with that of New York, Washington had stationed a brigade at Brooklyn; and an extensive camp had been marked out and fortified, fronting the main land of Long Island, and stretching quite across the peninsula occupied by the village of Brooklyn. When the movements of General Howe threatened an immediate attack on this position, Major-General Putnam was directed to take the command, with a reinforcement of six regiments; and the day previous to the action Washington passed entirely at Brooklyn, inspecting the works, and encouraging the soldiers.

The Hessians, under General De Heister, composed the centre of the British army at Flatbush. Major-General Grant commanded the left wing, which extended to the coast, and the greater part of the forces under General Clinton. Earl Percy and Lord Cornwallis turned short to the right, and approached the opposite coast of Flatland.

On the night previous to the action, General Clinton was successful in seizing a pass through the heights, leading into the level country between them and Brooklyn. Before this movement was completed, General Grant advanced along the coast, at the head of the left wing, with ten pieces of cannon. As his first object was to draw the attention of the Americans from their left, he moved slowly, skirmishing as he advanced, with the light parties stationed on that road.

This movement was soon communicated to General Putnam, who reinforced the parties which had been advanced in front; and as General Grant continued to gain ground, still stronger detachments were employed in this service. About three in the morning, Brigadier-General Lord Stirling was directed to meet the enemy, with the two nearest regiments, on the road leading from the Narrows. Major-General Sullivan, who commanded all the troops without the lines, advanced at the head of a strong detachment on the road leading directly to Flatbush; while another detachment occupied the heights between that place and Bedford.

About the break of day, Lord Stirling reached the summit of the hills,

[323]

VIEW FROM GOWAN'S HEIGHTS, BROOKLYN

where he was joined by the troops which had been already engaged, and were retiring slowly before the enemy, who almost immediately appeared in sight. A warm cannonade was commenced on both sides, which continued for several hours; and some sharp but not very close skirmishing took place between the infantry. Lord Stirling being anxious only to defend the pass he guarded, could not descend in force from the heights; and General Grant did not wish to drive him from them until that part of the plan which had been entrusted to Sir Henry Clinton should be executed.

About half-past eight, the British right having then reached Bedford, in the rear of Sullivan's left, General De Heister ordered Colonel Donop's corps to advance to the attack of the hill, following himself with the centre of the army. The approach of Clinton was now discovered by the American left, which immediately endeavoured to regain the camp at Brooklyn. While retiring from the woods by regiments, they encountered the front of the British. About the same time the Hessians advanced from Flatbush, against that part of the detachment which occupied the direct road to Brooklyn. Here General Sullivan commanded in person; but he found it difficult to keep his troops together long enough to sustain the first attack. The firing heard towards Bedford had disclosed the alarming fact that the British had turned their left flank, and were getting completely into their rear. Perceiving at once the full danger of their situation, they sought to escape it by regaining the camp with the utmost possible celerity. The sudden rout of this party enabled De Heister to detach a part of his force against those who were engaged near Bedford. In that quarter, too, the Americans were broken, and driven back into the woods; and the front of the column led by General Clinton continuing to move forward, intercepted and engaged those who were retreating along the direct road from Flatbush. Thus attacked both in front and rear, and alternately driven by the British on the Hessians, and by the Hessians back again on the British, a succession of skirmishes took place in the woods, in the course of which, some part of the corps forced their way through the enemy and regained the lines of Brooklyn, and several individuals saved themselves under cover of the woods; but a great proportion of the detachment was killed, or taken. The fugitives were pursued up to the American works; and such is represented to have been the ardour of the British soldiers, that it required the authority of their cautious commander to prevent an immediate assault.

The fire towards Brooklyn gave the first intimation to the American right that the enemy had gained their rear. Lord Stirling perceived the danger, and that he could only escape it by retreating instantly across the creek. After one other gallant attempt, however, upon a British corps under Lord Cornwallis, the brave men he commanded were no longer able to make opposition, and those who survived were, with their general, made prisoners of war.

The British army were masters of the field, but before morning, Washington had won one of his brightest military laurels in the safe withdrawal, unperceived by the enemy, of his defeated and dispirited troops to the opposite shore of New York.

View on the Susquehanna

(Above Owago, or at Grand Island)

THE spectator in this view looks up the Susquehanna, with the river behind as well as before him; for the mountain on which he stands is almost encircled by the bend with which it turns downward to Owago. It is, perhaps, the best view that could be taken to express the etymology of its name, (Crooked River,) besides being one of singular beauty. I regretted only when the artist was there, that the rafts and arks with which the river is for a great part of the year enlivened, were, from the low state of the water, entirely wanting. The wild navigation of these crafts gives the Susquehanna a picturesque character, which, to do it pictorial justice, should not be omitted in the drawing. Perhaps the amends may be partially made to the reader's imagination by quoting an account of the raftsmen, written in a letter to a friend: —

"This part of the country is not destitute of the chances of adventure, however; and twice in the year, at least, you may, if you choose, open a valve for your spirits. One half the population of the neighbourhood is engaged in what is called *lumbering*, and until the pine timber of the forest can be counted like the cedars of Lebanon, this vocation will serve the uses of the mobs of England, the revolutions of France, and the plots of Italy—I may add, the music and theatres of Austria and Russia, the sensual indulgence of the Turk, and the intrigue of the Spaniard; for there is in every people under the sun a *superflu* of spirits unconsumed by common occupation, which, if not turned adroitly

VIEW ON THE SUSQUEHANNA

(ABOVE OWAGO, OR AT GRAND ISLAND)

or accidentally to some useful or harmless end, will expend its reckless energy in trouble and mischief.

"The preparations for the adventures of which I speak, though laborious, are often conducted like a frolic. The felling of the trees in mid-winter, the cutting of shingles, and the drawing out on the snow, are employments preferred by the young men to the tamer but less arduous work of the farm-yard; and in the temporary and uncomfortable *shanties*, deep in the woods, subsisting often on nothing but pork and whisky, they find metal more attractive than village, or fire-side.

"The small streams emptying into the Susquehanna are innumerable; and eight or ten miles back from the river the arks are built, and the materials of the rafts collected, ready to launch with the first thaw. I live myself, as you know, on one of these tributaries, a quarter of a mile from its junction. The Owago trips along at the foot of my lawn, as private and untroubled for the greater part of the year as Virginia Water and Windsor; but as it swells in March, the noise of voices and hammering coming out from the woods above, warn us of the approach of an ark; and at the rate of eight or ten miles an hour, the rude structure shoots by, floating high on the water, without its lading, (which it takes in at the village below,) and manned with a singing and saucy crew, who dodge the branches of the trees, and work their steering-paddles with an adroitness and nonchalance which sufficiently show the character of the class. The sudden bends which the river takes in describing my woody Owago puts the steermanship to the test; and when the leaves are off the trees, it is a curious sight to see the bulky monsters, shining with new boards, whirling around in the swift eddies, and, when caught by the current again, gliding off among the trees, like a singing and swearing phantom of an unfinished barn.

"At the village they take wheat and pork into the arks, load their rafts with plank and shingles, and wait for the return of the freshets. It is a fact you may not know, that when a river is rising, the middle is the highest, and *vice versâ* when falling—sufficiently proved by the experience of the raftsmen, who, if they start before the flow is at its top, cannot keep their crafts from the shore. A pent-house, barely sufficient for a man to stretch himself below, is raised on the deck, with a fire-place of earth and loose stone; and with what provision they can afford, and plenty of whisky, they shove out into the stream. Thenceforward it is *vogue la galère!* They have nothing to do all day but abandon themselves to the current, sing and dance, and take the turn at the steering-oars; and when the sun sets, they look out for an eddy, and pull in to the shore.

[328]

The stopping-places are not very numerous, and are well known to all who follow the trade; and, as the river swarms with rafts, the getting to land and making sure of a fastening, is a scene always of great competition, and often of desperate fighting. When all is settled for the night, however, and the fires are lit on the long range of the flotilla, the raftsmen get together over their whisky and provender, and tell the thousand stories of their escapes and accidents; and with the repetition of this night after night, the whole rafting population along the five hundred miles of the Susquehanna becomes partially acquainted, and forms a sympathetic *corps*, whose excitement and *esprit* might be roused to very dangerous uses.

"By daylight they are cast off, and once more on the current; and in five or seven days they arrive at tide-water, where the crew is immediately discharged, and starts, usually on foot, to follow the river home again. There are several places in the navigation which are dangerous, such as rapids and dam-sluices; and what with these, and the scenes at the eddies, and their pilgrimage through a thinly-settled and wild country home again, they see enough of adventure to make them fire-side heroes, and incapacitate them, (while their vigour lasts, at least,) for all the more quiet habits of the farmer. The consequence is easy to be seen: agriculture is but partially followed throughout the country, and while these cheap facilities for transporting produce to those aboard exist, those who are contented to stay at home and cultivate the rich river lands of the country, are sure of high prices, and a ready reward for their labour."

BRIDGE AT GLEN'S-FALLS, ON THE HUDSON

Bridge at Glen's–Falls, on the Hudson

FEW of our readers who will not consider this subject as one of the most picturesque in our collection, and yet many of them we fear have passed over the
bridge in our View unconscious of the proximity of so extraordinary a scene
as the Falls of the Hudson at this spot.

This was, at least, our own case when first visiting Lake George, from Saratoga; and we would counsel every one to steal a few moments, even if travelling by the stage, to descend from the covered bridge to the rocky bed of the
river. Miss Martineau observes—"We were all astonished at the splendour
of Glen's Falls. The full, though narrow Hudson, rushes along amidst enormous masses of rock, and leaps sixty feet down the chasms and precipices
which occur in the passage, sweeping between dark banks of shelving rocks
below, its current speckled with foam. The noise is so tremendous, that I cannot conceive how people can fix their dwellings in the immediate neighbourhood. There is a long bridge over the roaring floods, which vibrates incessantly; and clusters of saw-mills deform the scene. There is stone-cutting as
well as planking done at these mills. The fine black marble of the place is cut
into slabs, and sent down to New York to be polished. It was the busiest scene
that I saw near any water-power in America."

Her description is excellent, but, as regards the mills, we cannot agree with
her; they certainly add much to the picturesque effect of the scene.

VIEW FROM MOUNT IDA, NEAR TROY, NEW YORK

View from Mount Ida, Near Troy, New York

THE scenery in this neighbourhood is exceedingly beautiful. The junction of the Mohawk and Hudson, the Falls of the Cohoes, the gay and elegant town of Troy, Albany in the distance, and a foreground of the finest mixture of the elements of landscape, compose a gratification to the eye equalled by few other spots in this country. "Think," says one of our noblest and best writers, speaking of a similar scene—"think of the country for which the Indians fought! Who can blame them? As the river chieftains, the lords of the water-falls and the mountains, ranged this lovely valley, can it be wondered at that they beheld with bitterness the forest disappearing beneath the settler's axe—the fishing-place disturbed by his saw-mills? Can we not fancy the feelings with which some strong-minded savage, who should have ascended the summit of the mountain in company with a friendly settler, contemplating the progress already made by the white man, and marking the gigantic strides with which he was advancing into the wilderness, should fold his arms and say, 'White man, there is eternal war between me and thee! I quit not the land of my fathers but with my life! In those woods where I bent my youthful bow, I will still hunt the deer; over yonder waters I will still glide unrestrained in my bark canoe. By those dashing waterfalls I will still lay up my winter's food; on these fertile meadows I will still plant my corn. Stranger, the land is mine! I understand not these paper rights; I gave not my consent when, as thou sayest, those broad regions were purchased for a few baubles of my fathers. They could sell what was theirs; they could sell no more. How could my father sell that which the Great Spirit sent me into the world to live upon? They knew not what they did. The stranger came, a timid suppliant, few and feeble, and asked to lie down on the red man's bear-skin, and warm himself at the red man's fire, and have a little piece of land to raise corn for his women and children; and now he is become strong, and mighty, and bold, and spreads out his parchment over the whole, and says, It is mine. Stranger, there is not room for us both. The Great Spirit has not made us to live together. There is poison in the white man's cup; the white man's dog barks at the red man's heels. If I should leave the land of my fathers, whither shall I fly? Shall I go to the south, and dwell among the groves of the Pequods? Shall I wander to the west? the fierce Mohawk—the man-eater—is my foe. Shall I fly to the east? —the great water is before me. No, stranger, here have I lived, and here will I die! and if here thou abidest, there is eternal war between me and thee! Thou hast taught me thy arts of destruction, for that alone I thank thee; and now take heed to thy steps; the red man is thy foe. When thou goest forth by day, my bullet shall whistle by thee; when thou liest down at night, my knife is at thy throat. The noon-day sun shall not discover thy enemy, and the darkness of midnight shall not protect thy rest. Thou shalt plant in terror, and I will reap in blood! thou shalt sow the earth with corn, and I will strew it with ashes! thou shalt go forth with the sickle, and I will follow after with the scalping-knife! thou shalt build, and I will burn, till the white man or the Indian shall cease from the land. Go thy way for this time in safety, but remember, stranger, there is eternal war between me and thee!'"

As the same writer afterwards observes, however, the Pilgrim Fathers "purchased the land of those who claimed it, and paid for it—often, more than once. They purchased it for a consideration, trifling to the European, but valuable to the Indian. There is no overreaching in giving but little for that which, in the hands of the original proprietors, is worth nothing."

View from Glenmary Lawn, the Residence of N. P. Willis

(At the Junction of the Owaga and Susquehanna)

THE Owaga here is scarce a quarter of a mile from its junction with the Susquehanna, and the lawn of Glenmary is the western limit of the star of interval land formed by the union of two broad valleys. The river here is a secluded stream, shadowed originally with dark forest trees, and running deep
and still. The farm of Glenmary, part of which is presented in the drawing,
was once an Indian burial-place—warrant enough for its possessing the highest rural beauty. The plough has turned up many skeletons in the fields above,
and a small museum of Indian weapons and domestic implements was collected by the gentleman from whom the land was bought by the writer. Off
to the left of the drawing, (too far off to be brought into the sketch,) a bright
and brawling brook comes leaping down from the hills, and passing by the
cottage door crosses the meadow to pay tribute to the Owaga; and back from
the meadow, by broad and easy terraces, the land rises to the summit of a
mountain ridge, crowned with primeval and gigantic forest trees. Having
possessed the reader thus of the principal features of the spot, I may be excused for filling a page from an epistle to a friend, descriptive of the artist's
visit to Glenmary.

"This is not a very prompt answer to your last, my dear doctor, for I intended to have taken my brains to you bodily, and replied to all your 'whether-
or-noes' over a broiled oyster at Downing's. Perhaps I may bring this in my
pocket. A brace of ramblers, brothers of my own, detained me for a while, but
are flitting today; and Bartlett has been here a week, to whom, more particularly, I wish to do the honours of the scenery. We have climbed every hill-top
that has the happiness of looking down on the Owaga and Susquehanna, and
he agrees with me that a more lovely and habitable valley has never sat to him
for its picture. Fortunately, on the day of his arrival, the dust of a six-weeks'
drought was washed from its face, and, barring the *wilt* that precedes Autumn, the hill-sides were in holiday green, and looked their fairest. He has enriched his portfolio with four or five delicious sketches, and if there were gratitude or sense of renown in trees and hills, they would have nodded their tops
to the two of us. It is not every valley and pine-tree that finds painter and historian, but these are as insensible as beauty and greatness were ever to the
claims of their trumpeters.

VIEW FROM GLENMARY LAWN

"How long since was it that I wrote to you of Bartlett's visit to Constantinople? Not more than four or five weeks, it seems to me; and yet here he is, on his return from a professional trip to *Canada*, with all its best scenery snug in his portmanteau! He steamed to Turkey and back, and steamed again to America, and will be once more in England in some twenty days—having visited and sketched the two extremities of the civilized world. Why, I might farm it on the Susquehanna, and keep my town-house in Constantinople, (with money.) It seemed odd to me to turn over a drawing-book, and find on one leaf a freshly pencilled sketch of a mosque, and on the next a view of Glenmary—my turnip-field in the foreground. And then the man himself—pulling a Turkish para and a Yankee shin-plaster from his pocket with the same pinch—shuffling to breakfast in my *abri* on the Susquehanna, in a pair of peaked slippers of Constantinople, that smell as freshly of the bazaar as if they were bought yesterday—waking up with "*pekke! pekke!* my good fellow!" when William brings him his boots—and never seeing a blood-red maple (just turned with the frost), without fancying it the sanguine flag of the Bosphorus or the bright jacket of a Greek! All this unsettles me strangely. The phantasmagoria of my days of vagabondage flit before my eyes again. This, 'By-the-by, do you remember, in Smyrna?' and, 'The view you recollect from the Seraglio!' and such like slip-slop of travellers, heard within reach of my corn and pumpkins, affects me like the mad poet's proposition,

'To twitch the rainbow from the sky,
And splice both ends together.'

"I have amused my artist friend since he has been here, with an entertainment not quite as expensive as the Holly Lodge fireworks, but quite as beautiful—the burning of log-heaps. Instead of gossipping over the tea-table these long and chilly evenings, the three or four young men who have been staying with us, were very content to tramp into the woods, with a bundle of straw and a match-box; and they have been initiated into the mysteries of 'picking and piling,' to the considerable improvement of the glebe of Glenmary. Shelly says,

'Men scarcely know how beautiful fire is,'

and I am inclined to think that there are varieties of glory in its phenomena which would make it worth even your metropolitan while to come to the west and 'burn fallow.' At this season of the year—after the autumn droughts, that is to say—the whole country here is covered with a thin smoke, stealing up from the fires on every hill, in the depths of the woods, and on the banks of the

[337]

river; and what with the graceful smoke-wreaths by day, and the blazing heavens all around the horizon by night, it adds much to the variety, and I think, more to the beauty of our western October. It edifies the traveller who has bought wood by the pound in Paris, or stiffened for the want of it in the disforested Orient, to stand off a rifle-shot from a crackling wood, and toast himself by a thousand cords burnt for the riddance. What experience I have had of these holocausts on my own land, has not diminished the sense of waste and wealth with which I first watched them. Paddy's dream of 'rolling in a bin of gould guineas,' could scarcely have seemed more luxurious.

"Bartlett and I, and the rest of us, in our small way, burnt up enough, I dare say, to have made a comfortable drawing-room of Hyde Park in January, and the effects of the white light upon the trees above and around were glorious. But our fires were piles of logs and brush—small beer of course to the conflagration of a forest. I have seen one that was like the Thousand Columns of Constantinople, ignited to a red heat, and covered with carbuncles and tongues of flame. It was a temple of fire—the floor living coals—the roof a heaving drapery of crimson—the aisles held up by blazing and innumerable pillars, and sometimes swept by the wind till they stood in still and naked redness, while the eye could see far into their depths, and again covered and wreathed and laved in ever-changing billows of flame. We want an American Tempesta or 'Savage Rosa' to 'wreak' such pictures on canvass; and perhaps the first step to it would be the painting of the foliage of an American Autumn."

View Near Anthony's Nose, Hudson Highlands

THIS mountain, "known to fame," serves as a landmark to the industrious craft plying upon the Hudson, and thus fulfils a more useful destiny than is commonly awarded to spots bright in story. It stands amid a host of interesting localities, marked with the events of the Revolution, and has witnessed, with less damage than other noses, many a conflict by land and water.

On the opposite side of the river from the base of the mountain, lie the two forts Montgomery and Clinton, taken by the British in October, 1777. The commander-in-chief at New York was prompted to this expedition by two ob-

VIEW NEAR ANTHONY'S NOSE, HUDSON HIGHLANDS

jects: to destroy a quantity of military stores which the Americans had collected in this neighbourhood, and to make a diversion in favour of General Burgoyne. For these purposes Sir Henry Clinton embarked between three and four thousand troops at New York, and sailed with them up the Hudson. On the 5th of October they landed at Verplank's Point, a few miles below the entrance to the Highlands. The next morning, a part of the force landed on Stony Point, which projects into the river on the western side, just below the mountains; hence they marched into the rear of the fortresses.

General Putnam commanded at that time in this quarter. He had one thousand continental troops, a part of which only were effective, and a small body of militia. He believed the principal design of the enemy to be the destruction of the stores; and when he was informed of their main purpose, it was too late for him to resist with success. He supposed that they were aiming at Fort Independence, and directed his attention to its defence; the heavy firing on the other side of the river gave him the first decisive information of their real intentions. Mr. Clinton, at that time governor of the state, placed himself at this post on the first notice that he received of the enemy's advancing. Having made the best disposition for the defence of the forts, he despatched an express to General Putnam to acquaint him with his situation; but when it reached his head quarters, that officer and General Parsons were reconnoitering the position of the enemy on the east side of the river.

Lieut.-Col. Campbell, in the mean time, proceeded with nine hundred men by a circuitous march to the rear of Fort Montgomery; while Sir Henry Clinton, with Generals Vaughan and Tryon, moved onwards towards Fort Clinton. Both fortresses were attacked at once, between four and five in the afternoon: they were defended with great resolution. This will be readily admitted, when it is remembered that the whole garrison consisted of but six hundred men. The conflict was carried on till dark, when the British had obtained absolute possession, and such of the Americans as were not killed or wounded had made their escape. The loss of the two garrisons amounted to about two hundred and fifty. Among the killed on the enemy's side was Lieut.-Col. Campbell.

It has been thought that an addition of five or six hundred men to these garrisons would have saved the works; the correctness of this opinion may be doubted. Fifteen hundred soldiers would have been barely sufficient completely to man Fort Montgomery alone. The works themselves were imperfect, and the ground was probably chosen rather for the defence of the river, than because it was itself defensible.

Governor Clinton and his brother, General James Clinton, escaped after the enemy had possession of the forts; the former by crossing the river. The latter had been wounded in the thigh by a bayonet.

On the 8th, the English forces proceeded to the eastern side, where they found Fort Independence evacuated. A party then burnt the continental village, as it was called, a temporary settlement raised up by the war for the accommodation of the army. Here had been gathered a considerable number of those artisans, whose labours are particularly necessary for military purposes; and a considerable quantity of military stores. They then removed a chain which was stretched across the river at Fort Montgomery, and advancing up the river, removed another which was extended from Fort Constitution to the opposite shore at West Point. General Vaughan then advanced still further up the Hudson, and on the 13th reached the town of Kingston, which he burnt. On the 17th, took place the surrender of Burgoyne, and he returned down the Hudson with his fleet to New York.

Count Grabouski, a Polish nobleman, was killed in the assault on Fort Clinton, while acting as aid-de-camp to the British commander. He was buried on the spot, but his grave is now undiscoverable.

Washington's Monument at Baltimore

THIS fine monument stands at the end of a long street, forming an ascending perspective; and as its base crowns the summit of a considerable hill, it is fully relieved against the sky, and shows very nobly. The square which immediately surrounds it is newly divided into building-lots, and is becoming the "west end" of Baltimore. The Monument and the handsome buildings which are going up around are a mutual improvement of appearance.

The design of this monument was conceived in 1809, when a company obtained leave of the legislature to raise 100,000 dollars for the purpose by a lottery. By the year 1815, funds sufficient to authorize the commencement of the work had been raised, and a plan had been furnished by Mr. Robert Mills. On the 4th of July, the corner stone was laid upon ground presented by Col. John E. Howard. The monument is a Doric column upon a square base, sur-

WASHINGTON'S MONUMENT AT BALTIMORE

mounted by a pedestal, upon which is placed a colossal statue of Washington. The base is fifty feet square, and is elevated twenty feet; the column, to the feet of the statue, is one hundred and sixty feet, and the statue is thirteen feet in height. The statue is the work of Causici, an Italian, and represents Washington at the instant when he resigned his commission after the Revolution.

There were three periods in Washington's life, and either of the two first would alone have placed him in the highest roll of the names of great men. The close of his military life (here represented) terminated the first period. His civil career in the presidency terminated the second; and here all comparison between Washington and any other man that ever lived ceases entirely. With a fame as complete as his, on his second retirement to Mount Vernon, a sincere and ardent wish to pass the remainder of his days in peaceful seclusion, and domestic ties and attachments of the strongest character; with all this around him, to come out once more from his tent of glory, and at his country's call to expose his bright name again to the hazards of failure, and to the eagerness of human envy and misconstruction,—this seems to me the sublimest moment of the life of Washington.

"You know, Sir," he says in his letter to the President, accepting the office of commander-in-chief of the army, "what calculations I had made relative to the probable course of events on my retiring from office, and the determination with which I had consoled myself of closing the remnant of my days in my present peaceful abode. You will, therefore, be at no loss to conceive and appreciate the sensations I must have experienced to bring my mind to any conclusion that would pledge me, at so late a period of life, to leave scenes I sincerely love to enter upon the boundless field of public action, incessant trouble, and high responsibility."

It is singular how all the contemporaneous judgments of Washington's character unite in ascribing the difficulty of drawing his portrait to the unity, harmony, and perfectability of his character. Chastellux says very forcibly, "If you are presented with medals of Cæsar, of Trajan, or Alexander, on examining their features you will still be led to ask, what was their stature and the form of their persons; but if you discover in a heap of ruins the head or a limb of the Apollo, be not curious about the other parts, but rest assured that they were all conformable to those of a god. Let not this impression be attributed to enthusiasm. I wish only to express the impression that Washington has left on my mind: the idea of a perfect whole, that cannot be the produce of enthusiasm, which rather would reject it, since the effect of proportion is to diminish the idea of greatness."

In a funereal eulogy pronounced by Mr. Ware at Hingham, occurs nearly the same sentiment.

"The image of this great man is not like that of most others who have shone with distinguished lustre in the annals of the world. It is not composed of some bright spots surrounded with dark shades, so as to dazzle without enlightening the beholder. His character is not an assemblage of great talents by the side of great defects, and splendid virtues contaminated by their vicinity to atrocious vices: he shone with a clear and steady lustre, which, if it seldom appeared with flashes of splendour to dazzle and astonish, was yet never mingled with shades, nor intercepted by clouds. The circumstance which seems to distinguish his name from that of all others, is not the preeminence of any one talent or virtue, but a unity of character resulting from the perfect combination and exact balancing of all those great and good qualities, which enter into the character of one who is to possess public esteem, guide public opinion, and command universal respect and confidence."

Eastport, and Passamaquoddy Bay

THE people of this beautiful State are just now enduring a double share of the evils of border location, having not only the ill-directed "*sympathy*" with the insurrectionists of Canada to repress, but the excitement of the newly-vexed question of *boundary*. As this last subject is one little understood, perhaps the history of the negotiations on the subject may not be unacceptable to the readers of the AMERICAN SCENERY.

"In their endeavours to bring about the settlement of another contested point, the two governments were less successful than they had been with respect to the commercial intercourse between America and the West India Island. This point related to the fixing the north-eastern boundary of the United States.

"By the treaty of 1783, which recognised their independence, it was declared that the eastern boundary of the United States, dividing them from Nova Scotia, should be 'a line to be drawn along the middle of the river St. Croix, from its mouth in the bay of Fundy to its source, and from its source, directly north, to the highlands, which divide the rivers that fall into the Atlantic Ocean from those which fall into the river St. Lawrence.' The northern line, separating Canada from the New States, was to commence 'from the north-west angle of Nova Scotia; viz. that angle which is formed by a line drawn due north from the source of the St. Croix river to the highlands, along the said highlands, which divide those rivers that empty themselves into the river St. Lawrence from those which fall into the Atlantic Ocean, to the north-westernmost head of Connecticut river; thence, descending along that river to the forty-fifth degree of latitude, thence due west on that latitude, until it strikes the river Iroquois or Cataruguy, thence along the middle of the said river into Lake Ontario,' &c.

"Being for the most part marked out by mathematical, or by well-known natural lines, the frontier between the head of the Connecticut and Lake Ontario afforded but little ground for dispute. But such was not the case with the boundary from the head of the Connecticut to the sea. Untrodden, except perhaps by the foot of the hunter, all the northern division of the country between the Bay of Fundy and the St. Lawrence then consisted of a dense forest, scattered over with mountains and lakes, and intersected by streams of considerable magnitude. No survey of it appears ever to have been made, and the British ministers were, consequently, ignorant of its topographical features. Yet, even under these circumstances, they can scarcely be excused for having admitted such a vague description of the future limits, since, without much difficulty, sufficient information might have been obtained to prevent this defect. Their negligence gave birth to a controversy, which, after the expiration of half a century, yet remains undecided. Only a few years elapsed before a doubt arose respecting the river which was meant under the name of St. Croix; the Americans insisting that the St. John was the river which was intended. By the treaty of 1794, it was arranged that this point should be left to the decision of a joint commission. In 1798, the commission decided that the extreme source of the northern branch of the Scoodic river was the source of the St. Croix designated in the treaty; and a monument was erected there, to indicate the spot whence the line was to be drawn to the north. Thus far the question was satisfactorily set at rest. Not such, however, was the result of the subsequent proceedings. For some years, no further steps appear to have been taken by either of the governments. While the territory in question continued to be a wilderness, there was not much temptation to discuss its limits; but when the new state of Maine, and the British province of New Brunswick, began to extend their settlements into the interior, the case was materially al-

EASTPORT, AND PASSAMAQUODDY BAY

tered. The line of demarcation claimed by the Americans would not only include an area of ten thousand square miles, but would entirely cut off all direct communication between New Brunswick and Lower Canada. From the source of the Scoodic river, they prolonged the line northward, as far as a chain of mountains distant less than thirty miles from the St. Lawrence; which chain, they contended, formed the highlands specified in the treaty of 1783.

"The British, on the contrary, maintained that the north-west angle of Nova Scotia was at Mars Hill, about forty miles from the source of the Scoodic; and that the northern frontier of Maine ought to pass from thence to the westward over a range of hills which lie at the sources of the Penobscot, Kennebec, and Androscoggin. Neither party would recede from its pretensions. In the treaty of Ghent, in 1814, it was agreed that two commissioners should be appointed to make surveys and settle the boundary. If they coincided in opinion, their decision was to be final; but if they disagreed, some friendly sovereign, or state, was to be chosen as umpire, and from his judgment there was to be no appeal.

"Affairs remained in this state till 1827, when the commissioners being unable to agree, and some disputes as to questions of jurisdiction having rendered it desirable to bring the frontier controversy to an issue, a convention was concluded between the British and American government, by which it was arranged that the king of the Netherlands should be requested to act as arbitrator. To this request his majesty assented; and their statements and surveys were accordingly laid before him. The award of the sovereign umpire was not delivered till the 10th of January, 1831. It was not calculated to satisfy either of the claimants. Considering the pretensions of the two powers to be equally balanced, it proceeded to lay down new limits, upon principles of mutual convenience. The British frontier was to commence at the spot where the line drawn due north from the source of the Scoodic intersects the St. John, and was to pass up the latter river and the St. Francis, to the highlands which run parallel with the St. Lawrence. Though this award assigned to the Americans seven-eighths of the district which was contended for by Great Britain, yet, as it gave a direct communication between New Brunswick and Lower Canada, it was accepted by the British government. The United States was not so yielding. The award was immediately protested against by the American ministers at the Hague, on the ground of the arbiter having exceeded his authority. The State of Maine also entered its protest, and denied the right of the federal government to cede any portion of the litigated territory. The matter was finally brought before the senate by the President, and that body decided that the umpire having gone beyond his powers, his award was not binding; and that a new negotiation must be opened with Great Britain. Since that period, however, no steps have been taken to accomplish an arrangement."

Cemetery of Mount Auburn

THIS picturesque and beautiful burial-place occupies a grove, formerly an academic and sylvan retreat for the students of Harvard College, near by. It is about five miles from Boston, and presents naturally a most agreeable mixture of hill, valley, and water, forming altogether the beau-ideal of a site for the purpose to which it is at present devoted.

If we are not mistaken, the people of the United States owe the most creditable and delicate taste, newly awakened throughout the country on the subject of sepulture, to one of their most distinguished poets, the Rev. John Pierpoint, author of the "Airs of Palestine." By his exertions, mainly, a society was formed for the purchase, appropriation, and improvement, of the beautiful spot represented in the drawing; and, at present, most of the wealthier citizens of the capital of New England are possessors of verdant and flowery enclosures, which are ornamented even more tastefully than the celebrated cemeteries of Père la Chaise. In doing away thus with the neglectfulness and dreariness of the outer aspect of the grave, death, it seems to us, is divested of half its terrors, while a refined and salutary feeling is awakened in the bosoms of the living.

The example of this cemetery has been followed in other cities; and at Philadelphia, particularly, there is a most sweet spot selected upon the banks of the Schuylkill, and appropriated to this purpose. The refinement has spread all over the country; and in a few years, probably, the burial of the dead will be associated in the minds of the people of the United States only with sylvan repose, and the sacred loveliness of consecrated natural beauty.

CEMETERY OF MOUNT AUBURN

NORTHAMPTON, MASSACHUSETTS

Northampton, Massachusetts

IT is recorded of the first settlers of Northampton, that in the tenth year of their establishment in the wilderness, in 1663, they paid for the support of a clergyman one hundred and twenty pounds sterling. According to the change in the value of money, and the circumstances of the persons who formed the congregation, this sum was equal to at least six times the amount of the present valuation. In this one fact is to be found a leaven which has pervaded the town ever since, preserving for its inhabitants the rigid morality, the religious feeling, and almost the stern manners of the Puritan pilgrims.

The inflexible justice practised among such men had its effect on the Indians among whom they settled; and Northampton, in consequence, was one of the last towns affected by the general hostilities of Philip's war.

In their first purchases, they secured no less their own rights than the rights of the natives; and the latter were always considered as having a right to dwell and hunt in the lands they had sold. In the year 1664, they requested leave of the settlers to build themselves a fort within the town; and leave was granted on the following conditions: —

"That the Indians do not work, game, or carry burdens within the town on the Sabbath; nor *powow* here, or anywhere else;

"Nor get liquor, nor cider, nor get drunk;

"Nor admit Indians from without the town;

"Nor break down the fences of the inhabitants;

"Nor let cattle or swine upon their fields; but go over a stile at one place;

"Nor admit among them the murderers, Calawane, Wuttowhan, and Pacquallant;

"Nor hunt, nor kill cattle, sheep, or swine, with their dogs."

There is in these conditions an attention to the sobriety and morality of the Indians, which has been very seldom regarded in compacts with this injured race. The consequence was, a perpetual peace between them and the Indians of their immediate neighbourhood. On the breaking out of Philip's war, however, they became liable to incursions from other tribes, and especially from the Canadians, French, and Indians. They fortified their "meeting-house;" and in every cluster of houses, one was fortified and pierced with holes for the discharge of muskets. The whole town was then enclosed with a palisado set up in a trench, and a guard of fifty persons perpetually kept.

It is scarcely possible to convey, to a mind that has not reflected on the subject, a fair idea of the difficulties, hazards, and horrors, that beset the first adventurers for religious liberty in New England. Beside all the usual evils of pioneering—the separation from friends, the hardships, the privations, the loss of all communication with the civilized world, these settlers had to encounter the most diabolical warfare recorded in history.

"The first announcement of an Indian war," says a diffuse writer on this subject, "is its terrible commencement. In the hour of security and sleep, when your deadly enemies are supposed to be friends, quietly fishing and hunting—when they are believed to be far off, and thoughtless of you and yours, your sleep is suddenly broken by the war-whoop, your house and village set on fire, your family and friends butchered, and yourself escape only to be carried into captivity, and wrung with every species of torture. If you go out to the fields, you may be shot down by an unseen enemy in the woods, or return in the evening and find your house consumed to ashes, and your family carried into captivity."

During the last part of what is called Philip's war, to the Indians' treachery, cruelty, and cunning, was added the instigation, the sustenance, and the wealth of the civilized French. A price was paid for English scalps; European officers planned and assisted to execute schemes of devastation and slaughter; and, in short, nothing was wanting to develop, in its fullest ferocity, the Indian's love of blood.

It is curious to reflect how wide and immortal would have been the fame of the king of the Wampanoags, had he succeeded, (as he came very near doing,) in exterminating the Whites, and restoring the land of his forefathers to his subjects and children. The experiment of settlement would scarcely have been soon repeated; and, perhaps, to this day, the Indian, confident in his tried strength, would have possessed and defended the lands from which he has so utterly disappeared; while the name of Philip would justly have been associated with those of Gustavus Vasa, and Alfred of England. The difference between him and these great lights of history, is, that he failed.

Chapel of "Our Lady of Cold Spring"

THE Hudson bends out from Crow-Nest into a small bay; and, in the lap of the crescent thus formed, lies snug and sheltered, the little village of Cold Spring. It is not much of a place for its buildings, history, or business; but it has its squire and post-master, its politics and scandal, and a long disappointed ambition to become a regular landing-place for the steamers. Then there are cabals between the rival ferrymen, on which the inhabitants divide; the vote for the president, on which they agree (for Van Buren); and the usual religious sects, with the usual schisms. The Presbyterians and Methodists, as usual, worship in very ugly churches; and the Catholics, as usual, in a very picturesque and beautiful one. (*Vide* the Drawing.)

It is a pity (picturesquely speaking) that the boatmen on the river are not Catholics; it would be so pretty to see them shorten sail off Our Lady of Cold Spring, and uncover for an Ave-Maria. This little chapel, so exquisitely situated on the bluff overlooking the river, reminds me of a hermit's oratory and cross which is perched similarly in the shelter of a cliff on the desolate coast of Sparta. I was on board a frigate, gliding slowly up the Ægean, and clinging to the shore for a land-wind, when I descried the white cross at a distance of about half a mile, strongly relieved against the dark rock in its rear. As we approached, the small crypt and altar became visible; and, at the moment the ship passed, a tall monk, with a snow-white beard, stepped forth like an apparition upon the cliffs, and spread out his arms to bless us. In the midst of the intense solitude of the Ægean, with not a human dwelling to be seen on the whole coast from Moron to Napoli, the effect of this silent benediction was almost supernatural. He remained for five minutes in this attitude, his long cowl motionless in the still air, and his head slowly turning to the ship as she drew fast around the little promontory on her course. I would suggest to Our Lady of Cold Spring, that a niche under the portico of her pretty chapel, with a cross to be seen from the river by day, and a lamp by night, would make at least a catholic impression on the passer by, though we are not all children of St. Peter.

Half way between the mountain and our Lady's shrine, stands, on a superb natural platform, the romantic estate of Undercliff, the seat of Colonel Morris. Just above it rises the abrupt and heavily wooded mountain, from which it derives its name; a thick grove hides it from the village at its foot; and, from the portico of the mansion, extend views in three directions unparalleled for varied and surprising beauty. A road, running between high-water mark and the

CHAPEL OF "OUR LADY OF COLD SPRING"

park gate, skirts the river in eccentric windings for five or six miles; the brows of the hills descending to the Hudson in the west and north, are nobly wooded and threaded with circuitous paths, and all around lies the most romantic scenery of the most romantic river in the world.

The only fault of the views from West Point, is, that West Point itself is lost as a feature in the landscape. The traveller feels the same drawback which troubled the waiting-maid when taken to drive by the footman in her mistress's chariot—"How I wish I could stand by the road side and see myself go by!" From Undercliff, which is directly opposite, and about at the same elevation, the superb terrace of the Military School is seen to the greatest advantage. The white barracks of Camptown, the long range of edifices which skirt the esplanade, the ruins half way up the mountain of old Fort Putnam, and the waving line of wood and valley extending to Mr. Cozzen's estate of "Stoney Lonesome," form a noble feature in the view from Undercliff.

I had forgotten that Cold Spring "plucks a glory on its head" from being honoured with the frequent visits of Washington Irving, Halleck, and other lesser stars in the literary firmament; when these first lights above the horizon shall have set, (Hesperus-like—first and brightest!) there will linger about this little village—by that time, perhaps, arrived at the dignity of a landing-place—many a tale of the days when Geoffrey Crayon talked in his gentle way with the ferryman who brought him to Cold Spring; or the now plethoric post-master, who, in his character of librarian to the village, enjoyed the friend-ship of Irving and Halleck, and received from their own hands the "authors' copies," since curiously preserved in the execrable print and binding then prevalent in America. Perhaps even old Lipsey the ferryman, and his rival Andrews, will come in for their slice of immortality, little as they dream now, pulling close in for the counter-current under our Lady's skirts, of working at that slow oar for posthumous reputation.

VIEW FROM THE MOUNTAIN HOUSE, CATSKILL

View from the Mountain House, Catskill

IN the following masterly description, by Miss Martineau, is said all, and the best that can be said, of the glorious view from the Mountain-House at Catskill.

"After tea, I went out upon the platform in front of the house, having been warned not to go too near the edge, so as to fall an unmeasured depth into the forest below. I sat upon the edge as a security against stepping over unawares. The stars were bright overhead, and had conquered half the sky, giving promise of what we ardently desired, a fine morrow. Over the other half, the mass of thunder-clouds was, I supposed, heaped together; for I could at first discern nothing of the campaign which I knew must be stretched below. Suddenly, and from that moment incessantly, gushes of red lightning poured out from the cloudy canopy, revealing, not merely the horizon, but the course of the river, in all its windings through the valley. This thread of river, thus illuminated, looked like a flash of lightning caught by some strong hand and laid along in the valley.

"All the principal features of the landscape might, no doubt, have been discerned by this sulphurous light; but my whole attention was absorbed by the river, which seemed to come out of the darkness, like an apparition, at the summons of my impatient will. It could be borne only for a short time—this dazzling, bewildering alternation of glare and blackness, of vast reality and nothingness. I was soon glad to draw back from the precipice, and seek the candle-light within.

"The next day was Sunday. I shall never forget, if I live to a hundred, how the world lay at our feet one Sunday morning. I rose very early, and looked abroad from my window, two stories above the platform. A dense fog, exactly level with my eyes, as it appeared, roofed in the whole plain of the earth—a dusky firmament, in which the stars had hidden themselves for the day. Such is the account which an antediluvian spectator would probably have given of it. This solid firmament had spaces in it, however, through which gushes of sun-light were poured, lighting up the spires of white churches, and clusters of farm-buildings, too small to be otherwise distinguished; and especially the river, with its sloops, floating like motes in the sun-beam. The firmament rose and melted, or parted off into the likeness of snowy sky-mountains, and left the cool Sabbath to brood brightly over the land. What human interest sanctifies a bird's-eye view! I suppose this is its peculiar charm; for its charm is found to deepen in proportion to the growth of mind. To an infant, a campaign of a hundred miles is not so much as a yard square of gay carpet. To the rustic, it is less bewitching than a paddock with two cows. To the philosopher, what is it not? As he casts his eye over its glittering towns, its scattered hamlets, its secluded homes, its mountain ranges, church spires, and untrodden forests, it is a picture of life; an epitome of the human universe; the complete volume of moral philosophy for which he has sought in vain in all libraries. On the left horizon, are the green mountains of Vermont; and at the right extremity sparkles the Atlantic. Beneath lies the forest where the deer are hiding, and the birds rejoicing in song. Beyond the river, he sees spread the rich plains of Connecticut; there, where a blue expanse lies beyond the triple range of hills, are the churches of religious Massachusetts sending up their sabbath-psalms—praise which he is too high to hear, while God is not. The fields and waters seem to him to-day no more truly property than the skies which shine down upon them; and to think how some below are busying their thoughts this Sabbath-day about how they shall hedge in another field, or multiply their flocks on yonder meadows, gives him a taste of the same pity which Jesus felt in his solitude, when his followers were contending about which should be greatest. It seems strange to him now that man should call any thing *his* but the power which is in him, and which can create somewhat more vast and beautiful than all that this horizon encloses. Here he gains the conviction, to be never again shaken, that all that is real is ideal; that the joys and sorrows of men do not spring up out of the ground, or fly abroad on the wings of the wind, or come showered down from the sky; that good cannot be hedged in, nor evil barred out; even that light does not reach the spirit through the eye alone, nor wisdom through the medium of sound or silence only. He becomes of one mind with the spiritual Berkeley, that the face of nature itself, the very picture of woods, and streams, and meadows, is a hieroglyphic writing in the spirit itself, of which the retina is no interpreter. The proof is just below him, (at least, it came under my eye,) in the lady (not American) who, after glancing over the landscape, brings her chair into the piazza, and turning her back to the campaign, and her face to the wooden walls of the hotel, begins the study, this Sunday morning, of her lap-full of newspapers. What a sermon is thus preached to him at this moment from a very hackneyed text! To him that hath much—that hath the eye, and ear, and wealth, of the spirit, shall more be given—even a replenishing of this spiritual life from that which, to others, is formless and dumb; while, from him that hath little, who trusts in that which lies about him rather than in that which lives within him, shall be taken away, by natural decline, the power of perceiving and enjoying what is within his own domain. To him who is already enriched with large divine and human revelations, this scene is, for all its stillness, musical with divine and human speech; while one who has been deafened by the din of worldly affairs can hear nothing in this mountain solitude."

Faneuiel Hall, from the Water

Two noble streets, and a market, perhaps the finest in the world, have been projected in front of the old Faneuiel Hall, which stood a very few years ago close to the water's edge. The new land was made, and the plan carried into effect during the mayoralty of Josiah Quincy, Esq., to whose enterprise and sagacity the city is indebted for these great improvements.

Faneuiel Hall, which in the view from the water stands in the rear of these fine structures of granite, is the dearest spot connected with American freedom. It was used as a town-hall in the time of the Revolution; and within its walls arose the first murmur, which, stirred by the daring eloquence of Adams and Otis, terminated in the Declaration of Independence. The name by which it is best known, is, *"The Cradle of Liberty."*

In the year 1740, Peter Faneuiel (a Huguenot) made an offer to build, at his own expense, "an edifice on the town's land in Dock Square, to be improved for a hall and market, for the sole use, benefit, and advantage of the town, provided that the town would authorize it, and lay the same under such proper regulations as should be thought necessary, and support the same constantly for said use." A vote of thanks was immediately passed to Mr. Faneuiel, the work was commenced, and two years afterwards, "Mr. Samuel Ruggles, who was employed in building said house, waited on the select-men, by order of P. Faneuiel, Esq., and delivered them the key of said house." A meeting was then held in the hall, and a motion was made that the thanks of the town be given to Peter Faneuiel, Esq., for his generous benefaction of the Market-House to the town; and resolutions were drawn up and passed to that effect. A large committee of the first citizens waited on him, "and, in the name of the town, rendered their most hearty thanks for so bountiful a gift, with

FANEUIEL HALL, FROM THE WATER

their prayers that this and other expressions of his bounty and charity might be abundantly recompensed with the divine blessing."

Another vote was then passed unanimously, "that, in testimony of the town's gratitude to Peter Faneuiel, Esq., and to perpetuate his memory, the hall over the market-place be named Faneuiel Hall, and at all times hereafter be called by that name." And as a further testimony of respect, it was voted "that Mr. Faneuiel's picture be drawn at full length, at the expense of the town, and placed in the hall; and the select-men were charged with the commission, which was accordingly executed."

"The building was of brick, two stories in height, and measured one hundred feet by forty. It was esteemed one of the best pieces of workmanship, and an ornament to the town. The hall would contain one thousand persons; there were convenient apartments for the officers of the town, besides a room for the naval office, and a notary public."

Mr. Faneuiel did not long live to enjoy the gratitude of his townsmen. He died suddenly, a year after the completion of the building. His funeral oration, delivered by Mr. John Lovell, Master of the Grammar School, was the first specimen of eloquence uttered in the "Cradle of Liberty." It was, in some of its sentiments, very unlike the orations which followed, and far from prophetic.

"What now remains," he concludes, "but my ardent wishes (in which I know you will all concur with me) that this hall may be ever sacred to the interests of truth, of justice, of *loyalty*, and honour. May no private views nor party broils ever enter within these walls; but may the same public spirit that glowed in the breast of the generous founder influence all your debates, that society may reap the benefit of them.

"May liberty always spread its joyful wings over this place—liberty, that opens men's hearts to beneficence, and gives the relish to those who enjoy the effects of it; and *may loyalty to a king, under whom we enjoy this liberty*, ever remain our character—a character always justly due to this land, and of which our enemies have in vain attempted to rob us."

The family of Faneuiel had been more than fifty years in America, and had fled from persecution in France to find a refuge in the wilderness. The Faneuiel arms were subsequently placed in the hall, elegantly carved and gilt.

Eight or nine years after the erection of Faneuiel Hall, it took fire from a neighbouring conflagration, and was nearly burnt to the ground. It was on one of the coldest nights of January, and the water froze so rapidly, that it was impossible to work the engines. The walls were left standing, and it was rebuilt and enlarged soon after.

Just against the end of Faneuiel Hall, in a broad dock, now filled up and built upon, used to lie a cluster of oyster-boats, that were half house, half vessel, floating oyster-shops—in short, of the most canonical rudeness and simplicity. It was as necessary to go to them to eat oysters in perfection, as it is to go to Blackwall for white-bait; and no true gourmand pretended to have elsewhere found the relish. They are gone, alas! and with the old hulks are gone the amphibious venders—the rude, high-booted, superannuated oyster-openers, dressing, for years after they had given up the vocation, just as if they were embarking for the mud-bank, and talking in the same hoarse tone as if their words were meant to struggle, as of yore, with a nor-wester. So flee away before the advances of improvement all that reminded us of other days; and it is by this resolute plucking up of old associations, and resolute modernizing and improving, even upon the most sacred habits and usages of our forefathers, that this new nation keeps its unchecked headway, with neither rooted superstition nor cherished prejudice to restrain it. When it ceases to be so, we shall have the age of poetry; but adieu, then, to the age of improvement!

AMERICAN SCENERY,

BY

N. P. WILLIS, ESQ:

ILLUSTRATED IN A SERIES OF VIEWS

BY

W. H. BARTLETT.

American Scenery; or, Land, Lake, and River: Illustrations of Trans-atlantic Nature, was first published in 1840 by George Virtue, London, and R. Martin & Co., New York. The Imprint Society reproduces all the original steel plate engravings described in the 1840 text, which is also included.

This edition was designed by Warren Skillings and composed at The Anthoensen Press in Portland, Maine, the city of author's birth. The fine-screen illustrations of the plates were reproduced and printed offset by The Meriden Gravure Company, Meriden, Connecticut, on Mohawk Superfine paper. The binding was executed by Stanhope Bindery of Boston.

This is copy number

987

THE
NORTH EASTERN PART
OF THE
UNITED STATES.

Engraved for N.P.Willis's "American Scenery Illustrated."

Scale of Miles.

0   20   40   60   80

78   76   74

Montreal
River S.t Lawrence
L.S.t Francis
L.S.t Louis
C A
L A
Malone
Plattsburg
Kingston
Black Lake
Iron L.
L. Saranac
Elizabe
Watertown
Sackets Harb.r
Source of R. Hudson
Long Lake
Schroon
Rogers's Slid
Ticond
E. Hudson
L A K E   O N T A R I O
Martinsburg
Caldwell
Glens Fa
Oswego
Pulaski
Queenstown
Brock's
N. Newport
Tuscarora Reservation
Lockport
Albion
Erie or
Falls of Niagara
Buffalo
Batavia
Rochester
Falls of the Genesee
Grand Canal
Lyons
Waterloo
Auburn
L. Oneida
Oswego
Rome
West Canada C.
Trenton Falls
Utica
Erie Can.
Herkimer
R. Mohawk
Little Falls
Saratoga Springs
Ballston Spr.
Mohawk & Hudson Rail.
LAKE ERIE
Aurora
Genesee R.
Canandaigua
Penyan
L. Seneca
Morrisville
Courtland
Cooperstown
Schenectady
Schoharie
Albany
N   E   W
Ellicotville
Angelica
Bath
Ithaca
L. Cayuga
Norwich
Chenango Canal
Susquehanna R.
Delhi
Catterskill Falls
R. Hudson
Cha
Che
Hinsdale
New York & Erie Railroad
Elmira
Oweg
Glennan
Binghamton
Susquehanna
Y   O   R
Kingston
Hyde Par.
Poughke
Alleghany R.
Coudersport
Towanda
Montrose
Gr. Bend
New York & Erie Rail.a
Hudson & Delaware Can.
Newburg
Crows Nest
Bull Hill
Cold Spring
Wellsborough
Beach
Monticello
Milford
Coshen
West Point
ckskill
Sing Sing
Sinnemahoning R.
Pine Creek
Williamsport
Susquehanna E. Branch
Wilkesbarre
R. Delaware
Newton
Clarkstown
Karthaus Falls
Susquehanna W.Br.
Danville
Vale or Wyoming
Lehigh Navigation
Morris Can.l
Passaic Falls
Weehawken
P   E   N
Clearfield
Bellefonte
Northumberland
Sunbury
Morristown
Somerville
Brunswick
Newark
NEW YORK
M.ts
Ebensburg
Lewistown
Liverpool
Orwigsburg
Easton
Flemington
Holidaysburg
Huntingdon
Juniata
Allentown
R. Schuylkill
Reading
Doylestown
Norristown
N   S   Y   L   V   A   N   I   A
Johnstown
Bloomfield
Blue Mountains
Union Canal
Harrisburg
Columbia
Columbia R.road
Philadel
Burlington
Freehold
Bedford
Carlisle
Bridge
York
Lancaster
Westchester
Chester
Woodbury
Bordentown
Alle
Chambersburg
Susquehanna R.
Wilmington
Elkton
N   E   W
Chesapeake R.
Gettysburg
Bellair
Chester
Salem
Bridgeton
Cumberland
M   A   R
Bath
Hagerstown
Delaware
Dover
Egg Harb.r
Potomac Riv. N.Br.
Ohio Can.
Fredericktown
Aqueduct
Baltimore
Centreville
DELAWARE
Delaware Bay
Romney
Harper's Ferry
Rockville
Denton
Cape May
Martinsburg
Winchester
Shenandoah R.
Leesburg
Georgetown
Annapolis
Georgetown
M.rfield
P   A   R   T   O   F
Woodstock
Alexandria
Washington
Chesapeake Bay
Easton
Georgetown
Kent
VIRGINIA
River
Warrenton
M.t Vernon
Potomac R.
A
Longit

78   76   74